W9-CFV-433

# Daisy Dooley does divorce

# Daisy Dooley does divorce

Anna Pasternak

Vermilion
LONDON

3 5 7 9 10 8 6 4 2

Published in 2007 by Vermilion, an imprint of
Ebury Publishing

Ebury Publishing is a division of the Random House Group



The Random House Group Limited Reg. No. 954009

Addresses for companies within the Random House Group
can be found at
www.randomhouse.co.uk

A CIP catalogue record for this book is available from the British Library



Printed in the UK by CPI Mackays, Chatham, ME5 8TD

ISBN 9780091917265

# Acknowledgements

There is a long line of inspirational, talented and encouraging people who make up the Daisy chain and to whom I owe my heart-felt gratitude.

Firstly, to Richard Addis who has been a brilliant mentor and incredible catalyst. To Paul Dacre, editor of the *Daily Mail* for backing Daisy and believing in me. I am indebted. Similarly, to Lisa Collins and Anabel Cutler and the rest of the Lifestyle team who have made working for the *Daily Mail* a weekly delight. To my fantastic agent Mal Peachey, who has made me laugh, kept me sane and inspired my creativity like no other. To Miles Ketley, my inimitable lawyer. To John Conway, Albert Fox and Damian Lally, all of whom have helped keep me afloat financially. To Clare Hulton, Julia Kellaway and Anabel Briggs at Vermilion, for their vision and passion for Daisy. To Robert Holden, Ross Clarke and John and Deborah Peters for being such incredible creative influences on me. To Wilfred, my beloved dachshund, who has been by my side for every written word. And lastly, but most importantly, to my mother and to my daughter, Daisy. Together they have supported me, loved me, inspired me and enabled me to follow my dream. I could not have written *Daisy Dooley does divorce* without their patience, humour, kindness and help. Thank you both.

# Prologue

# The PDD (Post Divorce Date)

There's only one thing worse than being thirty-nine and single. Being thirty-nine and divorced. The relief of getting married meant never having to date again. The subtext of 'I do' was: 'Thank you, hubby, from the bottom of my heart that I do not have to scan men at parties any more, I do not need to fire up my married friends' search engines for "eligible" or "available", nor suffer the angst of "will he call or won't he?"' A trip to the altar in Jamie's family tiara put paid to that. Or so I thought. Yet here I am, three years after I hurled my bouquet in the air – as if celebrating a win at sports day – about to go frog kissing. Again.

Turns out Jamie Prattlock wasn't my prince after all. I wanted the marriage to work – every woman does – but he was incapable of blowing my heart right open. On the honeymoon, I asked myself how long does it take for it to feel *right*? After a year of being Mrs Prattlock, I wondered how long do you *wait* for it to feel right? I stayed for another six months. In the end, it wasn't so much that I was unable to live with Jamie. I was unable to live with myself and the gnawing emptiness that something was missing. Something so much more.

My oldest school friend, Jess, says that even as a child I was overly sentimental. If we played near a blossom tree, I'd scoop up handfuls of pink petals and fling them over her, shouting 'It's your wedding!' (She's nudging forty and single. By choice – not chance or lack of it because with her lofty libido every man is a potential fuck, or even better, a willing fuck buddy to add to her Rolodex of sex.) Meanwhile, my chaste diet of soul-stirring, female-empowering, self-esteem boosting bestsellers, has, Jess believes, completely skewed my expectations. But doesn't it say everything about Jamie's blocked-off plight that I openly devoured *Should I Stay Or Should I Go?* before I left him?

My new bible is the *Little Book of Dating Dharma*. This precious gem guides me through the Post Divorce Date, or PDD. I don't enjoy being a relationship statistic now that I've got more emotional baggage than Heathrow handles in a day, but I press on because I know my soulmate exists. Otherwise I couldn't possibly be this lonely.

When my marital dreams went up in smoke, humiliatingly, I boomeranged back home to the country to Mum. Not only couldn't I afford to replicate our marital pad in town, I couldn't face purchasing a flat on my own, to live in alone, when all my girlfriends were looking to expand their properties along with their pregnant waistlines. Mum is a dotty divorced dog breeder – her logo is: Dooley's Dachshunds: Long and Strong. When she dropped me off at the station to go to London for my first PDD, she pulled up alongside a dishy bloke on a motorbike. My ring radar immediately alerted me to the fact he wasn't wearing one, just as Mum shouted out: 'Remember, Daisy, nice girls and divorcees don't.' He looked around, while Mum continued brazenly. 'And don't forget, princes get warts too.'

My friends, Lucy and Edward Primfold, set me up on the blind date with Troy Powers. I clearly wasn't thinking straight when I went to stay with them a couple of months after my divorce from Jamie came through. What was I thinking? When I had broken the blood vessels beneath my eyes sobbing over my unhitched and childless state, it was insanity to visit a picture-perfect family with angelic twin girls.

It was nursery tea when I arrived and the twins, Tabitha and Lily, aged six and dressed up as flower fairies, were tucking into homemade carrot cake and crudités. Edward, a suave public school type who moves through life with the languor only breeding and masses of inherited money affords, put his arm around me as he led me into the kitchen. 'Chaos as usual,' he said, gesturing to the girls quietly eating. They smiled up at me as if I was the photographer for a centre spread in the Mini Boden catalogue. Click. It was a Kodak moment of such domestic harmony that the bile of jealousy instantly soured inside.

Lucy was at the end of the table, stunning in a crisp white shirt and Chloe jeans, her short blonde hair expensively highlighted. I'd met Lucy at a freshers' drinks party in our first week at university and have marvelled at her composure ever since. Lucy never looked like a student even when she was one, whereas I can still pass for a mature student on a bad hair day. You always knew that Luce was going to waltz off campus and into the City, marking time until she fell into the eager embrace of a prospective husband because even when she was single she had the aplomb of a married woman.

'Darling Daise,' she said, hugging me. I wanted to bury my face in her smooth, scented neck and scream. Why me? I felt as if I'd walked into a scene of such purity and innocence that I should rip off my own failure riddled skin. As Lucy poured me a cup of tea, I stared at the parrot tulips billowing out from a crystal vase in the centre of the table and I wondered how come she got it so right? Not only did she sign up to the right life story at birth, she'd been hitting the bull's eye ever since. With her rock-steady marriage, her uber-earning hubby and angelic, well-adjusted kids, there was no need for her to obsess over 'what ifs?'. She had nothing in her past to regret, only well-rounded decades to reflect on with happiness and pride. Unlike me.

'Sorry to hear about the divorce coming through,' Edward said. 'I always thought Prattlock was okay.'

'Okay isn't always enough,' I sighed, but thought to myself, When have you ever settled for okay? The Chelsea townhouse with access to communal gardens is hardly okay, is it? Your collection of Old Masters, including a Veronese and a Frans Hals, those aren't merely okay oils to hang on your drawing room, are they?

Later, Edward happily let slip that he had bumped into Jamie at some arse-numbingly boring charity bridge tournament where Jamie had boasted about his new girlfriend. Talk about kicking a dog – or a divorcee – when they're down.

'So?' Lucy said gamely. 'Men always pull straight away to prove that *they* don't have a problem. It's just comfort sex at the end of a relationship.'

'You should try it,' Edward said, winking at me. 'Got a mucker who's moved back here from Bahrain. Bright bond trader. Successful, stinking rich and recently divorced; so at least you will have one thing in common.'

Yup. We both know what it is to feel irrevocably broken inside.

A few weeks later in Battersea preparing for the date, Jess opened a pack of fags – she's a pragmatic GP. As I stared at my reflection in the mirror, she stood behind me blowing smoke rings. With her liquid green eyes, strawberry-blonde Pre-Raphaelite curls and lightly freckled skin, she has an attractiveness and easy-going charisma that eludes me. It's not that I'm ugly; I'm just not a natural beauty either. I'm the type who's referred to as 'striking' when I'm all done up. My large brown eyes are probably my strongest point – even if they look sufficiently bulbous when I'm tired that my mother keeps asking me if I have a thyroid problem. Worse, I have an intensity that frightens men; I don't do light-hearted, particularly when it comes to flirting. (That's also partly due to Mum who wouldn't let me flick my fringe around when I was a teenager because she said it would make me look thick and my hair look thin.) Jess radiates sexuality because her agenda is upfront and uncomplicated. With the teensiest hint of a smile, her message reads: 'we both know that we want it so why pretend?' whereas I could wear a 'come hither' grin from ear to ear and I'd still come over as off-putting.

Infuriatingly, even though Jess lives like an errant teenager, smoking, rarely exercising outside the bedroom, drinking spirits and eating sugary food late at night – Krispy Kreme doughnuts are her favourite post-coital snack – she looks not exactly younger but fresher than me.

Angst is terribly ageing I thought, as I smeared a face pack on, carefully avoiding the crêpe-like skin around my eyes. Mind you, boredom is another zest zapper and while it's difficult to reconcile it with her personal irresponsibility, Jess thrives on the demands of her job. She is highly respected in her practice – and presumably responsible too. I, on the other hand, had injudiciously thrown my once promising future in publishing away when I got married and now had little left to show for it. After all, you can hardly have your decree nisi framed or inserted in your CV by way of explanation for a lengthy career dip, can you?

Jess warned me against shaving my legs: that way I wouldn't be tempted to go too far, too soon, but I got busy with the Bic. An insurance policy, just in case. I started cream bleaching my moustache, which she pooh-poohed as too high maintenance, but small beer when you consider that in New York they are into pre-date butthole bleaching. 'I can't do this any more,' I said, wiping the creamy gunk off my upper lip.

'Good, because he's unlikely to inspect your facial hair with a magnifying glass.'

'No, this!' I gestured to the beautifying paraphernalia spread around the room. Then, regardless of my carefully applied, non-waterproof mascara, I got weepy. Nearly twenty years, minus my fleeting marital break, of wondering if tonight's the night made me churn with despair. 'It still hurts that Jamie didn't fight for our marriage. I wanted him to fight for us.'

'No,' Jess said softly. 'You wanted him to fight for you.'

And there's the rub. I may be a Born-Again Single, I may be dolled up and drinking Rescue Remedy for Dutch courage but I can't override the fact that I feel a failure and a fool. I turned to *Dating Dharma*, held it against my chest and opened it at a random page. 'Everyone's story is completely different yet exactly the same. Isn't everyone searching for the same thing? To end up in the arms of the right partner?'

I got my coat.

# Chapter 1
# Sexual Sorbet

In the taxi en route to meet Troy Powers, I mentally ran through Jess's checklist of the Dos and Don'ts of the PDD. Do wear nice underwear, even though you don't intend to sleep with him. But if, God forbid, you do slip up and screw him senseless – at this point I had to interrupt and remind her that it was me we were talking about, not her – don't wear matching white bra and knickers, wear black.

I knitted my brows, confused. 'Isn't black shorthand for slut-speak?' I asked.

'That's the point. Men sleep with girls who wear black knickers, then marry girls who sport white. And you don't want him to marry you, do you?' asked Jess, fixing me with a stare.

I didn't dare admit that leaving Jamie hadn't put me off marriage – if anything it had made me even more determined to get my next marriage and underwear combo right.

'Do keep the conversation light and easy,' counselled Jess. 'Don't, whatever you do, swap divorce histories and notes on the final division of marital property. "I got to keep the champagne flutes but he took the Smythson albums once he had ripped out the wedding photos and torn my parents' faces to shreds." Do be upbeat, don't get maudlin. Don't give too much detail on anything and for God's sake keep away from personal revelation. Any Daisyesque: "my heart may be bleeding but inside there is a tiny throb of hope" is a complete and utter no-no. Men find that strain of emotional nuttiness as much of a turn-off as cuddly toys stacked on a chick's bed. But be yourself. Actually, don't be. Be a moderated version of yourself. Don't drink alcohol; you'll over-emote. Don't end up back at his place. But if you do, whatever you do, don't sleep with him because you can't handle anything as uncomplicated and gratifyingly good for you as slam-you-up-against-the-wall, no-strings sex.'

Twenty minutes later, sitting in front of Troy, having downed two vodka tonics in quick succession, I was in shock that the PDD would not only be this exacting but would make me feel so nervy and sad. It wasn't that Troy wasn't good-looking. He was. He had hazel eyes and grey – but zesty grey not over-the-hill dull grey – hair. He was fifty, which seemed sexy and seasoned to me. Like he was mature enough to know exactly what to do to you and how. His conversation was emotionally intelligent, which scores highly on my wish list. He seemed like the perfect Alpha Male. But he wasn't The One. I wanted that instant recognition because the thought of years of searching for my soulmate made me feel incredibly tired. I rushed to the loo and opened my *Little Book of Dating Dharma*. 'Rebound Relationships: Real or Revenge?' I read on. 'You may not be with your ex but are you still in competition with him?' Spookily accurate. I felt a surge of confidence. Sod the rules. If he wasn't The One, I was going back out there to enjoy myself.

I got the gory details of his divorce: his spoilt, stunning trophy wife thought he was married to his job and he was. They had everything except a relationship. He realised too late that the perfect union is more than money can buy. She left him for an accountant, which cut him deep, then cleared off with mega bucks. Work was his therapy.

'I made my first million by the time I was twenty-three,' said Troy, puffing out his chest. 'I had my own bond trading firm by twenty-nine . . . so you see, I've never failed at a job in my life and Amy quitting our "partnership" felt like being sacked from the biggest, most important job. Losing out on the best deal.'

'And it was something you couldn't control?' I added, helpfully.

'No way. Totally left field. So I studied the emotional paradigm. Spent a summer cross-examining myself. Troy Powers . . .' He put one hand up, then faced it with the other: 'On Troy Powers. What percentage of the breakdown was my responsibility?' He balanced his hands up and down as if they were weighing scales. 'Seventy thirty? Sixty forty?'

'Sixty-nine?' The words seemed to shoot from my mouth before I'd registered them. I also saw that I had linked my hands suggestively and was making a thrusting movement.

Oh God, what was happening to me? 'I'm sorry. I'm not myself . . .'

Troy gave me a wan smile, as if to say, forget about it. Moments of post divorce dating madness happen to us all.

Encouraged – clearly the trauma of divorce had softened him – I ignored Jess's dictum not to go into anything in too much detail and gave him a charged account of how I met Jamie.

*

I was working in the publicity department of a publishing company, Ludgate Press, organising book launches and press coverage when Candace, a girl in accounts, set us up. Jamie was a friend of hers who worked in a nearby advertising company. Although I initially resisted the idea of a blind date, Lucy and Jess forced me to go in a bid to purge Julius Vantonakis, my first love, from my system. Julius was the man I prayed I would marry but as he had spent my entire adult life messing with my heart and my head – saying he loved me yet screwing around with any top totty that wasn't me – I went out with Jamie Prattlock in a frantic bid to exorcise him.

We met in the foyer of Jamie's office on a Wednesday evening at six and the first time I set eyes on him, I didn't feel a connection. I didn't feel relief that the man I had been waiting for since I understood what a wedding was, was standing in front of me. I didn't feel that I knew him better than myself. I didn't feel as if my inner ache of loneliness was set to cease. I didn't want to get up, slap him, shriek 'What the hell took you so long?' and fall sobbing and laughing into his arms. There was no lightning bolt. No moment of recognition. There was absolutely nothing that I thought there would be. As he walked towards me, I did a quick inventory: nondescript black shoes; sexy long legs; badly cut navy suit; good Jermyn Street shirt with dreadful bulbous ceramic ladybird cufflinks; thick, brown floppy hair and great double-layered eyelashes. I remember thinking 'He's okay.' He's okay? Was my self-esteem in such freefall that I'd happily settle for okay? I wasn't choosing a sandwich filling or a new towel rail, was I?

My inner voice was screaming that chemistry was instant and we instantly had none but, for some reason that still poleaxes me, I said to myself that this could be the one. Why? Because on paper he was box-tickingly good? Was I was so determined not to disappoint my parents that I'd break my own heart, then theirs by default, by setting out to marry a guy who didn't touch the core of me but who did go to the right school? Yes, apparently I was that freaking shallow.

'Jamie Prattlock,' he said, extending his arm. I stood up and he confidently pulled me towards him. 'You must be Daisy?' He kissed me on both cheeks, then guffawed: 'Well, I bloody well hope you are.'

He smelt of strong lemony soap. I noticed he had cut himself shaving and the dried nick of blood on his collar was endearing.

'Sorry that I kept you waiting. Afraid am on bit of a deadline. Mind awfully coming up to the orifice?'

I followed him up the escalators and through to a vast open plan office. For such hives of activity, it's amazing that no one can ever enter an office unnoticed. Regardless of frantic deadlines, phones ringing off the hook, faxes jamming from over-use, people shouting, typing and swigging coffee from plastic cups, every time anyone new walks past the jumble of desks, everything goes into momentary slow mo as everyone automatically cops a look. I knew I was being clocked and so did Jamie. If anything, he moved with even more of a celebratory swagger.

'Piss off, Atkins, you common little creep,' he said, swatting an oily looking man who was sitting at his desk. 'Clear off and get Mizz Dooley a cup of tea.'

Jamie gestured for me to sit in his place. 'Just can't get the staff,' he said theatrically.

'Must file copy over here.' Did he always speak in this jaunty sing-song way as if he was dictating a memo? 'Why don't you email Candace first impressions?' he winked.

Jamie set me up with a blank email to fill in. While he typed away nearby, his long, artistic fingers darting impressively across the keyboard, I scanned his email address book. His friends all had names like Bunty and Joffy and Toadby and Fi-Fi and Wiggy and Minty, which should have been warning enough but then I saw we had a mutual friend, Mark Styles. Mark was a guy I'd known at university who was now working in New York. I quickly snuck into Jamie's inbox and saw an email from Mark with the subject: 'Doing Dooley (Doggy!?)' Naughtily but naturally I opened it.

*Jimmy, you sad fucker. Long time no hear. Yes, I do know Dooley. Snogged her once at a party but mercifully she was well pissed and is bound to have forgotten.*

*She's quite intelligent and not bad company – but very highly strung. Barking mad – her mother breeds mutts – but she's not a bad egg. She actually listens to what one says which I find discombobulating.*

*If you want to shag her, mention you're into the whole bag; family, kids, mortgage, etc. – she's big on commitment.*

*Good luck mate, you'll need it. See ya, Piles.*

I wasn't sure what shocked me more: how Mark Styles saw me or how Jamie and his mates corresponded. *Discombobulate*? As for *quite* intelligent? And 'big on commitment'? I knew the subtext – listen mate, watch out. She's past thirty and desperate to get hitched. I raked my fingers through my hair. Thing is, he was right. Mark blooming Styles, or Markie Piles or whatever nifty nickname these men-boys delight in calling each other, was bang on the nose. I *was* just like every other thirty-something bird for whom life wasn't hitting the spot. I was perceived to be successful enough with my trendy metropolitan job, respectable family, groovy friends and studio flat in Shepherd's Bush and yet inside I felt this huge gaping hole because I didn't Have It All. I didn't even have a boyfriend. I left every party and hailed a cab home, alone. Worse, I believed those *Cosmo* cover lines that it was possible to have the handsome hub and cracking career and for me, the race was on. Why was I in such a hurry? Why did I always have this fear that I was going to miss out on my own future? Why, instead of looking at Jamie Prattlock and running for my life, did I tap him on the shoulder and say: 'I didn't know you knew Mark Styles?'

'Marco Piles? Yah.' He swung around and glanced at the screen with the email still up.

I looked at him, then let out a mad bark. He started to laugh and in between my manic 'ruff ruffs' and 'woof, woofs', I laughed too.

'It only dawned on me when the decree nisi came through,' I explained to Troy, 'that he hadn't been laughing with me but at me. I thought we had bonded over a shared joke but the joke was always on me. In that moment, the pattern was set.'

I paused to register Troy surveying me, his head tilted to one side. Although it vaguely crossed my mind that he might be viewing me with disgust, it was too late. I had developed a verbal dating dysfunction, like a nervous tic that I simply couldn't control. I hadn't really tried to reign myself back in even though I had had an image of Jess, appalled, screaming: 'For fuck's sake, shut up *now*!' but nothing could have brought me to an emergency stop. I had hurtled down an icy highway of cringeable over-exposure. No detail had been too small or off beam to be overlooked.

I drained my glass. As the stunned silence enveloped us, I

didn't feel funny and vibrant any more. I felt unbearably silly and sad. Suddenly I knew the problem with the Post Divorce Date: you both told your story as that was all you had in common and then there was nothing left except the awkward emptiness of having told too much, too soon. Maybe Troy felt sorry for me because he said, not unkindly, 'Sounds like you two were a strange match.'

'Yes. We brought out the worst in each other,' I said lamely. 'Marrying Jamie didn't make me like him more; it made me like myself less. He bored me and once you bore someone, you can never unbore them, can you?' I looked up, barely able to make eye contact, as I knew that I had blown it. Troy must have been bored rigid.

He re-filled my glass. 'I can't imagine you boring anyone,' he said. 'You're so open, you need emotional contraceptive for protection.'

'It's the only contraceptive I do need right now.' I laughed bitterly. 'Men don't like candour. They find it threatening.'

Troy held my gaze. 'But I'm not most men.'

The minute Troy dropped me off at Jess's without attempting to kiss me or suggesting seeing me again, I fancied him madly. Was it because he was much richer than me? (Why do women feel that they have to hide their desire for a wealthy man as if it's demeaning to admit that actually, yes, we do get an erotic charge when he slaps his loaded Amex on the table because his ability to pay is part of his potency?) Or was it because Troy didn't make a play for me that I suddenly wanted him to? Either way, his air of controlled knowing was thrilling. His glinting eyes seemed to say: 'We both know I'll have you if I want you.'

I wanted him to want me more than anything because, even though I was the one who had walked out, the fact that

Jamie had let me go was a blistering rejection. That night, agonising over my date with Troy, I lay in bed and reflected that you have left a marriage long before you pick up your bag and walk out. Or in my case stagger down the stairs balancing an orchid, my wash bag and a plastic bag full of clean (greying) knickers. My legs were convulsing as I negotiated my way, not with nerves but from one too may sun salutations that morning. Did my body know before I did that I would return from a yoga class, eat a chicken sandwich and then leave my husband? Is that why I had trembled in 'downwards facing dog' and collapsed on to my head when trying to do 'bridge', arms shaking like jelly?

Where was the high drama? Shouldn't there have been shouting and sobbing? A few plates smashed and him on his knees, begging me not to go? Not to leave him. Not to crush the embers of our dream? But we both knew that the flame of hope was already extinguished and there was nothing real to fight for any more. Even though I wanted him to, he wasn't going to humiliate himself for me by lying on the floor and grabbing my calves like a child begging a parent not to go to the party. Not just because he was six foot two and could have dislocated my ankle had he tried but because he didn't care enough. That's what tore me apart inside. That he didn't come after me. Instead, he went into the kitchen and fried himself an egg.

My mother was waiting in the car outside. She gave me a brave nod of maternal reassurance. As I opened the boot of her mud-splattered station wagon, Donald and Dougie, her favourite long-haired dachshunds, jumped up, barking. I let them exfoliate my face with their tongues as I wedged the orchid against a giant sack of dog biscuits. I got in the front seat beside my mum. The car smelt of damp dog, urine-stained straw and dust. It was gag-inducingly familiar. I couldn't look at her. I didn't know what to say. I couldn't say: 'Sorry, Mum. You know that sixty grand you splashed out for the wedding of my dreams? Well, erm, there's been a bit of a cock-up. I forgot to marry the man of my dreams.' Instead, I said: 'Shit. I've left my handbag in the flat.'

'I'll go. You stay here.' As she got out, she knocked on the window of the boot. Donald and Dougie were staring motionless and wide-eyed with terror, as if certain they were never going to see her again, only the inside of a cage of Battersea Dogs Home.

'Wait here my angels,' she said in a loud voice. 'You keep Daisy company while Mummy pops out. Back in a sec.'

I took a deep breath. I felt sick. Not just a waft of nausea but a guttural, oh-my-God-I've-left-my-husband-what-the-hell-am-I-going-to-do-with-the-rest-of-my-life? vomit-making panic. Could this really be happening? Was I actually sitting in grubby yoga pants sweating pure terror? And if I was going to walk out on Jamie Prattlock on a Sunday afternoon in late April, why couldn't I at least look the part? Why couldn't I be pinging with energy, all honed and toned beneath my Juicy Couture tracksuit à la J-Lo or Jennifer Aniston? Why do I always compare myself to some A-list celebrity, as if I'm living my life under public scrutiny? There were no paparazzi waiting to snap my tear-stained face, no famous friends carrying out my belongings, no chauffeurs whisking me to a mansion in obscurity where I could get a face lift and face myself. It was the sudden realisation that it was my very ordinariness, my absolute everyday ability to fuck up like everybody else that made me want to weep.

And then I heard her. It was the wild, protective roar of a lioness whose cub is wounded and she's out for the kill.

'All I ever asked of you was for you to love Daisy and even that was too much for you.'

'Your daughter's a bloody lunatic . . . Her problems make . . .' My mother and Jamie were shouting so loudly you could hear them half way down the street.

'And your problem, young man, is that you never learned to give.'

'Who the hell do you think bought this flat?'

'Give of yourself. You haven't a clue what real generosity means. Daisy left because she couldn't stay but she's the most loving, decent girl around and you destroyed . . .'

The tears were coming so fast that I couldn't hear any more. My heart had split in two. Not because I had married a man who did not love me enough to fight for me, but because my mother did.

The morning after my first date with Troy, Jess and I met Lucy for cappuccinos and confession. I had given Jess a highly edited version of my conversation with Troy when I returned to her flat after my PDD. 'Late night?' Lucy pointed at my red-rimmed eyes. I admitted to an earlier avalanche of tears. 'So you didn't like him?'

No. I did. What I couldn't stomach was being in teenage angst mode, strung out about a man again. At first, I had relished the emotional drama of being in an unhappy marriage with Jamie. All the rows, hurt, deranged splitting of hairs, then passionate making up, was an antidote to my boredom. But then the drama became the most boring thing of all.

'But you don't have to get emotionally involved with Troy,' Jess said.

I explained that even though it petrified me, I wanted to sleep with him. Actually, I needed to sleep with him to eradicate Jamie from my system.

'A sexual sorbet.' We looked at Lucy blankly. Apparently,

in Los Angeles, this is how they refer to the first person you sleep with after a break-up; someone who cleanses away the after-taste of a bad relationship. Jess pointed out that you could still sleep with someone and not get emotionally involved. My inner jury is out on that one. I think it only works for angry men and mummy's boys.

I whipped my latest self-help fix from my handbag. A bestseller called *The Phoenix Syndrome: Rising from the Dust of Divorce.* Jess groaned. 'If you're going to start spouting psychobabble, I'm off.'

'It's all about erotic intelligence,' I said.

'Speak English, please.' Jess banged her fist on the table.

'Hush, you might learn something,' said Lucy, adding: 'I think I need a shot of this.' Jess raised an eyebrow. Lucy, noticing her reaction, said, 'There's nothing like married sex to make you lose confidence in yourself.'

But at least Lucy and Edward were happily married (weren't they?) so she didn't need to get up close and confident with anyone else again, and I did.

The whole gig with erotic intelligence is that it empowers you to emerge from a juicy encounter with your dignity intact. If you have low EI, you're so grateful to be fancied, you would do anything. Behind your back, or worse, to your face, it is clear your date thinks you are easy or ugly – or both – and he would never take you to meet his mates or his mother. A high EI is about maintaining steely self-esteem in the face of attraction. It is the Oxbridge of flirting; a Double First in seduction. Obviously, after last night's fiasco of getting hammered with Troy and verbally unpacking all my emotional baggage pronto, I scored perilously low.

'You didn't even kiss him, so how can you bang on about any erotic encounter?' snapped Jess.

I argued that the subtext of a first date is desire. What is left unsaid is what matters. You need to be wired to that invisible current of sexual tension to the point where you long to be touched.

'Well, he's obviously got high EI,' Jess got up to leave. 'He's got you exactly where he wants you.'

'Where, *exactly*?'

'On standby for his call. Ready to put out the minute he's ready to put you out of your misery. Gain some erotic advantage. Make him wait.'

Later, on the train going home back to Mum's, I was beside myself that I had bared my soul with Troy. He hadn't wanted to kiss me because I hadn't stopped mouthing off about myself and my marital mayhem long enough to let him. Had my instinct for verbal honesty become a dating disability? I used to give good date but now that I had Divorcee Despair tattooed on my forehead, I couldn't maintain an iota of feminine mystique. A few drinks and I became every man's confessional, not minx or mistress material.

Would I have been similarly wound up if Troy had been a road sweeper? Was I lusting after him or his lifestyle? I dipped into my *Little Book of Dating Dharma*. 'Don't measure your self-worth against someone else's net worth.' Spot on. My mobile rang. Troy? No. It was Mum, wondering when I'd be back.

It's not just being unsettled in life that wakes me early at Mum's, it's also the incessant yapping of dogs in the kennels. Mum's well known in the dog-breeding business because Diana Dooley's dachshunds have a certain cachet. They certainly project arrogance like no other dogs I've ever seen. It's incredible how a fat, stunted sausage dog – a melodramatic little log of fur – can look at you with haughty superiority as if raising a wiry eyebrow and curling a long snout in disgust. They just know that they are distinguished. Not just because they get full-page write-ups in *Dachshund Daily*, which, presumably, they can't read, but because they never let her down. The inference being: unlike your dad.

So Dougie and Donald and Dominic and Doughnut and Des and Deborah and Desdemona and Diandra and Dennis and Dusty and Daniel and Damon and Denny and Delia and Delphinium Desiree (an award-winning bitch – literally) and all the other bloody Dooley Dachshunds will never let my mother down. They can piss up against the beds and stain the valances, crap on her Aubusson rugs in the drawing room, dig up her favourite peonies, throw up acid-green grass-filled bile on the sofa and chew the few decent pairs of shoes she has to mulch, but they will never let her down. Emotionally, these wire-haired, smooth-haired and long-haired beasts are rock solid.

My scientist father, Derek, however, is not. Nearly two decades ago when emptying his pockets to take his jacket to the cleaners, Mum discovered that Dad was being unfaithful. When she asked him if he was having an affair, at least he had the decency not to lie. He was sitting at the kitchen table when she dangled two 'French Letters' (as she calls them) in front of him. He slowly looked up from his ploughman's, betraying no alarm. When she asked, 'Can you give her up?' he paused. Probably only for a few seconds but for my mother it was an eternity. He wasn't fighting for her. He wasn't stumbling over his words because he couldn't get them out fast enough to tell her that he loved her. That it was all a hideous mistake. No, in his very male, measured, academic way, he took his time. And in those few precious moments, he broke her heart. I think she could have got over the infidelity but it was during that hesitation before his reply that he lost her. When he finally answered, 'With difficulty,' their marriage of twenty-two years ended. Mum simply picked up her handbag and walked out of the house. She didn't return until Dad had packed his bags and left us and our family home. She carried on walking in court shoes (she never seems to have the right shoes at the right time – she once went to a wedding in an evening gown and Wellington boots) for over two miles until she got to a phone box and rang a girlfriend. My parents never spent another night under the same roof again.

When Dad tried to explain that the difficulty arose because his lover was a scientist with whom he was collaborating on an important research paper, unsurprisingly his defence didn't hold much weight. Did he honestly believe that my mother would understand that he didn't want to end the relationship because that might jeopardise his research? As usual, he put his career first. Needless to say, the fact that his scientific and bed partner happened to be twenty years Mum's junior, didn't endear us to him much either.

So now home feels like a hostel for brave women who haven't been fought for by their men. It's totally gloomy waking up in my childhood room with faded rose wallpaper and gymkhana rosettes hanging off the headboard, when my friends are pushing prams around the park. It used to be a treat to come home before I was married but being forced to live at home as a divorcee makes you feel retarded and claustrophobic. In a short marriage (or sorry mistake) like Jamie's and mine there is no great financial settlement; you get out what you put in. That left me with just enough money to live off for a year or longer if I lived with Mum. Unlike Jamie, I wasn't cushioned by inherited wealth and, again unlike Jamie, I had given up my job at the publishing house after we married – at his behest – so living back in the country was a lame last resort.

Everything in this house is tired and dusty but that's okay because the tag line screams old money. The chintz may be faded, the beds lumpy, the linen sheets partially threadbare but none of that matters because everything is *right*. Nothing jars because nothing is new. We're not *nouveau riche* but *nouveau pauvre*, which here in the Cotswolds is infinitely better. What does it matter if Mum can't afford to take a decent holiday or have hot water on tap (these gargantuan oil-fired boilers cost a fortune to heat) when she wears blindingly large diamond rings ingrained with dirt and dog hair to do the gardening? Her Hermès handbag is ancient and the leather is cracked but when she goes into town in her cheap catalogue fleece and M&S skirt, people who know, know in a nanosecond that she's one of them.

Whenever I come down for breakfast, Mum is never dressed. There simply isn't time. She's always in a thick, green dressing-gown, Wellington boots and pearls slung around her neck, a vivid slash of pink across her lips.

'So, how was the date with the bond trader?' she asked on that particular morning, boiling up some stinky meat on the Aga. 'What was he like?'

'Intelligent. Rich. Amusing. Successful,' I answered succinctly.

'Oh, dear,' she sighed. 'Best leave well alone.'

'I'm sorry? Have you got a dog biscuit lodged in your ear?'

'Don't think I don't see the attraction of a man like that,' she said, huffily. 'I was young once too, and of course, men like him – powerful men – have always been a temptation. But these are men who would hurt you, if necessary, to get their way.'

'In business, yes, but not emotionally,' I countered.

'He's a deal maker. For men like that their whole life *is* their business. They can't distinguish between one and the other.'

I stood up, agitated, because deep down I knew Mum was right. Troy said his wife had left him because he was married to his job. But I didn't want to marry him; I wanted to win him. To prove to myself that I could. Mum followed me into the hall. 'Don't make my mistake. There's no greater loneliness than being with a man who puts his career first. Playing second fiddle gets awfully demoralising over the years.'

I put my arms around Mum because I knew that nearly twenty years on there were pockets of tenderness that still hurt. 'I just want what's best for you, Daisy.'

'No,' I said, gently pulling away. 'You want what you think is best for me, not what I want for myself.'

I went upstairs. And what *did* I want? I wanted to be free. Free of my obsession with out-scoring Jamie. I wanted not to care that he appeared to have got ahead; that he was happier, more successful and more loved-up with a new partner than I was. I wanted to be happy for him, instead of bubbling up with rage and envy that he had a life. I flicked through my battered copy of *When Leaving Is Lifesaving*, hungry for a nugget of wisdom to enlighten me. 'When no one wins, both partners take the prize.' I had to walk away mentally, to finally let go. That would be my prize.

I sat on my bed and leafed through our photo album. Some loose photos from our last Christmas on holiday in Barbados fluttered out. Jamie and I, framed by a glorious blood-red sunset were on a boat to see the snapping turtles. (I couldn't get into the water as the turtles snap when you have your period, which, typically, I did.) God, on paper we looked effortlessly good. But I'll never forget lying on the beach, staring at the exquisite turquoise sea, able to see the beauty but being utterly depleted by it. Neither Jamie nor I had the energy to pretend any more; in fact we almost bonded in our inability to inject any life into our union. We were lolling in luxury but you could taste the deprivation. Jamie must have been as lonely and despairing as I was, I thought.

I knew that I may have regrets but I couldn't help myself. I started ripping pages out of the album as I was in a hurry to heal. I couldn't let this man and my wasted dreams take up any more of my time. (However, I was tempted to save a couple of snaps of me in my bikini in Barbados and a few of me in my wedding dress as the chances were that I'd never look that thin or my hair that bouncy and perfect again.) An hour later I was standing in front of a roaring bonfire, cheeks glowing from the heat. I hurled our wedding video, with the caption 'Daisy and Dickhead's Big Day' in Jamie's scrawl, on the fire, followed by boxes of photographs of us together. I watched the corners crinkle and the rivulets of coloured ink turn black as they dripped into the heat. Little pieces of charred paper floated up from the funeral pyre of my dreams. When I saw photographs of my hated ex-mother-in-law Lavinia Prattlock, I let out a whoop of joy. Hooray! I would never have to endure heavy roasts and endless games of Boggle at lunch with the Prattlocks again.

Suddenly, I plucked up courage and threw my wedding album into the centre of the flames. Finally, nearly a year after I left Jamie, I was burning off the karma of our union. Complete closure may not ever happen like it does in the movies but this felt close enough. I tried a little handstand of excitement but my arms gave way and I toppled sideways into the compost heap.

I was clutter-clearing my bedroom – yes, my worn Snoopy and my first Valentine's card had to go if I was to move on and get a life worth living – when my mobile rang. I saw Troy's number flash up but let him leave a message. 'Hey, Dooley. What's up? Listen, baby, your post-divorce dating defence was so good the other night, I want to give you a full cross-examination. How about meeting at my personal chambers, next Wednesday, at eight?'

I couldn't wait.

'Don't forget, men rarely appear as good-looking on the second date,' said Lucy, raking her fingers through my hair and jamming in heated rollers.

'We build them up in our minds in the space between dates,' nodded Jess, 'and then it's like "euch, what's with *those* shoes?"'

We were crammed into Jess's tiny bathroom – again – as Lucy tried to glam me up and Jess tried to calm me down before my all-important second date with Troy. Lucy tugged and teased my tresses, snipping off a few split ends, while Jess launched into a menacing monologue that would have raised the roof at any self-empowerment seminar for staying single.

'Get this straight in your noodle, Daisy. You are not looking for love. You are looking for a good time.' She grabbed a make-up brush and started jabbing it against my arm. 'If a good time involves a one-night stand, you must, at all times, keep your emotional distance. If you can't remain detached, he will think you are a needy, easy lay . . .'

'If she sleeps with him tonight, he'll have a point,' said Lucy, busily backcombing.

Jess threw her a look before continuing her diatribe to me. 'If, God forbid, you are immature enough to resort to beer goggles – remember it doesn't matter if they slip off, as long as the condom stays on.'

'I won't sleep with him as I've got my period,' I said.

Jess shrugged. Since when was that a deterrent to any action in her book?

'Well, at least you can't get pregnant,' Lucy said.

I sighed. Post Divorce Dating suddenly seemed so tacky and undignified. 'Don't you understand?' I said as Lucy continued her ministrations. 'I don't have time for a good time. I'm nearly forty.'

Jess jerked her head backwards in horror. 'Haven't got time for a good time? You really are a saddo, Daisy.'

'Look, I know how to give good date,' I tried to explain. 'I know how to be witty but not so funny as to be threatening. How to challenge yet not dominate. How to hold my knife properly' – do men notice or even care? 'I'm a sophisticated neurotic, if nothing else. I know how to eat a globe artichoke, how to fish out meat from lobster claws, but the point is that I'm too tired to play these mating games any more. I just want to find The One and get on with the rest of my life.'

Lucy put down the comb and grabbed my copy of *Dating Dharma* from my handbag. She held the book against her chest, then opened it randomly. 'Perfect! This was meant for you. "Live out the glory of your imagination. Not your memory."'

'And your point is?' harrumphed Jess.

'It's telling me that my past – my painful divorce – does not have to govern my future,' I said sheepishly. 'That I can create something meaningful in my life if I believe in it enough.'

'Right,' Jess slapped me on the back. 'Then go out and practise having something meaningful with Troy but don't be stupid enough to believe it'll mean something to him.'

Lucy turned me towards the mirror. 'Goody. You've got artfully dishevelled Come-To-Bed-Because-I've-Just-Got-Out-And-Look-How-Fabulous-I-Look hair.'

'So, I'm supposed to look like a slut yet act chaste, but if I do slip up, I'm to take it on the chest – I mean, chin – like a man?'

'You got it,' smiled Jess. 'Casual sex is meant to satisfy the libido not engage the heart.'

Lucy raised an eyebrow. 'You should know.'

'I've had roughly fourteen partners in five years,' said Jess. 'That is not promiscuous, it is spaced.' She opened the door and pushed me through it. 'Okay, ditsy Dooley. Ready for anything.'

What Jess didn't understand was that as much as I wanted to move on, I was scared of physical intimacy. After a brief monogamous marriage to Jamie and over a year of celibacy, I felt as inexperienced and ill equipped as a Born-Again Virgin when it came to hitting the high notes in the sack. I longed for teenage-style affection, where snogging wasn't a means to an end, it was an end in itself. In those sepia-toned, inexperienced days, there was no such thing as a good Merlot, a brazen double entendre and a swift transition to the bedroom. But now, when I was old enough to have the menopause in sight, I couldn't exactly fob a guy off with only hitting first base after an expense account dinner, could I?

The fact that Troy didn't take me out to some swanky restaurant but cooked me dinner at his home threw me completely. His bachelor loft cum lair was intoxicating. He had a good eye; vast canvases were strategically placed around the expanse of white walls. I couldn't stop staring at one of a rugged slice of Cornish coastline, near where his parents lived. The sea, a deep lavender colour, swirled angrily against dark jutting rocks. There was passion and poetry in the painting – which I instantly read to mean that Troy had taste and sensitivity. He also cooked girlie food: swordfish with puy lentil and beetroot salad, scattered with tufts of fresh parsley, which I found strangely touching.

When I went to 'wash my hands' – i.e. check my hair and reapply spot concealer – I did a quick snoop and mental inventory of his pad. He got full marks for reading matter – along with business tomes, weighty classics and dodgy thrillers, he had a well-thumbed copy of *Chemistry Or Karma?*, the new bestseller on sex and spirituality on the bedside table. Hmm. Promising. Maybe Jess was wrong and he *was* looking for a soul connection, too? In the bathroom he had thick, matching white towels, decent French soap and when I came back to the dining table I saw that he had laid the table with linen napkins, water glasses and serving spoons, which men always forget.

The champagne was chilled, a Coldplay CD was spinning and Troy's conversation was smooth and funny. He asked me when you know you've become a woman, which I thought was a great, incisive question. I said, 'When you realise Daddy isn't a god or Mummy's first choice, after all,' and we fell about laughing.

I don't know if I was wearing beer goggles, or just alcoholic pince-nez, but I found Troy seriously attractive. He was bigger set than Jamie, not fat but broad, and seemed such an open, unedited person. After Jamie and his emotional constipation, it was an incredible relief. That Troy had a pulse and seemed sensitive – and was plying me with champagne – sent me into another orbit. I was desperate for him to take me in his arms and hold me tight.

'So Daisy,' he said, adopting an authoritative tone, 'tell me what you hate most about dating?'

I giggled. 'Am I under oath?'

'Yeah, you're under an obligation to tell me the truth, the whole truth . . .'

'And will it lead to a full examination later?' I ventured bravely.

Troy grinned, 'You bet, baby.'

'You'd be shocked,' I said.

'Really?' he said, excitedly, scooping his last mouthful of chocolate pudding on to his spoon. 'Try me . . .'

I leaned towards him and said in a loud whisper. 'Secret shitting.'

Troy put his spoon down. 'What?'

I explained I hated the artifice that when you first went out with someone you had to pretend that you were too perfect to poo. You may have spent the night with them and they had probably navigated the contours of your naked body inch by inch but there was still that insurmountable intimacy barrier to conquer of them knowing that you were in the loo, doing a 'big job' or a 'jobby' as my mother still insisted on calling it. Many is the time I've held it in and suggested we go for a morning coffee, only to hurl myself down the stairs and into the loo the moment we hit Starbucks.

Troy was wiping tears of laughter from his eyes. 'Well, I guess I asked for that. You're quite a character, Daisy Dooley.'

He stood up and put his hand out. I took it and the next thing I was in his arms and he was kissing me. I could feel the energy of his heart melting into me like warm honey. There was something strong and reassuring in the way we moulded together. Well, it felt meaningful enough to me. He stopped kissing me but I didn't want to let go. I hadn't realised how lonely and bereft of physical affection I was. I started to cry. At first it was a mute snuffle, which gathered pace into full sobbing and runny snot.

Troy nuzzled my neck. 'Listen, if it's too soon . . .'

'No, no, you don't understand. I'm crying because . . . because my husband never once held me like that.'

*

'I can't believe you slept with him.' Lucy shook her head.

'I can't believe you didn't use a condom,' hollered Jess. Did the whole coffee shop really fall silent, swivel and stare, or did I imagine it? Either way, my cheeks were puce and my head was pounding.

I closed my eyes and plunged my fingers into my sockets. Quite how I could have lost my emotional foothold so soon – on the second date – and tumbled into bed with a virtual stranger, was beyond me. I had never behaved so badly before I was married to Jamie, so why did being a divorcee make me unstable and erratic, as opposed to seemly and erotic?

When Troy had led me to his bedroom, I had followed in a daze. Because he had seemed so nurturing when I was crying, soothing me and stroking my hair, I trusted him. 'We don't have to do anything,' he said. 'I just want to hold you.'

Ah yes, that old chestnut. In my state of addled naivety, I fell for it as fast as the conker falls from the tree. At first, when we lay together, whispering and giggling, it felt safe and romantic. But I had forgotten how predatory a man in boxer shorts in the dark can be. Before I knew it, he was coaxing me here, easing underwear off there, kissing me, caressing me, turning me on. When it came to the crunch, I protested that we should use a condom but he was going in all guns blazing. 'Ah, baby, I just want to fill you up,' was his jarring *cri de cœur* as he came.

I suppose, pathetically, I was partly flattered. I assumed that a man of his substance knew full well the consequence of crossing the line of no return. It even occurred to me that he had made a deliberate decision – let's roll the dice of life and see what happens.

I tried to protest to Lucy and Jess that the situation wasn't irredeemable. Clearly, Troy held me in high regard. Despite the fact that he was in the middle of a large deal and had to take some important sounding calls during dinner, when we retired to bed, he switched the phone to silent. All night it rang, but only the lights twinkled on and off, like fireflies glowing in the dark. It was kind of romantic.

'Being with Troy felt truly intimate,' I argued. 'When he held me, I felt like I was lying in the arms of a mature man who could take my emotional weight.'

'Not to use a condom is hardly mature.' Lucy looked away, disgusted.

'I know, but Troy got all macho and urgent about it.'

'Daisy, your gullibility is a dangerous liability,' said Jess.

'Has he called?' Lucy raised an enquiring eyebrow.

'No!' I said, as if I didn't expect him to – yet. 'It's only eleven and he's doing some massive deal.'

I didn't dare admit that I had my mobile in my pocket on silent and vibrate and had been waiting to hear from him since the moment I left his flat. Each hour that passed without a sexy little text spoke volumes. Who was I trying to kid? No man is that busy that he can't type two words which will change a woman's whole emotional landscape. 'Miss you.' 'Call later.' 'Call me.' 'Big kiss.' 'Great evening.' 'Great tits . . .' Well, maybe that wouldn't be as reassuring but it would be something. And anything is better than nothing in the contact stakes.

I felt terrible. The whole brouhaha of the Post Divorce Date had got me in such a tizzy that I had blown everything. Could Lucy and Jess be right? Was Troy just seeking some naughty heat, while I was craving the reliable warmth of a relationship?

As a teenager, Mum had drummed into my head the mantra that with men you had nothing to lose and everything to gain by resisting. I knew full well that a woman asserts her self-respect and subsequent standing if she makes a man sing for his supper. In fact, I had taken her dictum to heart to such an extent that I remained a virgin the whole way through university. I had underfloor heating in my college room and guys would come back after supper and we'd lie on the floor, close enough for me to feel their breath on my face, and while I longed for them to make a move, they never, ever, even kissed me. My body language was so buttoned up that while I was dying of celibacy inside, berating myself for my total inability to exude the slightest whiff of come-hither (let alone cum-thither) they were writing me off as the starchiest girl on the campus. No wonder I was the student that they all took home for Sunday lunch to meet their parents. They could be fully secure that with a repressed bluestocking like me lunch would go without a hitch, but as soon as they'd dropped me back after tea, they'd swing by some other chick's room and pin her to the floor. I'd be left alone, pining.

So what the hell was happening to me that at nearly forty, I had offered myself up on a plate to Troy? The neediest dish on the menu?

I tried to lighten things up by revealing that Troy was into manscaping.

'I must get Edward on to that. Our laurel hedge has gone crazy,' said Lucy.

'No, men who wax their chests and even . . . elsewhere,' explained Jess. 'Did he have a back, crack and sack wax?'

Lucy and I winced. 'No,' I said.

'Don't look so shocked. That's what modern women expect nowadays,' said Jess. 'Men who shape their pubic hair.'

'So Troy's a metrosexual?' asked Lucy.

'Nope, but he's into his home comforts and himself. Big time.'

'He's selfish?' Lucy laughed. 'Then he's definitely heterosexual.'

If it wasn't bad enough facing Lucy and Jess for coffee, I then had to go and meet my father. Ever since Mum and Dad divorced, my regular lunches with my father had all the levity of a tax inspector's coffee break. It was as if since he had betrayed Mum, the knowledge that he had let himself down too meant that he couldn't quite face me. Before Dad left, I wasn't really aware of his presence, but his absence in my life became deafening. As a child, he was just there; not centre stage like Mum, but in the background, hiding behind a newspaper or in his study reading or in the garden badly pruning the roses. He had this strange aloofness that meant that he didn't like us to engage with him outside mealtimes, so we never did. This disjointed communication, which felt slightly false then, even under the same roof, felt unbelievably stilted now. I never looked forward to going to see him but I always left tinged with sadness for what might have been or, on a good day, still might be. In some sadistic way, I held him partly responsible for the fact that I chose to marry a man like Jamie. After all, it's not as if I had the perfect male role model to emulate, is it? Recently, it dawned on me that despite their intellectual differences, Jamie and Dad are not cut from too dissimilar a cloth.

One thing that unites them is their steadfast devotion to their mothers. I knew from a young girl that if my mother, my grandmother and I were drowning in a river, it was a no brainer for my father whom to rescue first. His mother. Jamie would be just the same. If Lavinia Prattlock were in some churning swell, head bobbing about, gasping for air – freeze that glorious frame for a second! – Jamie wouldn't give it a second thought. Mater would triumph.

On the tube to South Kensington, I tried not to think about Jamie and replayed the night before with Troy in my mind instead. God, it was true that he *had* been less lovey-dovey in the morning. He hadn't wanted to spoon or snuggle but he did run me a shower and offer me some expensive herbal shampoo. When he packed me off into a taxi, he blew me a kiss and mouthed that he'd call. Yeah, right.

Walking to the restaurant, I tried to bolster myself up. Well, who wanted to date a guy who made funny putt putt noises when he kissed, anyway?

Dad was already seated at his usual banquette in Thai Temptations, the Thai café where you could eat all you wanted for £7.99. We had been meeting in this depressing joint with its formica tables; red ripped plastic banquettes; fake lotus flowers; unflattering, concentration-camp bright lighting and tired Thai waiters for years now. Somehow, it had become an intrinsic part of the ritualistic discomfort of seeing my father. Amongst the students hoovering up the ghastly, greasy grub, there was always some reedy chain-smoking chap trying to cop off with an acne-ridden tart in the corner. Dad remained oblivious. In a crumpled suit, soup-stained tie and plastic shoes, he managed to retain a patrician bearing, despite the flecks of prawn cracker falling from his lips.

'Ah, Daisy,' he said, rising to greet me.

A bit like Jamie, Dad speaks in a theatrical way but his manner is even more clipped. That's because he's used to lecturing his science students, so he speaks e-m-p-h-a-t-i-c-a-l-l-y, to ensure you fully comprehend everything he is trying to say.

'I walked here from the London Library,' he said, unprompted. 'Took a bit of a detour round Green Park and then came via Victoria. Obviously not as scenic as walking through Hyde Park but I estimated it shaved three, maybe four minutes off the journey.'

As usual, as he rambled on, I looked as if I was listening when in fact I was deaf from the tedium. When he asked me what I was doing in London, I gave another highly edited, rather depressing version of the night before. 'Yes,' he said. 'I'd imagine that at your age, being single again, especially if you want children, is quite difficult.'

Bingo! 'Everything is difficult,' I said.

Oh shit. I could feel myself welling up. I dug my spoon into my acidic Tom Yum Gong soup and took a slurp. Phew, it was spicy. I wafted my hand in front of my face, as if chilli were the culprit.

'You're a very brave girl,' Dad said, his pale eyes steady.

'The soup's not that hot,' I replied, but I knew what he meant. Why did I pretend to misread him? Because I don't know how to handle any expression of his love as it comes so rarely? Because I'm so accustomed to fighting men that I don't know how to acquiesce? To let any man, least of all my father, help me shoulder the strain?

'I admire your courage,' he continued. 'Most people settle in life because they don't have the energy to seek something more. They don't believe that they will find, let alone deserve, anything or anyone better. You do. I'm proud of you, Daisy.'

I concentrated hard on my tears as they fell into my soup. Had I really just heard the words that I had craved from my father for my entire adult life?

# Chapter 2
# The Sperminator

It was over a month since my sexual slip-up with Troy and he still hadn't called. Simply beside myself, I had written a myriad of elaborate 'Hey, remember me, big boy?' texts which I deleted as Jess had forbidden me to contact him. Every time I was tempted to call, I had to ring her instead. She had even added a caveat to her answerphone message: 'And if it's Daisy calling, leave him alone. You're a fully consenting adult who willingly spread her legs. No man revisits a needy lay.'

Jesus! It was the only time that I thought the unthinkable when I heard it – thank God that both her parents were dead. I mean, imagine facing them for tea after they'd rung their daughter for a chat, only to discover *that* about you?

Smarting from the sting of rejection, I had taken to my bed at Mum's, a library of self-help books to hand. Although I kept reading and repeating to myself rousing truths, like,

'It's not the world around that causes pleasure or pain, it's your reaction to it', I couldn't help reacting to the fact that I had fallen into the arms of the first cad looking for a frolic. I had thought that fellow divorcees spoke the same language. When we first kissed, I imagined that beneath the passion lay mutual understanding. Tread carefully, was the subtext; emotionally, we've been derailed. Clearly, Troy was back on track, intent on getting the first available, hare-brained fool into the sack. There was no alliance, no emotional empathy in his mind. No doubt deranged divorcees were considered wincingly easy prey.

Felled by my sluttish behaviour, most days I felt too humiliated to move. Mum regularly found me sobbing on my bed or hyperventilating on the bathroom floor. As my Pavlovian response to stress is to pick my face, I had hacked at non-existent pimples, leaving angry, red craters on my forehead.

Mum came in with a dachshund-shaped hot water bottle and a cup of soup. 'Oh Daisy, not again,' she said, gesturing to my face. I shrugged. What did it matter if my forehead resembled a war zone? I couldn't have felt any more ashamed. 'Nothing lasts for ever,' she soothed, stroking my limp hair.

'They'll be gone by tomorrow,' I said, applying toothpaste to the spots which now looked like white mini molehills.

'No,' she said. 'I mean the pain.'

That weekend, she summoned Jess to lift my spirits. Jess, who was born in South London and is a smog-riddled townie through and through, just doesn't do the country. She looked absurd in black opaques and a purple mini, legging it across the fields, while I trailed behind in an old 'Dooley's Dachshunds' sweatshirt, the dog logo stretched too tight across my chest, and a pair of faded cords. 'At what point do intelligent, educated women wake up to the fact that the knight in armour just ain't gonna show?' she shouted, before crouching by a hedge to pee. 'Why do you buy into the dream, Daisy?'

'So I can feel even more inadequate than I already do?' I managed a weak laugh. 'I mean, I know what's important in life – loyalty, a giggling fit with a girlfriend, a sense of spiritual connection, being able to communicate with your Guardian Angel' – Jess grimaced as she came back from behind the hedge – 'okay, okay,' I teased, 'enhancing your intuition or listening to your spirit guide,' – she pretended to throttle me, 'wait,' I shrieked, 'honouring kindness, practising patience, caring how you feel inside instead of obsessing about how you look on the outside, blah, blah, blah. But I still feel a failure because I can't get the right man. Sure, I got *a* man to marry me. Just not *the* man I wanted to be married to for the rest of my life.'

We sat down on a stile. Jess lit a fag. 'Why have you always been in such a rush?'

'I don't know. I was so hung up on having the big wedding, I overlooked the marriage.'

Jess threw her head back and screamed: 'Why, oh why, Jamie Prattlock?'

'Don't you think I haven't asked myself that a thousand times? Why did I marry a puzzle-book addict pushing forty, who thought that whacky clothes gave him a personality.' I turned to Jess. 'Because I wanted to belong.'

'To that prank-playing type?'

'I know, okay. I somehow thought that if I got married, I'd feel like everyone else. I'd feel normal.'

'No chance.' She patted me on the back. 'You need a fuck buddy.'

'Why?'

'Because you're not getting any and it's safer and less tacky than a one-night stand.'

Oh, please, I thought to myself. A free-love friend? Free love or loveless freedom? 'But is it any more thrilling or emotionally captivating than using an animated vibrator?' I replied.

'Probably not,' said Jess. 'But look at me. I have enough sex to stay single. It feels safer that way.'

'Does it really?' I raised an enquiring eyebrow. 'Is loneliness safe?'

'I'm not lonely,' she countered. 'I just haven't got time for emotional intimacy. Getting to know someone is so all-consuming and often a waste of time because they're not all they're cracked up to be. I like my job and my life and I love sex. But I'm not bothered if I have a boyfriend or not. I need servicing and regular re-fuelling, not connecting on all levels with a bloke.'

'So you never feel empty after a one-night stand?'

'Hardly, if he's worth his salt or his seed,' she giggled.

'No, I mean emotionally empty,' I said.

She shook her head. 'Usually, I feel relieved when they leave so that I can get some sleep. I hate spooning, men snoring, the way they get sweaty and push the covers off leaving you cold, then leave little chest hairs all over the bed. And unlike you, I certainly don't want to lie entwined, discussing meaningless guff until dawn.'

'I don't believe that if the right guy came along, you wouldn't trade independence for interdependence.'

Jess groaned: 'No. How often do I have to tell you? I'm not like you, Daisy.'

'But you don't take any real risks and is a life without risk a life worth living?' I stood up.

'Oh, cut your Californian crap,' she said. 'Have you got over your risk of unprotected sex with Troy?' I looked away. 'Tell me everything is okay.' Jess grabbed my arm. 'It is, isn't it? No false alarms . . . now you're scaring me. Daisy, everything *is* okay. Isn't it?' I didn't know if everything was okay and while I reassured Jess it was, I had a funny feeling it wasn't.

It was weird that before I married Jamie, we never discussed having children. We didn't do that gaga googoo baby speak, in which we fantasised that we'd have cute mini mes in our offspring of potential Poppy or Piers Prattlocks. We didn't lie in bed discussing what schools they'd go to and Jamie never once grabbed my tummy muffin hanging over my jeans and called me Mumpty, but still, I always assumed I'd have kids. Or rather, it never occurred to me that I wouldn't. Once the engagement ring was on my finger, I didn't give it much thought but in the back of my mind must have been the latent belief that, one day, I'd give birth to a Prattlock. Everything changed on the honeymoon, however, as I knew the moment I'd shaken the last speck of confetti from my hair that I'd made the biggest mistake of my life.

At first, I couldn't give vent to the notion. I couldn't admit to myself that I had been *that* silly and short-sighted, could I? Like a spoilt child who asked for a Barbie for her birthday, only to realise the minute she started brushing Barbie's hair that what she really wanted was a Snoopy. Needed Snoopy, even.

We were sitting on a chairlift in Colorado where we were skiing, it was Christmas and on the surface, all was idyllic. The wide skies were sea blue and the snow-capped mountains took my breath away. Literally. I couldn't breathe. Here I was snuggling up to the man whom three days earlier I had professed to love in front of four hundred people and I couldn't get my breath. Nothing to do with the altitude, I felt as if I was suffocating.

I looked across at Jamie. He was wearing a red wool Santa's ski hat with a long dangly bit that wound round his neck as a scarf. Jiggling his legs so that his skis swung back and forth, he took his poles in one bulky mitten and tapped my arm with the other.

'Okay, old girl?' I managed a smile. No one would have thought that I was crying on my honeymoon because it's normal for your eyes to water on the chairlift. The wind does that. But in fact, I was winded by my own stupidity. I wanted to feel happy. Christ knows, in that moment I would have given anything in the world to feel that this was right but it didn't *feel* like a honeymoon was supposed to feel.

We played the part of British newlyweds with award-winning zeal. On a mountain peak or outside a chalet-style café, Jamie would hand a stranger his camera. 'Would you mind?' He would pull me into the frame, wrapping an unfamiliarly protective and presumably husband-y arm around me. 'Would you mind awfully taking a picture of the *wifey and me*?'

As we stood smiling polished smiles, I ached inside. More than anything I wanted to feel proud of Jamie. I wanted to feel like a newly minted wife should feel; high on hope and expectation. I wanted to be able to squeeze his hand – admittedly, difficult through Gore-Tex gloves – and for that squeeze to mean everything.

How could I admit to Jamie I'd got it all wrong when I couldn't stomach the truth myself? Deep down, did he know? Did we both recognise that we had not married our soulmate? Did he feel lonely too? It sounds laughable, lonely on your honeymoon? The very place that you are supposed to feel absolutely at one, alone, together. But that was the point. I didn't feel united. I didn't feel that the man larking around in the snow, pelting me with snowballs and trying to do silly turns was my other half. My better half.

How could I have been so foolish? By the time I married him, we had been together for a year, so I knew that he felt he could express himself in garish floral shirts and themed hats instead of opening up emotionally. I knew he was saying, 'Hey, I'm a pretty witty laid-back kinda guy,' as he put on his felt 'bone head' hat before he went off to ski each morning. I knew by then that he wasn't what I wanted. And vice versa. That we weren't ever going to look like a power couple, him in a soft navy cashmere overcoat, underneath which he was slick and Armani clad. I'd offered to buy him a jacket for Christmas and he'd chosen a cherry red duffel coat with a hood instead. Obviously, when we walked down the street, people weren't thinking, 'what a striking couple', they were trying to fathom what the hell I was doing with a six foot two Little Red Riding Hood in drag on my arm.

Perhaps if I hadn't been so wrapped up in the mire of my mistake, if I hadn't craved Jamie to be something he wasn't, I could have shared his humour. Or at least I could have *tried* to find the hilarity in a man in his fourth decade in a green Kermit sweatshirt with a padded frog sewn into the front pocket. It wasn't as if I didn't know the code among these public school types. The point they are making by their whacky paisley waistcoat or purple velvet suit is that they can afford to stand out sartorially because, background-wise, they fit in. If you come from the right family, what does it matter if you go to the cinema or the supermarket in ethnic mustard-coloured tapestry slippers?

Regardless of Jamie's pantomime persona, everyone we came into contact with in Colorado bought into the marital dream. Who wouldn't see a honeymoon couple as if through gauze, marvelling that they must be *so* in love? No. Why should anyone else spot the fault lines of pain already pushing to the surface of our fractured story?

*

A couple of months after the honeymoon, Miles, one of my oldest friends from university, came over for coffee. He was then living in Hong Kong where he had become rollickingly rich as a banker and was on a fleeting visit back home. From the moment I had set eyes on Miles Kingly nearly twenty years earlier, seeing him drunkenly stagger across the quad in dishevelled black tie, I had fancied him. Even watching him puke into a fountain, then snog a slutty student in a strapless dress with one tit falling out, didn't put me off. Miles, the son of a stockbroker, had that boyish yet manly appeal; long limbs, scruffy hair and sunburned forehead, usually from doing something sporty like sailing or windsurfing. He sweated sex appeal. He was one of those men who have always been funny and good-looking enough to know that from pubescence to the grave, and probably beyond – with the undertaker or embalmer if she was female – he was going to pull. As I had all the sexual charisma of a dead snake, it never occurred to me that Miles would look at me *like that*. No, my only redeeming feature was that I could tease with the best of them. So, if I wasn't going to get laid, at least I could get the laughs in.

Miles, who still had that youthful appeal in his late thirties with his short, tufty hair, suggestive smile and crinkly laughter lines, surveyed the neat-freak perfection of my marital abode. With a vase of white lilies on the table and proudly displaying my new Limoges wedding china on the coffee tray, I felt a moment's smug pride. He sank back against the chocolate suede cushions on the sofa, his fingers nagging at the chenille throw carefully positioned on the arm. 'It's like a museum in here,' he said. 'I'm surprised Prattfuck can get it up in there,' he said, gesturing to the bedroom. 'Does he dare ruffle the covers?'

'He does on both counts,' I said.

Miles shook his head in disbelief and told me that his latest shag was unable to have an orgasm. 'Yeah, she's on Prozac.'

'Why?'

'She can't deal with her anger.'

'What about? Not being able to have an orgasm?'

He laughed.

'Oh, Miles,' I said, 'you do pick 'em.'

'And you don't?' I looked away. He leaned towards me. 'Marital bliss or marital hiss?'

'It could be worse,' I said. 'I just have to accept that Jamie will never understand me. Anyway, I adore this flat. I'm incredibly happy here.'

'When Jamie isn't?'

'Yes,' I giggled.

Miles's eyes danced and he looked at me with such warmth. 'You know what your problem is, Daisy? It's the sort of thing you'd say yourself: you sacrificed your emotional state for a piece of real estate.'

And he was right.

How long could I go on deluding myself that because the flat was Feng-shuied to death, because I had pink crystals in pairs in our relationship area, because I had red geraniums for fame and fortune in the window boxes, because I had done abundance rituals burning balls of sage and incense and forced Jamie to clap out old spirits from the corner of the room, then crouch and chant with me at dusk and dawn, that we were going to be okay? We were already running on empty, our relationship was in the red. There was no couple's credit in the bank.

This was finally driven home to me when I asked Jamie almost a year into our marriage if he thought we'd have children. We were having coffee on a chilly Saturday morning, sitting outside by the Serpentine in Hyde Park. When I broke the heavy silence by asking about potential parenthood and what might our plans encompass, he put his cup of coffee down and stared ahead: 'Daisy,' he said, wearily. 'Unlike you, I try to live in the present. And frankly, it isn't that great from where I'm sitting between us right now, so I prefer not to think beyond this cup of coffee.'

I was stung by how little he cared. It's one thing living in the present but how can you build a future with someone, let alone your husband, who has no dreams to share?

This wasn't really happening, was it? I would do anything in the world for this not to be true. I would never again wilfully gossip and say bitchy things in my regular rap 'n' yap sessions with Lucy and Jess. I would make a concerted effort to give Mum a hand in the kennels and muck them out at least once a week. I would let Mum's dogs, Donald and Dougie, sleep on my bed with their smelly snouts on my pillow, never pushing them on to the floor. I would never pick dry skin off my heels again or squeeze my blackheads. I would listen to people on the phone doing telesales or surveys. I would do whatever it took to pay off my karmic debt. Anything, anything but this.

I had prayed that it was a false alarm but having watched the indelible blue line creep up five pregnancy kits, on five consecutive days, who was I fooling? I was pregnant. I had to face it. The shock immobilised all sensation, as if I was having an out of body experience, yet I was burning up with heat and freezing cold at the same time. I lay back on the bathroom floor. It wasn't supposed to be like this. This didn't pay tribute to the fantasy script I had played out in my mind for years. Where was the husband – now the second husband but obviously the soulmate – who would come home from work as I smiled ecstatically from the top of the stairs? He would call out, 'Darling, I'm home,' and I would reply, 'Darling, I'm pregnant.'

He would roar with joy and bound up the stairs and take me in his arms. At that moment, he would never have loved me more and I would never have felt more adored, or stronger or more vulnerable in my intoxicating fertile state.

But this . . . there was no husband, no soulmate. I was a thirty-nine-year-old divorcee living back at home, lying on a dog-hair-covered bathroom floor, feeling cold and sick, pregnant after a post divorce one-night stand. It couldn't get any worse, could it? How on earth did my life CV, which once looked so promising, get so stained? I crawled back to bed and called Jess, who insisted I come straight to London.

On the train, I tried to make sense of my splintered scenario, dipping into *Faith in the Future*, a new book about trusting life. 'Life is unpredictable . . .' No kidding. I read on. 'We get tripped up when we are most convinced our foothold is sure. It is not what happens to us, it is how we deal with it that counts.'

How was I going to deal with this? I wasn't ready for a baby, was I? My life was shot to pieces. But an abortion? At thirty-nine? What if this was my only chance? What would I tell Troy? And my parents? They were going to go berserk. The stupidity, the irresponsibility. Sorry, Mum and Dad, a year ago I had a nice home and a husband and a decent life and now look!

Lucy collected me from the station and took me to Jess's. By the time I arrived I had cried so much, I had tiny shreds of tissue sticking to my blotchy face. 'I thought you said you had your period when you slept with Troy?' said Lucy.

'I did,' I sobbed.

'You can't have done,' said Jess. 'It must have been break-through bleeding.'

'Does it matter, doctor?' I said, tetchily. 'Because the fact is that I'm bloody well up the duff.'

Jess hugged me as she led me to the sitting room, which, typical of her Bohemian style, was awash with mounds of stale newspapers, overflowing ashtrays, stained coffee cups and dusty plants in dire need of water. What raised it from feeling like a careless student abode were the decent antiques dotted around and the wildly expensive French tapestry hanging above the fireplace.

'It could be a sign,' I said as I slumped on the kilim-covered sofa.

'Sick joke of fate more like,' spat Jess.

'Maybe a baby could bring me the inner peace I crave.'

Lucy almost choked. 'The one thing a baby won't bring you is peace.'

'But how do we know that this isn't meant to be?' I wailed.

'A marriage didn't save you, a baby won't either,' said Jess.

Lucy sat beside me. 'Listen, Daisy. Goodness knows you've had a rough ride. But a bad marriage you can undo. As you know, that's difficult enough. But you can never undo having a baby with the wrong man. A baby is a lasting commitment. It is real till death do us part.'

Lucy handed me more Kleenex. 'I'm not saying don't have this baby . . .'

'Well, I am,' interrupted Jess.

'Jess,' said Lucy, archly, 'just because you're a doctor and trained to take a clinical approach, you mustn't over-ride Daisy's emotional state.'

'Daisy's emotional state is what got her into this in the first place,' said Jess, clearly put out.

'I'm merely saying . . .'

'And all *I'm* saying . . .' continued Jess, throwing Lucy a look.

'Hey, you two, I'm still here,' I sniffed.

'All I'm saying is that you must make the right decision for you, for the right reasons. This is your call, Daisy,' said Lucy firmly.

Jess gave a 'whatever' shrug but her lips were pursed.

Oh Jesus, I thought, how am I ever going to survive this? Especially as the next call I needed to make was to Troy.

As I stood outside Troy's front door, I wondered how I was going to break it to him that I was pregnant. I knew I had to tell him face to face – you can hardly drop the baby bombshell over the phone – but it was torture. Breaking the ice of my own shock was bad enough without having to face his terror too. 'Hello, Troy. Remember me? The needy divorcee? We only met twice and the second time I fell into your arms, then into your bed and guess what? I'm knocked up.' I was dreading the sight of the anguish ripping across his features.

He buzzed open the door and was standing in running gear, a small towel around his neck. Flushed and dishevelled, with a thin shadow of stubble, he looked athletic and sexy. His face cracked into a wide smile, which stopped me in my tracks. 'Daisy Dolittle. What a surprise! Come on in.' He seemed genuinely delighted to see me. So why hadn't he called?

He beckoned me to follow him into the kitchen and opened the fridge. Devoid of food, it contained bottles of champagne, beer, wine and water. 'What can I get you?' Troy grabbed a bottle of Evian and gulped it back.

'Nothing, thanks. Erm, Troy, we need to talk.' I was desperately trying not to stammer.

'Indeed we do,' said Troy, putting his arms around me and guiding me to the sitting room, towards the sofa. He smelt great; slightly sweaty yet manly. He threw on a shirt – his chest looked buffed, so he needn't have bothered. 'Daisy, I owe you an apology. I've been so caught up with this damn complicated deal that I never called. I've betrayed your trust. Forgive me.' He took a white amaryllis from the arrangement on the glass coffee table and handed it to me.

My heart was beating so fast that I thought the sofa might begin to shake. 'Troy . . . I'm . . . well . . . I'm . . .' I said, laying the amaryllis back on the table as bits of water were dripping from the stem on to my skirt. 'Troy, I'm . . .'

Troy was looking at me, as if seeing me for the first time. Staring into my eyes with patience and interest, as if to say: 'Go on, I'm here. I'm hearing you.'

'Actually, I'm . . . I'm . . . pretty thirsty after all. Can I have a drink?'

He returned with a bottle of champagne and filled two glasses, handing me one. I guiltily knocked it straight back. (One glass couldn't do much damage, could it?) My hands were trembling. 'Troy . . . I'm . . . I'm . . .'

Suddenly, he leaned across, put his fingers to my lips to quieten me and kissed me. I felt instantly relieved – and massively turned on. Must have been all the new hormones flooding through me. I could feel myself wrapping myself around him, tighter and tighter, unable to let go.

Laughingly, he gently disentangled himself and pulled away. 'Hey, what's with you?' He stared at me. 'Actually, you look great, Dooley. Really pretty. I don't remember your tits looking this hot.'

Oh God, I couldn't string this out much longer. Perhaps there was nothing to fear after all and I'd got it all wrong? Maybe there was a teensy smidgeon of hope that he might be into me after all? 'Troy, I'm, I'm . . .'

'Not ready to date? I figured as much.' He nodded knowingly. 'We went too far too soon. I'm sorry. It was my fault. I couldn't resist you.'

'No, Troy, listen.' I stood up.

Troy got up, too, and stood before me, cupping my face with his hands. 'You're a great catch, Daisy. Original, oh *so* sexy. So when you're ready to settle down again, just let me know.' He tucked a stray wisp of hair behind my ear. I thought I was going to explode.

'No. Look, there's no easy way to say this . . . I'm . . . I'm pregnant.'

Troy froze. 'You're *what*?'

'You heard.'

'*Pregnant*?' The silence was deafening. And endless. 'Pregnant?' He turned and walked away, his back to me. I don't know how I managed to stay standing as my knees were quivering so much. Then, he turned around to face me. 'Pregnant?' he hollered. I stared past him, out of the huge glass windows, and fixated on the view of surrounding rooftops. Time stood still. I could hear a funny whooshing in my ears. It must have been the pressure.

Suddenly, Troy leapt into the air and punched it with his fist. I couldn't believe it. He whooped and shrieked with joy. He even did a cartwheel. Then he scooped me up into his arms. 'Honey, this is fantastic. Unbelievable.'

'You're pleased?'

'Ecstatic! Aren't you? Boy, I've always wanted to be a father.' He gestured towards his crotch. 'Wow, at least I know it works. I was beginning to wonder.' He gave a throaty laugh and a thumbs-up sign. I sank back on the sofa. My whole body seemed to collapse, freefalling with relief.

'Daisy,' Troy knelt before me and took my hands in his. 'This is just the beginning for us. A new start. After all we've been through . . . This was obviously fate, meant to be. We've both had a bad relationship experience. We've been hurt and this is the reason that we've met. To help each other heal and to eradicate the past. And what better way to do that than with a new life? This is incredible!'

I was staring at him, mouth agape. He began to stroke my cheek, running his fingers lightly across my face. 'I know that it must be frightening for you. After all, you're going to have to bear the brunt of this but I want you to know that I'm going to be here for you every single step of the way. I know its unconventional having a kid before a relationship but with enough effort we'll make it work. I promise you, I'm going to do everything in the world I can for you and our sprog.'

I tried to get up but I couldn't move. I wasn't in Troy's flat at all but sitting on a bench in the park nearby, dreaming of Happy Ever After. I looked at my watch. Troy said he would meet me at seven in a nearby wine bar. He sounded short on the phone but didn't ask why I needed to see him. Probably too busy to care. He said he could give me twenty minutes before an important work dinner. I felt sick. Not just a wisp of ante-natal nausea but a deep, guttural panic.

I was quaking with fear and unbearably hot, as the wine bar was packed. In my terror, I wondered if I had BO? I tried to surreptitiously sniff my armpits but couldn't get close enough, without being too obvious, to tell. Fingers crossed not. All I knew was that sweat was coursing down my back and my cleavage felt sticky. I sipped a bitter lemon to appear occupied. Bad choice. It made me even queasier. In despair at the sluggish passing of time – every second seemed an eternity – I got my copy of *Faith in the Future* from my handbag and opened it. '"Your vision will become clear only when you can look into your heart. Who looks outside, dreams; who looks inside, awakens." Carl Jung.' Tears began to prick. My heart was hurting so much all I could see was my stupidity. All I could feel was my pain. And still part of me couldn't believe that this was happening to me.

I looked up. Troy was real enough, walking towards me in an expensive-looking grey suit. Power and success emanated from him. Women turned to look at him as his magnetic appeal, like heady cologne, wafted in his wake. He seemed so sure of himself, so intact and unburdened by life, that I had a stab of jealousy. I had never felt less sure. He checked his Blackberry, quickly tapping something in before he even looked at me. Then, he sat down and said, 'So shoot.' He leaned back and waited.

I felt a flush of panic. Colour rose to my cheeks. The pressure was worse than being interviewed for my dream job, whatever that might be. In that moment, I realised that I wanted Troy to want this baby. Not just because it would mean that he wanted me, but more because then he would make the decision for me. For us. Rather than against us. Until then, the thought of having an abortion had never really been a possibility for me. Terminations happened to other girls. To stupid sluts. They didn't happen to dopey divorcees like me.

'There's no easy way to say this. I'm pregnant.'

Troy gulped. 'You're *what*?' Troy began drumming his fingers on the table. 'Is it mine?'

''Course,' I said, insulted.

'Have you done a test?'

I put my hand out, stretching my fingers and mouthed 'Five.'

'I thought they were only ninety-seven per cent accurate?' he said, swiping his hand across his forehead.

'Troy,' I said slowly, trying to get the notion into his head. 'I. Am. Pregnant.'

For such a cool customer, who was presumably used to

dealing under pressure – the man was a top bond trader, for Christ's sake – he lost it. 'This can't be happening . . . I'll do anything in the world for this not to be true.'

'You're not the only one, kiddo.'

Troy put his hands to his ears and started shaking his head from side to side, like a child refusing to listen. 'I can't deal. Can not deal. No deal. No deal.' His leg, jigging madly up and down, kept hitting the edge of the table.

The waiter, who was passing, gave Troy a quizzical look. 'Double vodka. No ice,' snapped Troy.

I batted away a plume of smoke that wafted over from a neighbouring table. Troy leaned in towards me, his eyes narrow. When he spoke, his voice was ice cold steel. 'You were out to trap me all along, weren't you? You selfish, bitter bitch. I should have listened to Edward Primfold. He warned me you were mad.'

I'm sorry? Was I really hearing this? I stared back, mouth hanging open. He paused, while the waiter gave him his vodka, which he downed in one.

'What is it with you crazy divorcees? You don't want men, do you? You just want walking wallets. You, with your wound-up body clocks and shrivelled ovaries. All you want is some decent seed and for us to shell out for the rest of our lives. You don't want husbands,' he was spitting now, 'you just want sperminators.'

'Are you out of your mind?' I shouted as tears of shame and temper coursed down my scarlet cheeks. 'What was with the "I just want to fill you up, baby"? You weren't accusing me then, were you? When you wanted to ride me bareback?' He narrowed his eyes. I raised my voice above the din of the bar. 'You were the one who refused to fuck me with a condom,' I screamed. Troy put his hand out, as if to shut me up.

'It may surprise you, Troy, but it doesn't fit my game plan to get pregnant right now,' I continued, vaguely aware that the couple at the next table had stopped talking and the woman was staring at me. 'But it's happened and yes, it's a bloody shock but it's a new life and you'd be prepared to throw that away without consideration?'

'I've got nothing to offer you,' he said. I let out a bitter laugh. Nothing to offer? 'Obviously I'll pay for the . . . erm . . . you know.'

The woman at the next door table interjected, 'Abortion, dickhead.'

Relishing her sisterly support, I stood up and shouted: 'It's all about the money with you, isn't it? Don't you get it? I don't want your money you pompous prat.' I threw my glass of bitter lemon in his face. He jerked his head in shock. Two women at another table clapped and cheered. 'All I wanted was some support.'

I turned, broken inside, but tried to hold my head high as I walked steadily towards the door. Once outside, I hurried around the corner and was violently sick in the gutter. Afterwards, shaking, I leaned my forehead against the cool of a nearby brick wall. I had never felt more alone or out of control in my life.

When Edward Primfold opened the door and saw me, he visibly shuddered. Mascara streaked my cheeks, my eyes were red and bulbous, I was puffy with tears and my skin was blotchy from stress. 'Daisy, what on earth's happened?'

I pushed past him. 'Why the hell did you set me up with Troy in the first place, if you think I'm mad?' As I caught a glimpse of my tortured face in the mirror, not a million miles from Munch's *Scream*, it briefly occurred to me that he had a point.

Lucy rushed into the hall. 'What's happening? Daisy, whatever is it?' She put her arms out and I fell against her, hysterical.

Edward, snug in olive green cashmere, stared at me, trying not to wince, as if I was not human at all but some sort of violent species. I felt a surge of anger. How dare he stand there in judgement? How lucky for him that in his smooth life path mapped out at birth: private prep school, public school, Cambridge, the City, along the way picking up the pretty wife who pushed out some perfect kids, he had never succumbed to anything as unruly as angst. Why has it all been so easy for them? As Lucy led me to the calm perfection of their first-floor drawing room with the heavy Old Master oils, over-stuffed sofas and matching side-tables with jasmine plants wafting heady scent, I felt ruptured to the core of my being. Edward and Lucy, sitting on their damask sofa, eyeing me with silent horror, had always expected to be happy. They had been fully secure in their destiny, whereas I must have doubted mine somewhere along the line or I wouldn't have been sitting there, the savage outsider, sobbing into my sleeve over my monumental mishap.

'For your information, Edward, I am pregnant. Your friend, Troy, is the father. Apparently, you told him I was mad. I'm not mad enough not to sleep with, it seems, just too mad to call afterwards. Apparently, with bonkers bitches like me, you can refuse to use a condom and then blame the consequences on the old bag for being so batty in the first place.'

Edward leaned away from me, visibly disgusted. 'Well, let's face it, Daisy, you are rather highly strung. You've always been a drama queen.'

Taken apart by his callous comment, I managed to blurt out, 'No, Edward, it's called having a pulse.'

'Edward,' snapped Lucy. 'Go and get us a drink.'

'So Troy freaked out?' asked Lucy, when Edward had left the room.

'Yup. Pinned his colours right to the mast. Doesn't want to know.' I sighed. 'Oh God, Lucy, what am I going to do?'

'I don't know, darling,' she said softly. 'Listen, take your time to think about this. There's no rush.'

'Oh, but there is,' I said, deeply pained. 'Every day that I'm pregnant it makes the decision more difficult. I'll get attached. If I'm seriously going to consider an abortion, I'm going to have to do it sooner rather than later.'

'You're in shock,' said Lucy. 'Or knowing you, denial.'

'Maybe,' I sighed. 'But part of me feels almost detached. It's as if the only way for me to deal with this is to make a brutal decision and not allow myself to get over-emotional. I feel quite unlike I've ever done before. As if I've gone into some weird survival mechanism. Perhaps that's the only way for me to stomach the shame.'

'It's Troy who should be ashamed not you,' Lucy pointed out.

'But to have an abortion. It's so . . . so . . . ugh, undignified and awful.'

'You'd be surprised who's had them,' said Lucy. 'I'm constantly amazed by girlfriends' revelations after they've had a few drinks. Most have had them in their early twenties before they were ready to settle down, when they had years ahead to try for another baby with the right guy. This is a tougher call for you when you're nearly forty.'

'Can you believe that Troy thought I was out to trap him?' I said, starting to cry again.

'Rich men always do,' said Lucy flatly.

'How come you got it so right?' I whimpered.

Lucy paused. 'It's not always what it seems.' I had never heard her sound hollow like that before. 'Listen, Daisy, I know you're hurting and your life seems a mess but please, don't envy me.'

'But I do,' I wailed. 'You've got everything. A good marriage, two beautiful kids, this house, a great life. You've got it all.'

Lucy stood up and shut the door. 'And you've got choices. That's the greatest freedom of all.'

'Are you saying you feel trapped?' I said, shocked. We could hear Edward walking back up the stairs.

'Believe me,' whispered Lucy, 'nothing comes without a price.'

In the taxi on the way back to Jess's flat, where I was staying as I couldn't face being at Mum's, I couldn't get over what Lucy had said. If she wasn't happy, what hope was there for the rest of us? Jess, who was away at a medical conference, called as I was scanning the empty, alcohol-filled fridge wondering what on earth I could eat. 'Baked beans and a bagel from the deep freeze?' she offered helpfully.

I told her about Troy. 'No surprises there,' she said.

Then I told her about Edward and Lucy. 'I've always had my doubts about steady Eddie,' she said. 'He's so squeaky clean. He probably buffs his own balls.' I managed a weak laugh. Then Jess asked: 'How are you doing?'

I stared into the unappetising pan of beans. 'I've never been more scared. I'm afraid to have this baby. Look at me: I'm in no state to be a mother.' I choked back grief. 'But I'm even more afraid that this will be my only chance to have a child.'

'That's not a good enough reason to go ahead,' said Jess. 'You know, our biological clocks speed up when we perceive time is running out. But they slow down when we believe we have all the time in the world. You have plenty of time, Daisy. You must remember that.'

'What if this is my last chance?' I asked, pressing my hand against my heart.

'You just have to trust that it won't be.'

I suppose I knew before I received Troy's email saying, 'If you have this child, I'll fight you every single day' that I wasn't going to keep the baby. Although the decision was agony, I felt it was right – for me – to make it. Of course, I wanted a baby but more than that, I wanted to be a good mother. I wanted to be like my mother, who was patient, centred, kind and wise – not scatty, selfish and unsure of herself and her future, like me. I honestly didn't think it was fair to a child to bring him or her into my anguished world. And as I didn't feel the feral kick of maternal desire above all else, I had to trust my instinct that for me, the time was not right.

Jess drove me to a private clinic in Chelsea. Troy has sent me a conscience-salving cheque for five grand, so at least I could have my insides hoovered out in safety and style. 'That was an expensive date for him, then,' she said.

'Hardly. He got off light. It was a lot cheaper than a lifetime's child maintenance and care,' I pointed out.

'Does he know you're doing it today?'

'No. He's so callous. What does he care, as long as it's done?'

Eva Cassidy was singing 'Over the Rainbow' on the radio and as I stared out of the car window, the streets seemed to be teeming with pregnant women and couples pushing prams. Were there always this many mums-to-be staggering around that I had been oblivious to, or had I only just woken up to the fact that every other woman in the world was breeding but me? We stopped at a zebra crossing and a man lifted a baby up in his arms, blowing kisses. Eva was singing 'and wake up where the clouds are far behind me . . .' and I was crying inside. Tears were shedding from my heart, flaking off like shards of glass.

Everyone in the clinic was frightfully proper and polite which made it worse. I made my payment at the desk by credit card and they assured me that it would appear discreetly on my bill. Like pay-per-view hotel-room porn. Behind the atmosphere of studied calm, amid the glossy magazines, the elaborate flower arrangements and strategically placed brochures about contraceptives and sexually transmitted diseases, the air was one of unmistakeable sorrow. As I sat in the waiting room I could almost feel that the women who had waited on these leather seats had similarly been silently screaming with future regret. There was an expensively dressed City type in her early thirties, next to a pin-stripe suited man, who at least had the decency to look ashen. Neither made eye contact with the other. It was the wedding ring that gave him away while she wasn't wearing one. It gave me strange comfort to imagine him bricking it – what if his wife found out? At least he, too, could be reassured that she wouldn't suss it if she was poring over his credit card statements. The man was holding his lover's hand – well, his sat limply in hers – as they stared tensely ahead and I wanted to shout, 'At least you could hold it like you mean it. You meant it when you were banging her, didn't you? I bet you had a bit more lead in your pencil then.'

The silence was suffocating and as I was in danger of losing it, I rushed into the loo and dry heaved over the sink. I stood there gripping the side of the porcelain, staring at my face in the mirror. This couldn't be me, could it? When was I going to wake up and be in another life? My rightful, easy, uncomplicated, much-to-be-proud-of life?

Jess came in and stroked my back. 'I want to kill that man

out there,' I said. 'Happily screwing her with no thought for the future or his wife. Sitting there all meek and terrified, when in an hour he'll probably be some big swinging dick in the boardroom, masterminding some massive takeover.'

'Come on, Daise,' Jess said gently. 'That City slicker played her part too. She knew what she was doing.'

'That's just it,' I said, tears splashing into the sink. 'She may be qualified to the hilt and a total star at work but we're all capable of making these terrible mistakes, aren't we? I mean, the university degree or the great job doesn't qualify you for a successful love life, does it? There's no guarantee against this sort of pain.'

Jess took me in her arms and held me tight. 'I love you, you mad bugger,' she whispered. 'You didn't deserve this.'

I stayed with Jess afterwards, sleeping fitfully. I lurched forward, my head pounding with pressure. 'Daisy, wake up, it's okay. It's just a bad dream.' Jess was shaking me by the arm. I looked around her spare room and wished it was just a bad dream. The surreal horror of the clinic and the termination I had had the day before came flooding back.

The doorbell rang and Lucy entered, her face full of tenderness and concern.

'Are you okay?' she kissed me, then handed me a bunch of daffodils.

'Yellow. The colour of hope,' I said, bleakly.

Jess and Lucy smiled nervously, as if to say 'It'll be okay.'

'It was supposed to be different,' I said, staring at the flowers. 'My life wasn't supposed to be like this. I no longer feel like I know who I am or how I should be.'

'Give yourself time,' said Jess, pouring me a glass of water. 'It takes a while for the anaesthetic to wear off.'

'I'm still not speaking to Edward for setting you up with

Troy,' Lucy said, sitting on the bed. 'I had no idea Troy Powers was such a complete cowardly, craven, condom-eschewing . . .'

'Cunt?' interrupted Jess.

Lucy pulled a 'you've got a point' face.

'What does Edward think about Troy?' asked Jess.

'Oh, nothing bad. He feels sorry for *him*,' said Lucy. 'Men never judge their male friends. Haven't you noticed?'

'You're right,' agreed Jess. 'Men totally accept their male friends. Women always want to change men, whereas men buy into "what you see is what you get, dude".'

'That's because men are too short-sighted to see the beauty of potential,' said Lucy.

'But at least they're not disappointed when that potential goes unrealised,' I said, bitterly.

When Lucy left to go and collect her girls from school, Jess followed her – they obviously wanted to talk about something – clearly me. I got up and wandered aimlessly around the room. Standing by the door, which was ajar, I heard Lucy and Jess whispering urgently in the hall outside. I edged closer to the door and stood, straining to listen.

'It's un-bloody-believable timing. I daren't tell Daisy, but Katie is pregnant,' hissed Lucy.

'Who's Katie?' asked Jess.

My stomach did a sort of lurch cum spasm. I knew exactly who Katie was.

'Jamie's girlfriend.' I heard Lucy answer.

'Jamie's girlfriend is pregnant?' repeated Jess, incredulous. 'Crikey. She didn't waste much time.'

'She's forty-one. Enough said,' sighed Lucy.

Jess tut tutted: 'Honestly, the childless women I see in my surgery amaze me. Don't they realise that if you are a woman with a brain, you are a mother in conflict?'

'No, because you don't realise that until you've had the child and it's too sodding late,' snapped Lucy.

I didn't hear the rest of Jess's tirade against the barmy biological clock brigade because I fainted. The next thing I knew was that I was sitting up in bed and Jess was administering an ice pack above my right eye. Apparently I hit my forehead on the door handle as I fell. 'Your bruise is going to be a beauty,' she said, proudly.

'I can't believe that Jamie is having a baby with Katie, when he never wanted a baby with me,' I wailed. 'I feel I did the right thing by not backing Troy into a corner, when Jamie is probably having his baby because he's too weak to fight.'

'No surprises there. You've always gone for men who need women to give them back their balls,' said Jess, carefully reapplying ice.

'Are you saying I'm not turning into my mother but my father with ovaries?'

She nodded and I managed a laugh.

Later, I couldn't sleep because I felt so empty and alone. I wanted to cry but no tears came. I tossed and turned for hours, before it dawned on me. There was only one man I wanted to talk to. I needed to hear it from him that everything would be all right. I picked up my mobile and dialled his number. When he answered, his voice reassuringly slow and thorough, I went to pieces inside. 'It's Daisy. I need to see you . . . No. Everything is not all right.'

# Chapter 3
# Raising the Rasa

I was convinced that the only person liable to break my heart on my wedding day to Jamie was my father. Surely this was going to be our once in a lifetime chance of emotionally bonding because it was such a momentous occasion? I had worn waterproof mascara because during the drive to the church, I just knew that Dad was going to tell me the words I longed to hear. Wasn't he? Fathers and daughters on their wedding day? Bring on the Kleenex! I'd had the whole thing scripted for twenty years.

*Act One*

*The bride gets into the car with her father. She is beautiful; in a full-length satin dress and glittering tiara. He is bursting with pride. He takes her hand.*

*Father*
*Daisy, I've never seen you look more radiant than you do today.*

*The bride beams.*

*Father (cont.)*
*I know I've never been that good at expressing myself . . .*

*The father's voice falters . . .*

*Father (cont.)*
*But I want you to know how proud I am of you.*

*A tear trickles from the corner of the bride's eye. Her father leans over and gently wipes it away with his handkerchief.*

*Father (cont.)*
*I know we've had our ups and downs over the years but I've never stopped believing in you.*

*The bride muffles a sob.*

*Father (cont.)*
*You're a one-off. I love you, Daisy Dooley.*

*Bride, her eyes glistening, looks at her father.*

*Bride*
*I love you too, Daddy.*

*The car draws up at the church. The peal of wedding bells fills the air. The photographer captures the bride's smile as she beams at her father.*

*Father*
*Jamie is a very lucky man.*

*Fade out.*

Actually, it went like this.

*Act One*

*The bride gets into the car with her father. She's not sure if she looks beautiful because her father hasn't said anything except 'wow!' wide-eyed like an owl. 'Wow!' fabulous? Or 'wow!' freaky and thoroughly over the top? The father sits, looking very tense. He obviously hates all of this. The train is folded into the car and the door shuts. The car gently motors forward. The bride leans forward to speak to the driver.*

*Bride*
*Would you mind opening the window? It's so hot in here.*

*The driver nods and opens the window. A gust of icy wind blows wisps of hair from the bride's chignon, untangling it from her tiara.*

*Father*
*I shouldn't do that, Daisy. It's messing up your hair.*

*The bride snaps, tense.*

*Bride*
*I know but I'm on fire. My mouth has gone completely dry.*

*Father*
*It's nerves. Actually, I was pretty nervous myself at one point this morning. I was driving here along the M4 and heard on the radio that there was a terrible crash on the M25. I looked at my watch and thought 'I don't want to get caught up in that jam as I could be late for my own daughter's wedding!' I was so agitated I ate a whole pack of Fisherman's Friends, so my mouth was on fire, too. I took a calculated decision to get to the M25 at Junction 16, then go the other way and cross over to the M40 so as to miss the problem. Obviously not a direct route as the crow flies but as there was a five-mile tailback and by this time . . .*

*Bride (screams)*
*Dad! Can you please be quiet? This is the most important day of my life and I've got to get my head together.*

*Bride thinks bitterly: if you're not going to tell me what I've waited the last two decades to hear, you can at least shut the fuck up.*

*Father, unfazed by acutely agitated state of bride:*

*Father (absentmindedly)*
*Yes, you are right. It IS an important day. Because whatever happens, marriage is never quite the same second time around.*

*Bride looks at father, stunned. Freeze frame on that image. Car pulls up at the church. Wedding bells peal. Click. Photographer captures bride's look of horror.*

*Fade out.*

Perhaps it was because I had never been a daddy's girl, reared to bask in paternal adoration, that despite the fact that I was now divorced and despairing, I still craved Dad's reassurance. I had always longed to be one of those smug daddy's girls, utterly secure that they could get what they wanted from a man because they had always had what they needed from Daddy. Sure, they were manipulative but they were fearless when it came to men because they had never suffered a moment's self-doubt. I grew up aware that I was loved, which differed from that Teflon feeling that my Dad adored me. It was almost love by proxy, taken as read but without much supporting evidence. If I walked into Dad's study as a child, he didn't look at me as if his world had just lit up, he merely held his pen aloft and said: 'Yes?' It wasn't that Dad was unkind, more that I never felt he had time to understand me. He didn't know what to do with me, any more than I now knew how to relate to him.

I may have been sitting on the tube, resembling an adult – albeit not a very sophisticated one with my black eye – but inside I was in pieces. It was all I could do to stop from shouting, 'I want my dad. I need a man to tell me he loves me because I can't cope with myself or any of this.'

Dad was sitting at his usual banquette in Thai Temptations. He motioned to the groaning, grease-laden buffet. 'Come on, stoke up. You look like you could do with a decent meal.'

'You call this food decent?' I muttered, but followed him up to the buffet anyway. Dad piled his plate while I toyed with some noodles. He pointed to my bruised eye.

'Oh, it's nothing,' I said. 'Just larking around.'

After a while, he gestured to my untouched food. 'Are you sick?'

'Not exactly.' I watched my father eat his green curry, then I let out a half moan, half sigh. 'Actually, Dad, yes, I am. I'm sick. Very sick in the head. Do you know, in the last year, I've walked out on my marriage, had a disastrous rebound fling, got pregnant and to cap it all,' I let out a manic laugh: 'I've just had an abortion.'

He didn't raise his head but kept quietly chewing. 'And guess what? Jamie's girlfriend is pregnant and they are keeping *their* baby.' I pointed to my blackened eye. 'When I heard I fainted and hit my head.'

Dad finished his mouthful, then looked up from his plate: 'How's work?'

I blinked, incredulous. 'Actually, I've just won the Booker prize.' I let out an irritated sigh. 'I gave up work at the publishing house when I married Jamie. Remember? Jamie didn't want me to have a life – or at least not a life worth living.'

Dad balanced his chopsticks on the edge of his empty plate. 'I do agree,' he said, ponderously. 'That it does look as if you've pressed the self-destruct button wantonly. But you see, Daisy, real life is about birth, death, marriage, divorce, termination even. You've had to make some challenging decisions of late, which means you are finally growing up.' He dabbed his lips with a paper napkin. 'And that, my dear, can only be a *very* good thing.'

'So you're not shocked?'

'Shocked? No. Naturally, I want to see you settled and happy. But you have a fresh start now, so I expect you to turn your life around.' He leaned over and kissed my cheek. 'You know, the most painful thing about loving someone is that you can't do their journey for them.'

My heart soared. He'd said he loved me. Maybe I was a daddy's girl, after all?

After lunch with my father, I felt buoyed up and optimistic about my future. I didn't even let living back at home with

Mum, who was coping with two litters of puppies, dent my determination. Everything was going to get better, even if my self-help addiction was getting worse. I spent my days devouring spiritual texts and scouring the Internet for a fast track to enlightenment. I was particularly taken by a website on ancient wisdom. Apparently, the Chinese believe that there are three mirrors that form a person's reflection. The first is how you see yourself, the second is how others see you and the third mirror reflects the truth. To know yourself, you must know the truth.

The truth was that, however much of a hash I felt that I had made of my life of late, at least it felt real. When I was married to Jamie, I didn't feel as if I was living the life that was meant for me. It felt like a two-dimensional, more contained version. Strangely, it didn't feel safe because not living one's dream isn't safe, is it? It's a crime against your own spirit. A road-block in your journey of hope.

Now, I had to work out what my dream for my future was. In yogic terms, apparently, all I had to do was connect to my 'rasa', my 'spiritual nectar', whatever that was. As I found meditation bottom-numbingly boring, I decided to start by cleansing my aura. I had read that Mayan tribes believe that covering your whole body in honey then washing it away sweetens you after a bitter experience and gets rid of all that negativity. Perfect! I decided to give it a go.

I stood naked in the freezing bathroom, slathering myself with sticky goo, rubbing great globs across my face, body and into my hair. While I was waiting for the bath to run, staring at the rust marks on the tired old tub, Donald and Dougie pushed open the door. Before I could escape, they started licking my ankles, exfoliating my embarrassingly hairy legs with their rough little tongues. Yelping, I managed to leap free of them, into the bath. They barked angrily, impatient for more honey, so I threw a wet flannel in their direction. They looked at me, utterly indignant, then flounced off to find Mum.

I lay back, eager for contemplation. I could see that I had got the balance of my life completely wrong. I had spent two decades wasting precious energy on relationships with unworthy blokes, when I should have been focusing on my relationship with myself. I used to repeat the mantra: 'I want to be a better woman, so I can attract a better man.' How sick and co-dependent is that? Something Jess said to me when I gave up work during my marriage to Jamie kept popping into my mind. 'You'll live to regret this, Daisy,' she had said, 'because the one thing career girls have promised themselves is self-fulfilment. We know that the more you demand from a man, the lonelier you are likely to be made.' She was right. I felt so blocked by unhappiness when I was with Jamie that I willingly gave up anything creative for myself in order to make my marriage work. The result was that I became lonelier, needier and more insecure – and doubtless more irritating by the day.

During my marriage, I was consumed with my own misery, at the expense of anything else. You know how when you read a rousing book, leave the theatre after a heart-jolting play or see a profoundly moving film, you either feel more alone or less alone? I always felt more alone. Now, more than anything else in the world, I wanted to feel less alone.

Mum knocked loudly on the bathroom door. 'Get out,' she said, excitedly, 'you've got a visitor.'

A visitor? In the country? On a weekday? I dried myself off, put on my faded flannel pyjamas, covered with a hearts and puppies motif, grabbed my ugly old sheepskin slippers and bumped into Mum on the landing.

'You can't go down looking like that,' she said. 'You look a fright. What's with your hair?'

I put my hand into the clumps of honey and laughed. I ran downstairs, with Mum in hot pursuit.

'Daisy, wait. Why not get dressed?' she called after me.

'Where is he?'

'He's in the drawing room,' she said. Only grown-ups were ever invited into the least dog-hair-covered room in the house. Hooray! It must have been Dad. He had obviously braved Mum's icy glare to check I was all right. My heart sang in delight.

I pushed open the door, my arms flung wide and did a double take. I couldn't believe my eyes. It wasn't Dad. It was Troy.

I stared at him in shock as Mum bustled past, a plate of pâté and crackers in hand. She put them next to Troy, who flashed a devastating well-practised-with-mothers smile. Donald and Dougie came snuffling in after the pâté. I could tell by Troy's overly anxious-to-please manner and the way he gingerly patted them as they sniffed his shoes that he didn't like dogs. That he was nervous gave me a joyous edge. Suddenly, I began to think that there was justice in the world, after all.

When Mum went off to re-fill Troy's drink, he turned to me and said: 'Daisy. I'm not asking you to forgive me. I know I've made a terrible mistake.'

I raised an eyebrow and gave a sarcastic smile, as if to say: 'You said it, buster.'

To my delight, Dougie began humping his ankle. At first Troy tried a snort of amusement, then he kicked Dougie off, a tad too aggressively, I noted. 'When you told me you were pregnant after our brief liaison, I panicked. I was scared,' he said.

'You weren't the only one, mate.' I retorted.

'But don't you see? This changes everything.'

Slowly and theatrically, I shook my head. 'No, Troy, there is absolutely nothing that can be changed about an abortion.'

Troy moved towards me: 'You don't get it. You see, I thought you were like the rest of them but you're not. You're different.'

As he spoke, he caught sight of a dog hair on his black jacket and meticulously picked it off his sleeve. I watched him, thinking, 'How could I have ever been interested in such an anal idiot, even as a sexual sorbet?'

Troy took another step towards me. 'Daisy, now I know for sure that you *are different*. You are not like the rest of the desperate single women out there. You are not a gold digger, trying to trap me, after all.'

Incredulous, I remained rooted to the spot, while Troy put his hand inside his jacket pocket and pulled out an envelope. 'I know I've messed up but let's face it, we didn't know each other well enough to have a baby.' He handed me the envelope, with a smile as if I'd just won the lottery. 'But who knows what the future could bring? I'd like us to get together. I'm going to give you another chance.'

In that moment, I felt as if I was standing outside my own body. I had a perfect flash-forward vision of what I would have liked to have done. I would have liked to have surged forwards with a roar of fury and with all my force, pushed Troy backwards on to the sofa. I would have then grabbed the slab of pâté, stuffed it down his trousers and motioned for Donald and Dougie to leap on to his lap. Once they got stuck into the pâté and Troy's private parts, he would never have had to have worried about getting a gold digger pregnant again, would he? Instead, I took the envelope. 'What's this?'

'A week in the Caribbean, all expenses paid. I thought we could go away together. Start again. Wipe the slate clean. We could have time to relax and really get to know each other. After all, this whole business has been pretty stressful, hasn't it?'

I nodded, thinking, and how exactly has it been stressful for you? All you had to do was write a cheque, draw a veil over your conscience and consider the case closed.

I smiled at him and said quietly, 'That's really kind, Troy. What an amazingly thoughtful gesture.'

Relief flooded his features. He put his arm out to touch me. 'Daisy, you're so cool. It's great that you understand.'

I batted his arm away. 'What you must understand though, is that us mad, bitter bitches, with our wound-up body clocks and shrivelled ovaries, us desperate divorcees, who according to you, don't want real men but only crave walking wallets and sperminators, well, we don't give guys like *you* a second chance.'

Troy looked away: 'Daisy, I was . . .'

'Funny, I don't see this powerful, successful, "catch",' I continued, relishing every second of my moment, 'I see a pathetic, deluded little man who's got a great, big . . . wallet in his pocket but who never knows whether people like him or what he's got.' I ripped the envelope in two and threw it in the fire. 'Do you honestly think that a couple of extra noughts on your bank balance make you a better person?' I shook my head. 'You know, the only time you told me the truth of who you are?' Troy, like a schoolboy on detention, remained silent, staring at the floor. 'When you said you had nothing to offer me. You were right.' With a triumphant flourish, I walked out and shut the door.

Catching my reflection in the hall mirror, I wondered if my hair, dripping gobs of honey on to the collar of my flannel PJs had diminished the impact of my outburst, but I reasoned that he got the message, nonetheless. As I rushed into the kitchen to find Mum, I knew I believed in karmic debt. That Troy had offered himself up so willingly for humiliation seemed more than a fantastic quirk of fate. A part of me knew that the higher path would have been to say nothing and walk away but who needed the wings of an angel when I was floating on air? Anyway, this wasn't cold revenge, it was altruistic punishment. Who could resist such an empowering opportunity when it came along, that fantastic fuck-you frisson of being an out and out bitch?

Mum was all of a flutter by the Aga. 'He's awfully good-looking, your rich fellow.'

'You've changed your tune,' I said. 'Remember, you told me not to get involved?'

'I just wanted you to be careful. That was all, but he was charming when I showed him round the kennels.'

'Mum. You were right. Don't be fooled. He's a bastard.'

'Oh?' she looked concerned. 'So it's over between you two?'

'It never began.'

'You've had a row? Is that it? He came to patch things up?'

'Sort of.' I shrugged, eager to change the subject. Suddenly Mum let out an anguished cry. 'He hit you, didn't he? That explains that black eye and the terrible bruise you had.'

I went over to her. 'No, no, it's nothing like that.'

Mum sat at the table. 'What happened, then?'

I sighed: 'You don't want to know.'

'Daisy,' she said, firmly: 'I am your mother. Out with it.'

I took a deep breath. 'I got pregnant.'

'How did *that* happen?'

'How do you think? Troy didn't want to know, so I had an abortion.' Mum clasped her hand to her mouth, as if to contain her shock. 'Then Troy turned up today with his yucky guilt gifts.' I shook my head.

Mum lurched towards the sink. 'Oh my God, I think I'm going to be sick.' She bent over, heaving. 'I can't believe I gave him my best pâté! What a terrible waste.' Mum started wailing, 'This is my worst nightmare for you come true. I can't believe it. This can't be happening.'

I went over and gently rubbed her back to stop her hyperventilating. 'This is exactly why I didn't tell you, Mum. I didn't want to upset you. Look, it's not your drama, it's mine.'

Mum tried to pull herself together. She looked me squarely in the eye. 'Never tell your father about this. He'd be so disappointed. Shocked.'

'Actually,' I said gingerly, 'he already knows. It just came out at Thai Temptations recently. He was surprisingly cool about it.'

Suddenly, we heard the loo flush – good, I *had* unnerved him – and then the front door shut behind him. The next thing, Troy was revving up the engine of his car. Before I knew what was happening, Mum sprinted from the kitchen and through the back door. Troy was carefully reversing his car – something black and swanky that looked as if it was fuelled by testosterone alone – down our narrow drive. Mum picked up the huge stone the postman uses for anchoring letters by the back door. With all her might, she ran forwards and hurled the stone at Troy's sports car. I screamed – not sure if from terror or elation. Fortunately her aim wasn't that good, so it missed the windscreen and bounced off the bonnet, leaving a satisfyingly large dent in the immaculate gleaming bodywork. Troy's eyes bulged with fear as he quickly manoeuvred the car out of the drive and up the lane.

Mum and I were doubled up with laughter. I put my arm around her touched, as always, by how much she loved me.

It was Lucy who told me. She had come to spend a couple of days with me at Mum's house. She wanted to escape the exhausting humdrum of running a home, a husband and two kids. She said that she needed to remind herself who *she* was, as the strain of holding her life together meant that sometimes she was straining to breathe. As we lounged around in our pyjamas or went for long, rambling walks, we dissected our lives. While Lucy was up for a girlie gossip and a giggle, there was something fractured about her that I had never sensed before now.

One afternoon, she was painting my toenails as she ran through a list of her husband's most infuriating characteristics. 'The way he reads the newspaper, clicking his tongue against his teeth and pedantically folding back the pages instead of flicking through them. The way he's incapable of neatly folding a towel so that the edges touch, but always flings it over the towel rail at a wonky angle. The way he stands in front of the fridge door, peering in and says "Have we got any butter?" as if I'm expected to have a mental inventory of our dairy products running through my brain at all times.' She clenched her jaw. 'Just once, I wish he'd ask me, "What can I do for you, darling?" He never says, "Let me take the girls to the play date, buy the party gift, collect the dry cleaning, phone the dentist, see if the car needs an MOT, stock up on rinse aid or fabric conditioner or book you a relaxing massage." Oh, no, because he earns so much money, his life is deemed more important than mine.'

'But isn't that true of all men?' I said.

Lucy sighed. 'I don't know but I do know that the reality is that over the years, Edward and I have stopped seeing each other. We've become like the furniture of married life. The thing is, I don't want to replace the furniture or re-upholster it, I just want to remember why I liked it in the first place.'

I nodded. 'So Edward bores you?'

'It's not really that,' she said, 'it's more that there is a part of him that I can't access any more. Perhaps the problem is that *I* bore *him*.' She put down the varnish. 'All I know is that I go through the motions of a good life but I'm dying of loneliness inside.' She let out an agonising sigh. 'How did this happen? One minute I was the sexy catch, dreaming of this great, fulfilling life, and a decade later, I'm just a boring old wife and mother with nothing to say.' She snorted. 'Oh

God, I *am* boring, aren't I? I mean, I even bore myself, most of the time.'

Lucy was silent for a while, carefully applying the top coat. 'Do you love Edward?' I asked her, finally.

'Everybody loves Edward,' she said, flatly.

'That's not what I asked. What does it matter what everybody else thinks? They're not there at two in the morning when you are being sick and you want Edward to hold your hair back.'

When Lucy spoke, it was in slow, hushed tones, as if admitting her deepest, most filthy secrets.

'Daisy, Edward has never once held my hair back.'

'Oh,' I said, utterly shocked, 'that's terrible.'

Lucy shrugged. 'You are so idealistic, it's frightening. Do you honestly think that Alpha Males, who earn mega bucks for their wives to spend, bother to get out of bed to hold our hair back when we are puking? They don't. Any more than they would contemplate missing a work meeting when we are laid up with flu to lay flannels on our foreheads and feed us chicken broth. It doesn't work like that.'

'So you're saying: if he's paying, he doesn't have to pay attention?'

'Right. They don't consider little nurturing things part of their remit.'

'So,' I said, 'let's get this clear: rich, powerful men short circuit when it comes to our emotional needs but it doesn't matter because they are footing the electricity bill?'

'Exactly!' Lucy carefully applied pale pink varnish to her fingernails. 'That's why it would never have worked between you and Julius. Marrying Jamie was a mistake but it didn't destroy you. If you had married a great catch like Julius, you wouldn't have been able to stomach the disappointment. It's the little things that would have broken you. After a while, even the flowers they send are a letdown because they never choose them themselves. You just pray their PA has good taste.' Lucy paused, and looked me in the eyes. 'Daisy, did you know that Julius is getting married?' My heart seemed to lurch, then plunge deep into the pit of my stomach. 'To Alice Randolph. She's a young American heiress. It's not a marriage, it's a merger,' she concluded.

So Julius Vantonakis, my first love, was getting married. I hadn't seen him for seven years and I felt the news as keenly as if we'd said goodbye only yesterday. Hearing this news was like having poison injected into my veins. He was the ultimate catch, *my* Mr Big, who had ignited a thousand dreams in my heart.

I was twenty-two when I met Julius, then twenty-nine, at a society party in London. We were introduced by one of my university friends, Natasha – a sensational looking Sloane with killer cheekbones – who had just started going out with Julius's oldest friend, the equally eligible Peregrine. They had an innate sense of belonging; they knew that their birthright had given them immediate entrée into a world of unparalleled privilege. They were the eighties version of the twenties Bright Young Things. Glossy, rich, carefree and enviable, they spent their lives in pedigreed packs. Staying in weekend house parties in crumbling country piles, skiing en masse and living it up in sprawling alpine chalets and summering in midge-ridden turreted castles; everyone was vaguely related. All they cared about was keeping it in the family and discussing who was doing what with whom and where. Everyone was 'a cousin of' or 'the sister of' as if you didn't merit a mention unless you were part of the right clan.

As the daughter of an academic, I certainly didn't share their aristocratic ancestry and I wasn't a trust-fund babe, but because my parents were offbeat and old-fashioned, I was deemed suitable enough to fit in. True, I knew the form; you didn't wear too much make-up, anything new or anything bling. You only wore hand-me-down jewellery – so I had some old pearls of Mum's – you had to make jolly conversation with the batty great-aunt over wincingly strong Bloody Marys before Sunday lunch and you always left a good tip by the bed for the cleaner, the cook, the housekeeper, or even the mother, if the family had fallen on hard times. Sure, I was a creditable enough imposter – I never looked or acted out of place – but I never felt at home. Amidst the utter frivolity and endless extravagance of the black-tie dances and champagne-cocktail parties, I always felt alone.

The minute I looked at him, it was as if I stared straight through his sad brown eyes into a similar private well of loneliness. I've never had that experience before or since; that instant recognition. A deep cellular knowing, when I knew nothing concrete at all. Of course, everybody knew who Julius Vantonakis was because he was a scion of one of the richest Greek shipping families in the world. The press was always full of tales of the family's derring-do on the international stage. The reason that Julius cut a swathe through the aristo scene was because his mother was a society beauty who gave her family entrée into this rarefied world where money alone could never cut it.

The whiff of scandal had permeated almost a decade before when Julius had fought his brother, Piers, for control of the empire. Staggeringly, he was only twenty yet after a bitter, public feud, he had won. Most people were scared of him because he displayed brutal business acumen, as if when it came to screwing people over, he had a morality chip missing. From the moment we met, I wasn't frightened of him because I felt this strange intimacy between us.

One of the first things I said to him at that party was: 'What's it like to be so successful?'

He replied, his eyes flat, 'I can't tell you because I don't know what it's like to be a failure.' He paused. 'I always get the deal I want because I can smell blood in the water.'

If it was meant to put me off, it didn't. 'Don't you think sharks have feelings too?' I asked. 'I mean, why shouldn't they, when even camels cry when they're lonely?'

He looked at me, intrigued. But all I felt from him was his unhappiness. Unlike the glossy beauties fawning all over him, I could sense his shame.

His mother, Amelia, a fragile English rose, had committed suicide when Julius was nineteen. I always thought that the reason he fought shy of love was because his mother's death felt like a betrayal to him. If she could leave him, when he loved her so much, then any woman could.

You never knew where you stood, emotionally speaking, with Julius, and perhaps, for me, that was part of the attraction. One minute he could be so open, free and giving, a second later he would close off. His loneliness was palpable. We were true friends – not just on/off lovers – because there was a silent knowing between us, as if we had a secret code which meant that we felt the same about life, as no one else could. Because we trusted each other, it should have felt safe. But for Julius, the risk was too great because I reminded him of his mother. Not physically speaking. Good grief, no! I may have passable hands and elegant ankles but with the wodge of fat at the top of my thighs and my bouncing persona, fragility doesn't figure. More, it was my romantic optimism which touched him. He once told me that I felt familiar to him, then immediately brushed the compliment aside by saying that was probably because his mother, like my mother, dead-headed daffodils early in spring mornings in her dressing-gown, always swam in a large straw hat and sunglasses in the summer, and adored dachshunds, too.

Julius toyed with me for a decade. He would never fully commit to me, yet he never let me stray. I always felt that he didn't want me enough, yet he didn't want to let me go either. I'd try to move on, date other men, but the moment I thought I might be interested enough in someone else, Julius's antennae were up. He'd appear and whisk me to dinner and on to romantic oblivion. Sure, it would be lavish with vintage champagne and shellfish on ice but none of that was what sealed it. It was his intuitive knowledge of me, his ability to ferret out my secrets and toy with my dreams, his cleverness and sudden soft touch. It wasn't even about sex for us; it was the real thing. I had fallen in love.

I had always hoped that one day he would come and claim me and yet he never did. All those years that he was single, toying with various vacuous posh totty, I could kick up my heels in hope. He took up so much space in my head that in my heart I believed it was our destiny to be together. Even when I stood at the altar and turned to face Jamie, it was Julius whom I prayed would show up.

'I've got to see him,' I said to Lucy.

'Are you crazy?' Lucy was aghast. 'You know the first rule of life: never go back.'

'Actually, I'm trying to move forwards. By seeing Julius I can finally close this whole chapter once and for all and let go. The timing is perfect. I can see it all so clearly now. It's not Jamie that's holding me back from getting my life together, it's Julius. What have I got to lose? If there's one thing I know from bitter experience, it is the things that you *don't* do in life that you end up regretting, more than the things you do.'

# Chapter 4
# Emotional Contagion

I may have looked a picture of professional calm, sitting in Julius's London offices, waiting for my 'interview', but inside I was churning. I had picked up a newspaper to appear occupied, but far from reading it my eyes were skating over words, hurrying past headlines and briefly registering photographs in a bid to focus. I was wearing a high-necked top under my jacket as I knew that nerves would force a livid flush across my chest.

A week earlier, busy Googling Julius, a small item in one of the gossip columns had caught my attention. Apparently, as part of his burgeoning property portfolio, he had acquired a boutique hotel in New York and was looking for a new PR. I decided that I would apply for the job under a pseudonym. That way, my cover would not be blown until we were face to face. I set about concocting a CV, confident that I knew enough about the media and marketing to give good enough copy to guarantee an interview. Sure enough, not long after, I got the call. Julius's PA wanted to fix up a meeting.

When I told Mum that I had faked a job application to come face to face with Julius, she crumpled into a chair. 'Oh Daisy, why do you always have to swim upstream?' I looked at her blankly, so she spelt it out. 'Is there some congenital fault in your makeup that means you have to make life difficult for yourself? I read in the gossip columns that Julius is engaged to an American heiress. Why on earth would you look him up now? Do you enjoy getting hurt?'

I wondered how Julius would view me now. I envied him his clean, as yet unmarried, slate. Divorce sullies one with its suggestion of stupidity and recklessness. I hated to be thought of as an emotional lightweight but that's the implication when you 'fess up to marital failure.

I watched his secretary, a clear-skinned, tight-lipped, efficient brunette in her early thirties, answer the phone, write memos and send emails. As Julius abhorred clutter, she, too, had the bare minimum work-wise on her desk but, as always, there was an impressive vase of white lilies. Julius only ever had flowers in white.

After a bell buzzed and she motioned for me to go inside his office, I realised Mum had a point. My stomach was flipping over and over. I wanted to leg it but then I saw him. He was sitting behind his desk, his head bent over paperwork. The office was just as I remembered. Sleek, modern and swimming in sunlight. His glass desk boasted an extravagant basket of white gardenia. Behind him was an enormous canvas of a midnight blue butterfly, fanning across the white wall. French doors led out on to a rooftop patio, where box hedges in aluminium containers stood in rows. He didn't look up immediately and I could see distinguished flecks of grey peppering his dark hair. He looked astonishingly good for forty-six. I should have slunk away before he recognised me but I knew before it happened that it was too late. Just being in the same room as him, inhaling his air of studied concentration, was enough. I still loved him just as much as I had ever done.

When he looked up and saw me standing there, he stared straight through me, his eyes completely glazed. I wasn't sure whether to rush over and give him the kiss of life or the Heimlich manoeuvre. It seemed ages before he caught his breath. 'My God, Daisy, what are you doing here?' He stood up and walked around the desk. He was thinner than I remembered and his olive skin more sallow, but he had an assurance that suited him. He didn't seem to be as burdened as before.

'I'm sorry. It's madness, I know,' I stuttered. 'I wanted to see you, so I pretended to apply for the PR job you advertised.'

He let his head fall to one side, still eyeing me, amused. When he came over and brushed his lips against my cheek and I smelt his aftershave – the same Penhaligon's Blenheim Bouquet he wore when I had first met him – it was as if time concertinaed into nothing. The past decade melted into a split second and that intense feeling of knowing was as keen as if I had made love to him that morning.

Julius shut the door and beckoned to a pale suede sofa. He sat opposite me on a chair, neatly folding one leg over another. 'How are you?'

I nodded. 'I'm good.'

'No,' he said, vaguely irritated. 'How *are* you?'

So nothing had changed. We were going to cut straight to the truth and avoid the social carapace of pretence like we always did. This nod towards our former intimacy delighted me. I knew I had to keep myself in check though, as Julius hated – and feared – unruly displays of emotion.

'I feel that I have caught up with myself at last,' I said.

'You've been through a lot,' he said, his brown eyes boring into me.

'Question or statement?' I asked.

'Both.'

Nervously, I ran my fingers through my hair in exactly the sort of weakly flirtatious gesture he hated. He raised a not-so-mock disapproving eyebrow and I laughed. 'You've changed,' he said.

'Obviously not enough,' I joked, holding my hand theatrically to my hair.

He smiled, still appraising me. 'No. You're calmer. More grown-up.'

'Disappointment does that to you,' I said.

'Disappointment or divorce?'

So he knew all about Jamie. Natasha must have said something to him. 'Sadly, they tend to be inextricably linked.'

'Did you love him?' Did I detect a shard of jealousy in his voice?

'Pathetically, I loved the idea of marriage more.'

'Did he hurt you?'

I had to pull hard on my emotions to get a grip. That Julius was asking these deeply personal questions, his manner still protective, must mean that he still cared. 'It hurt me that he didn't fight for me,' I said, then looked away. I couldn't hold eye contact for fear that I would betray what I really meant. But he knew. He knew that by not coming after me all those years before, he had hurt me more than Jamie ever could.

'And you?' I asked. 'How are you?'

'I'm getting married,' he said, matter-of-factly.

'Do you love her?'

He paused, then leaned forward and whispered suggestively, 'Come on, Daisy. What the hell do *you* think?'

*

Lucy and Jess were waiting for me in an Italian restaurant near Julius's office. When I walked through the door and Jess clocked my ecstatic glow, she slumped forward and groaned: 'Wake me when this nightmare is over. I don't know if I have the strength to go through another Julius saga.'

Lucy eyed me eagerly: 'So? How did it go?'

'I had forgotten that being with Julius feels like having front row seats on life,' I said.

Jess put her hands to my throat, pretending to strangle me. 'No, honestly,' I continued dreamily, 'he's so sharp and exciting. I feel like he's sprinkled magic dust all over me.'

'Well, after lunch you can have a cold shower, wash it off and come back down to earth,' said Jess.

Lucy threw her a censorious look. 'What is with you?'

Jess ignored her and snapped at me. 'Julius is about to get married. Remember?'

'Let's order a bottle of wine,' I said, beckoning the waiter. When our glasses were full, I proposed a toast: 'To best friends and . . . soulmates.'

Jess lit a cigarette and inhaled deeply. 'Daisy, please don't do this. Don't ricochet off into some fantasy state. I can't bear to see you getting hurt again.'

Irritated, I scanned the menu. Jess pulled it away from me and tilted my head to look at her. 'Julius is engaged to a very rich, very beautiful and frighteningly young woman. You can't match her. Let's face it, if Julius had wanted to marry you, he would have asked you a decade ago.'

Ouch. That hurt. 'He wasn't ready,' I sniffed. 'We've changed. We've both grown up.'

Jess turned to Lucy, exasperated: 'You talk some sense into her.'

Lucy put down her glass. 'Listen, Daisy, I know that you've

always dreamed that one day Julius might be The One but I don't think that even if he were available, he would be right for you long term. You're so romantic, but you don't realise that successful, independent people like Julius don't want love, they just want admiration.'

'What do you mean?'

She paused before saying, 'The fact is that the really rich are afraid of love. They shy away from getting close to anyone because a part of them always questions whether you love them, or what they've got.'

Jess nodded. 'Alice Randolph, Julius's heiress, feels safe because he knows that she's not after him for his money.'

'Well, nor am I,' I said, indignantly. 'I love him. I always have.'

Jess softened. 'We know, and Julius knows that too. That's the problem.'

'What do you mean?' My voice was quivering with disappointment.

Lucy gently patted my arm. 'There's a part of Julius that is untouchable, you know that. He's learned to isolate himself.'

'What from?'

'From love. From real life.'

'Why?' I whined.

'Because he's afraid.'

'Afraid?'

'Yes, of being found out.' Lucy let out a troubled sigh. 'Rich, powerful men like Julius are afraid that we'll discover that inside they are just like the rest of us.'

'Exactly,' said Jess, crisply. 'Their biggest fear is that they will disappoint us.'

'Oh God,' I said, rubbing my temples, knowing they were right. 'It's all so complicated. What do you do? Do you go for the ambitious, exciting but blocked off and selfish Alpha Male . . .'

'Or the kind, considerate beta guy?' interrupted Jess.

'Who's boring because he doesn't have the killer instinct.' I said combatively.

'Eventually that killer instinct kills a part of you,' said Lucy.

Jess and I stopped and stared at her. There was something unbearably hollow in the way she spoke.

'How are things with Edward?' I asked.

'Not great,' she said.

'Are you still having sex?' trilled Jess in her unshockable let's-lance-that-boil-on-your-bottom-now doctor's voice.

Lucy said nothing.

'So you're not?' Jess lit another cigarette.

Lucy batted the smoke away. 'Marriage, children, domesticity, familiarity, hormones . . . they all have a deadly effect on sexual expression. You should try it, Jess.'

'No way. I prefer Friends With Benefits.' We looked at her. 'Casual sex, of course. Got a great guy, Phil, on the go at the mo. He's an anaesthetist from work. Knows exactly how much to administer and where.' Jess let out a raucous giggle.

'Don't tell me, it was so good you were swinging from the ceiling?' I said.

'No, but it did hit the ceiling . . .'

'What did?' asked Lucy.

'Luce,' I said, 'you don't want to know.'

'Actually,' smiled Lucy, 'even I managed to eke out an orgasm the other day.'

We laughed.

'This is what I tell my patients about making marriage last,' lectured Jess. 'Go home every night. Find things to cherish. Rituals. Shared humour. It's the little things that grow into something big.'

'You hypocrite,' screamed Lucy. 'Do they know you're a resolutely single slut, incapable of monogamy?'

''Course not.'

'I think I'll give Julius your moving marriage monologue when I see him next week,' I said.

Jess and Lucy turned on me: 'No! What's happening?'

'Julius is taking me out to dinner.'

Obsession skewers our take on everything so that meaning can be derived from the most mundane detail. When Julius sent me an email confirming dinner, the mere fact that he addressed me by my initial gave me an erotic charge. Suddenly 'D' seemed intimate and suggestive, as opposed to hurried, pared-down, email speak. I read, re-read, deleted, retrieved from the delete box and read Julius's email until I was dizzy with delusion and desire. 'D. Why now? Everything in my life was easy . . . See you thurs. J.'

His missive was so laden with promise that there was no knowing what would happen. Inevitably, I played out every conceivable conversation in my mind, running a fairy-tale ending in my head. My fantasy script was rather like *Brief Encounter* but with a Happy Ever After finale. Julius would turn up at the restaurant and once the drinks were served, would lean in towards me, his head bent low. 'We both know what's happened,' he would say.

'Yes,' I would nod, adding: 'Actually, I've always loved you.'

'So nothing has changed?'

'Everything has changed. You're engaged to be married.'

He would reach across the table for my hand. 'You're different,' he would whisper.

'No, I'm still me.'

'I didn't realise until I saw you the other day how much I need you.'

'But Julius,' I would say, 'What about your fiancée, Alice Randolph? It's too late.'

'It's never too late for true love,' he would reply, kissing the back of my hand. 'Alice is young. She'll get over it. But I would never get over losing you again.'

Cue lights, camera, kissing, action . . . eventually the aisle, the altar, the ante-natal delight . . .

Mad, destructive, romantic love was injected like dye through my entire nervous system. It haunted my psyche, it was like an ache in my bones. I so wanted it to work out with Julius that the minute he started deviating from my prescribed script at dinner, I began to feel quite hostile.

We were sitting in a chic French restaurant in Chelsea, all hushed tones, starched white linen, crystal goblets and wafting garlic. Julius felt at home here because the male clientele were all power brokers obsessed with their bulging financial portfolios. Even the air smelt expensive. At first, I couldn't hear what he was saying as I was so busy at war within. I knew I only had myself to blame for imagining and worse, believing, my sentimental scenario, so when he was speaking, I considered firing my inner voice on the grounds of misleading flights of fantasy. Eventually, I managed to hone into the reality of what was happening.

'I thought success would be so much easier,' he sighed, after a gulp of vintage red. 'I mean, I suppose I thought if I was successful in business, it would automatically translate to the rest of my life.'

I wasn't sure exactly what he was alluding to, so I nodded.

Suddenly, he turned on me, a blaze of anger. 'You're so naive, Daisy. Don't you realise that if you want to be a success in life, you can not afford to marry someone you love. It is too dangerous.' Was he saying he loved me? I stared at him, speechless. 'If you want power, you can't afford to lose control.'

He seemed so tortured and impassioned that I realised to envy the mega rich is a mistake. We think that wealth gives people a glossy sheen which enables their troubles to slide off them, when in fact that amount of money creates myriad potholes of its own. 'Don't you get it?' he said, his voice shaking with temper. 'I can't allow myself to get distracted by you.'

I could feel tears welling up, so I looked away. 'Daisy,' pleaded Julius, in a voice that seared my heart, 'your spirit frightens me. Your emotion always pushes to the surface, ready to be aired. You're so honest and I don't know how to deal with that.'

I let a tear fall. Julius handed me his handkerchief. It was ironed into a perfect square, with JV initialled in tiny navy letters in the corner. 'Can't you be ambitious and intimate?' I asked him. He seemed relieved to have an intellectual hair to split, instead of watching me spiral off.

'What do you mean by intimacy?'

'Intimacy requires vulnerability even when we don't feel safe. That's what trust is. It's like love. It's a risk.'

'I can't afford to take that risk with you,' he said.

I wanted to scream, 'Why not?' but said instead, 'And Alice?'

'There's no risk with her,' he said. 'She's young yet she's more knowing than you. She understands the deal.'

'The deal?' I repeated.

'The deal is that we will get married and live this great big glamorous life . . .'

'Glamorous lie, you mean?' When Julius laughed, his eyes crinkled with delight.

'Yes. It was all going according to plan,' he said, 'until you showed up.'

I knew that things must be bad between Edward and Lucy because Lucy wanted to stay with me at Mum's, even though the dusting of dog hair had suddenly given her an allergic reaction. It made me think she must be under added stress. Handkerchief glued to her runny and reddening nose, Luce sat for hours at the kitchen table, openly dissecting her plight, even relishing Mum's offbeat input.

'Do you think a marriage can survive an affair, Mrs Dooley?' asked Lucy.

Mum stopped stirring her vat of damp dog biscuits and sighed. 'When the chips are down, dear, you have to believe the person you are with is on your side. That becomes difficult when someone else is lying by their side.' She began thrashing the mixture again. 'Some people survive infidelity but I'm afraid I couldn't make do.'

'Why? Do you think Edward is having an affair?' I asked Lucy, astonished.

'No. His big passion is his bank account. Some guys sniff glue, Edward sniffs wads of crisp fifty-pound notes.'

'An expensive way to get high,' I said, as I pushed the plunger into the coffee, 'but at least it's clean.'

'Actually,' said Lucy, twirling her fingers suggestively round a lock of hair, 'it's me that fantasises about having an affair.'

Stunned, I spilt the coffee. A few drops splashed on to Dougie's head, so the deranged dachshund ran yelping from the room. Mum hurried after him. 'Lucy, are you joking?'

'Sort of,' she said, sneezing. 'My biological clock may not tick any more but my life clock is chiming loud and clear. I keep asking myself over and over "Is this all there is?"'

'But why do you want an affair?'

'Oh, I don't know if I do really. But I can't stop thinking that there is no greater feeling in the world than when a man pursues you with complete conviction.'

'Even a creepy stalker?' I laughed before adding: 'Or a married man?'

'You should know,' Lucy batted back. 'Sorry, I forgot Julius is only engaged.'

I let her comment slide. 'Wouldn't it be more honest to leave Edward?'

Lucy looked at me with horror. 'And go through everything you have gone through since leaving Jamie? I can't think of anything worse than being single again. Worse: a single mother with two kids in tow. What man is going to look at me?'

Mum bustled back with Dougie wrapped in her arms. 'Love begins as a sonnet, but marriage turns it into a shopping list,' she said, apropos of nothing. 'Don't forget, Daisy, you need someone with whom you can go to the supermarket.'

'I'll remember to take my next wedding vows in Waitrose,' I said, beckoning for Lucy to leave the room.

Upstairs, lying on my bed, I turned to Lucy. 'Are you really capable of an affair? The lies, the deceit?'

'I don't know but Edward and I live a lie already,' she said. 'Everyone thinks we are this golden couple but we live in an emotional coma. Have you noticed that Edward never touches me? He only ever rubs my back when he wants sex. Then, he turns over afterwards and goes to sleep without even kissing me. I'm forty years old and I need to feel desired.'

'All marriages go through dead zones,' I said. 'But I don't think that having an affair is the way to perk it up.'

'You're right. I'm just hankering after that electric moment before a man kisses you for the first time.'

I frowned.

'I hardly think that you can take the moral high ground, Daisy,' said Lucy, poking me in the ribs.

'True,' I said, then beamed. 'Did I tell you that Julius is taking me away next weekend? To meet his grandmother.'

Lucy sat up. 'Has he called his wedding to Alice Randolph off then?'

'No,' I sighed. 'If only it were that simple.'

I knew that I should have felt guilty as I counted down the days before seeing Julius again but I didn't. The morning that he came to collect me from Jess's dragged interminably because I had been awake with excitement half the night. Jess was away working in another practice in Bristol, so I had her flat to myself. Just before eleven, after I had checked and re-checked my make-up and fluffed up my hair – again – I leaned against the front door and took some deep breaths. It was pathetic, I knew, but I felt like Cinderella. Part of me was fully aware that this was a day on loan before I returned to my drab, lonely, single life but who in their right mind would turn down time with Prince Charming?

When he rang the bell, I waited for a beat before answering. It gave me an erotic charge to sense him standing on the other side of the door. As he walked me to his car, a nippy green Mercedes, I thought that he may have been engaged to be married but I was the one slipping into the seat by his side, not Alice Randolph. I knew that my triumph was hollow because there wasn't a cracking carat on *my* third finger – yet it felt so right to be with him, that I couldn't really see that I was doing anything wrong. That's probably the excuse most people use to justify their behaviour. If you know you've met your soulmate, don't you owe it to yourself to follow your heart, regardless of whose you break in your wake? Obviously this was a ludicrously selfish and self-serving formula but sod it, that day – with a liberal sprinkling of denial – it worked for me.

Although Julius and I had not yet kissed after all these years apart, the atmosphere in the car was electric. He looked very European and gorgeous in a muted suede jacket and caramel-coloured cords. I kept staring at his hands resting on the steering wheel. I longed to be held by him, to feel his touch but I knew that the key to success with him was to be intimate without being intrusive. We didn't need to speak because the mere fact that Julius was driving me, and not Alice, to Somerset said it all.

Ever since his mother had died, his grandmother, Grace, had been the most influential woman in his life. I'd heard him mention her many times before; he clearly loved her dearly and held her in high regard. I'd never been asked to meet her before, so this trip seemed spine-tinglingly significant. As he drove, I thought of an article I had read on emotional contagion, whereby you pick up on each other's feelings without speaking. Was Julius receiving my psychic emails? Was he fully aware that without opening my mouth, I was imploring him to ditch Alice, whom I knew he didn't love and declare himself to me? As Julius was obviously deep in thought, I couldn't help fantasising that by introducing me to Grace, he was seeking her tacit approval and that the writing was on the wall for Alice.

Urgh, perfect, bloody Alice. Ever since Jess had pointed out a photograph of her in a society magazine, I had been consumed with fury, stung by how young my rival was. She was only in her early twenties, practically jailbait. Standing at a polo match, her whippet-thin legs looking infuriatingly endless in white jeans (whereas my stumps resemble those of a stocky Shetland pony in tight white). Alice had that unfeasibly translucent skin that comes with being well-bred. She looked like the sort of girl who was always cold: not frigid, just never warm. She had fine, flyaway blonde hair and glittering eyes. My only consolation was that she was the type of identikit arm candy who wouldn't age well. She didn't have enough substance in her features. What drove me to distraction was the fact that intelligent men like Julius tend to shy away from bright girls, writing them off as manipulative, when it is girls like Alice, who cultivate fey, simple exteriors, who are the ruthless ones. Why couldn't Julius see that behind the ready smiles, sweet with adulation, lie game plans of breathtaking complexity?

Suddenly Julius broke into my acid little reverie and I prayed that we weren't connected via emotional contagion or he'd know what an Alpha Bitch I could be. 'The dead gain such importance by dying, don't they?' he said, with unbearable sorrow.

I nodded, berating myself for not cottoning on to the fact that driving to his mother's family home stirred up emotion. When was I going to grow up to the fact that not everything was always about me?

'Every day since my mother's death, I've thought of her, yet when she was alive I didn't think much about her at all,' he said. 'Now, every time someone at work says "It's your mother on the phone" or "I'm off to have lunch with my mother", I miss her.'

I couldn't begin to envisage Julius's pain, as the thought of losing my own mother, however batty she was, was both a real and unimaginable fear for me. Before I knew it, Julius had swerved across the motorway and stopped on the hard shoulder. He cupped my face with his hands: 'Daisy, you must understand that my loss is so great that the only way I know how to cope is to shut off.'

'No,' I said, 'that's not the way to cope. The way to heal this pain is to open your heart and let someone in.' Inside, I was imploring, 'Me, me, me.'

We were in dangerous territory and I don't know whether I was picking up his despair – emotional contagion again, where one person can torpedo another's spirits – but suddenly I wanted to put down my head and howl.

It made me realise that we all live so close to the line; that every one of us is pressed up against the edge of life at different times, for different reasons and it is so easy to cross over and so terrible if we do.

'Don't you get it?' he said sadly, 'I'm incapable of having a proper relationship. I don't know how they work.'

'Most of us think that relationships are about taking responsibility for someone else's happiness but they're not,' I said. 'We're only responsible for our own feelings. That's not to say we can't share our hopes and fears but we can't make anyone else happy and vice versa.'

Julius turned on the engine. 'I can't afford to feel this,' he said. My heart was pounding.

'This what?'

He looked at me, then winked: 'This . . . distracted. Come on, we're going to be late.'

Standing in Julius's grandmother's drawing room, a grand, stately affair with gilt mirrors and massive crystal chandeliers, Julius beckoned to a pair of louvred doors with strange shafts of light filtering through the slats. He pulled them apart to reveal another set of doors covered with thin plastic panels. When he opened them, I gasped, unable to believe my eyes. Ahead lay a vast conservatory with Gothic windows reaching up to a large, glass-domed ceiling. Beneath the dome, tented netting created a colonial effect. Gravel paths ran through flowerbeds bursting with tropical plants and, in the centre, a fountain trailed water into an oval pond. Water lilies danced on the surface, while huge banana leaves hovered over deep pink hibiscus mingled with pale pink Busy Lizzie. Bougainvillea, heavy with red and purple flowers pushed for space among crimson rhododendrons, while oleander shrubs snuggled next to avocado trees. The riot of colour was breathtaking, but what made me cry out in amazement were the hundreds of butterflies soaring up to the ceiling and hanging off every plant.

'This is why I wanted to bring you here,' Julius said. 'Breeding butterflies is my hobby. This is my escape.'

I had always suspected that to protect himself, he had sought refuge somewhere but to have kept this passion hidden from me for this long was astounding.

Julius bent down to place a small brightly coloured pad in one of the many low trays filled with water that littered the gravel paths. 'What's that?' I asked.

'It's called a scouring pad. The butterflies are attracted to the colour and land on it to feed. It's to supplement their diet during winter when there isn't much nectar about.' He gestured towards the ceiling. 'There are more.' I craned my head back to look at the clear round trays shaped like flowers, hanging from the ceiling. 'The butterflies drink through holes in the lid. Here, come and look at this.' Julius led me towards an oleander tree and motioned to its leaves. Off it hung metallic drops, which looked like tiny nuggets of gold. 'This is the pupa of the Striped Blue Crow butterfly. The pupa hopes to be mistaken for a drop of rain. You can get up to fifteen on a bush in the summer, when it literally shimmers.'

I peered at the oleander bush. 'Butterflies are such delicate creatures,' he said, staring up at the tiny flecks of colour heading for the netting beneath the dome. 'So many things can go wrong that it always amazes me that they emerge from their chrysalis at all. Too much heat, not hot enough, too moist, too dry – at every stage they can die or become deformed. You should never touch a butterfly with your hands because the acid from your skin can destroy them. You have to use a paint brush. Everything in here is monitored with precision; we keep the air between seventy-five and eighty degrees Fahrenheit.'

As I watched Julius carefully tilting leaves and admiring them, I was beside myself. There is nothing like a man doing something with expertise – skiing, dancing, leaping over a fence or reversing into a tight parking space – to turn a woman to mush. Actually, physical attraction can grow from the most mundane contact as you can suddenly find a bloke sexy when he hauls out the rubbish, does the laundry, chops wood or shells peas but this . . . it was unbelievable. That Julius could be such a ruthless operator yet have this secretive, sensitive side made him all the more special.

'Did you know that the principal task of the butterfly is to reproduce?' he said. 'They have a fantastic mating ritual. The male dance is made up of movements and wing beats because his forewings have androconial scales which release aphrodisiac pheromones or love dust. So just before he wants to mate, he'll close his wings over his female's antennae and give her a blast. He then moves in a semi-circular direction around her. If she's up for it, she'll raise her wings and expose her abdomen.'

He moved around me in a semi-circular direction and I lifted up my jumper and gave him a flash of rounded tummy. His eyes crinkled and we laughed in total togetherness. For a moment, I knew that I had full advantage over my opponent, Alice, because I had the ability to amuse Julius. He looked at me with tenderness as he gestured to the door. 'Come on, it can get awfully heady in here. I want to show you something else before we meet my grandmother.' As if to guide me, he put his hand lightly on the small of my back and I let my body soften into his palm. 'Do you know one of the reasons why I was drawn to butterflies as a child?' he said.

'Because butterflies are fragile survivors. They exhibit virtually no parental concern for their offspring.' He eyed me levelly. 'Save choosing a safe place to leave their eggs.'

Tears sprang unexpectedly into my eyes. I quickly brushed them aside.

Julius led me upstairs, past rows of doors, some of which were ajar giving glimpses into well-appointed bedrooms with chintz-covered headboards, puffy silk eiderdowns and dressing-tables on which lay old-fashioned tins of shortbread, crystal water glasses and matching water jugs. Everything was luxurious without being ostentatious. Old money combined with immaculate taste. Julius led me into his room. He sat on the bed and motioned for me to join him. He was sitting so close that his scent of Penhaligon's wafted over me. I half closed my eyes in anticipation when I realised that he was putting something in my hand. I looked down. It was an ice-blue Fabergé egg.

'My God, this is incredible,' I said, stunned.

'Open it,' he said, putting his fingers over mine. My heart was beating so fast, I wondered if he could hear it. He pressed a tiny mechanism and a bejewelled butterfly rose up. I had never seen anything like it – or come close to anything so precious in my life before. The light from the window picked out the dancing colours of the rubies, sapphires and emeralds.

I stared at it, holding it up and examining the exquisite detail of the craftsmanship. Then I carefully placed it on the bedside table. Julius lay back against the pillows and I joined him. We lay side by side and he took my hand.

'Do you know the history of the Fabergé egg?' he asked.

'I know they're Russian,' I said.

'Yup. In 1885 Tsar Alexander III commissioned the first Imperial Easter egg for his wife, the Empress Maria

Fedorovna. This initiated a tradition that continued until the revolution. The romance of the egg is the element of surprise – the gift inside.' He squeezed my hand.

'What was inside the first egg?'

'A tiny golden hen with ruby eyes. The shell was gold and matt white enamel. After the first, each egg took about a year to make and was designed to reflect the previous year's important events. All in all, fifty Imperial eggs were made by the House of Fabergé.'

'Is yours an Imperial Egg?'

'No. Other rich Russians started to commission them when they realised that it was the fashionable thing to do. My father bought this from a dealer in New York in the early sixties.' He paused. 'It was his gift to my mother for giving birth to me.'

I turned on my side to face him. 'And that's why she left it to you?'

He turned to face me; we were breath-smellingly close but our faces were not actually touching. I could see a small speck of sleep still lodged in the corner of his eye.

'I suppose she left it to me,' he said, slowly, 'instead of a suicide note.' The way he said 'suicide' sent a jolt of shock through me. 'She left this by my bed and left my brother, Piers, a note.'

He was staring right through me, scanning me for the correct response. I knew I had to judge the moment with extreme delicacy; a sudden move in the wrong direction and I would have frightened him, a deer darting off into the undergrowth.

'She chose a safe place to leave her egg,' I said, gently. Did I detect a hint of a smile?

'She didn't leave me a note,' he repeated, gently, again driving home that this was the most revelatory detail he could ever give me about himself.

'Julius,' I said, 'she didn't need to.'

He grabbed me and hugged me, burying his face in the crook of my neck. He sighed deeply, full of relief and regret.

'Sometimes,' I said gingerly, 'we decide to bury a longing that seems impossible to fulfil because we cannot bear the pain. The danger is that if we forget that longing and cannot access it again, we lose a piece of ourselves.'

He looked at me and he knew. He knew I was saying: 'You're worthy of your longing. Don't be afraid. Choose me.' I waited for him to agree or at least to kiss me but, as always, with my emotional candour I'd gone too far, too soon. He pulled away and said: 'Come on, we're going to be late for lunch.'

All through lunch, I felt I was in an out of body bubble. I heard Julius and his grandmother but I could not connect. Instead, I watched them through the filter of my despair. Bringing me to see his butterflies was Julius's way of explaining why he wasn't going to jettison Alice and marry me. He had his work, his secret passion and that was enough. It was safer that way.

I looked at Grace, at her high cheekbones framed with elegant pale grey hair, at the diamonds dancing at her throat and I envied her. Not just her frail beauty – I noticed the trellis of veins running across her hands and how her rings, now too big, hung to one side of her fingers – but her poise. She had an inner stillness, a complete acceptance, as if she had learned early on in life not to wear herself out fighting the incoming tide. As she listened to Julius talk, her blue eyes radiated warmth. She clearly loved him dearly. I wondered if she thought it strange that he had brought me and not Alice to see her? Did she understand? Beneath her charm there was a knowing. When she lightly rested her hand on my arm as I thanked her for lunch, was she subtly urging me to let her grandson go? But could I let my battle go? Finally, give up on Julius? We drove back to London in silence; it wasn't tense but it wasn't easy either. It was the worn stillness of defeat. What more was there to say?

Lucy and I sat in the Jacuzzi, bubbles exploding in our faces. We were at an expensive, state-of-the-art spa in the countryside, an adjunct to a fashionable hotel among an achingly self-conscious metropolitan crowd. The other female guests, all honed and leggy, were the type that considered pampering their birthright, as much a part of their beautifying ritual as pre-shower skin brushing or daily flossing, whereas I winced at the extravagance and their sense of entitlement. Luce had booked us a girlie weekend on Edward's credit card as a mini act of empowerment. I was in such a state about Julius that I told her I needed help 'diffusing my inner invalidator'. I explained that I couldn't stop chipping away at my self-esteem as I was full of gnawing self-reproach.

'Whenever a relationship, or in this case the promise of a re-relationship, is over, I always go into a charged celibate state, where I cannot envisage anyone ever kissing me or holding me again,' I said to Lucy. 'Apart from that ill-fated night with Troy, I haven't had sex for thirteen months.'

'Not counting, then?' she laughed.

It was easy to remember the last time I got jiggy with Jamie, as I slept with him ten days before I left him. That was the one unfathomable as far as I was concerned: the sex was good right up until the end. Chemistry is inexplicable. He bored me senseless, yet the moment we got horizontal, he could reach me. I often thought that we showed the best of ourselves to each other in bed. Not in terms of flipping each other over like kippers but in acrobatic feats of honesty. I think it was the only place we felt safe with each other because, bizarrely, lying naked, we never had to pretend.

Real passion borders destruction because in relationships we believe we need to sacrifice part of ourselves. That was true with me and Jamie. We were passionate and antagonistic towards each other and we went on sacrificing our happiness until something broke in the end. But we never ran out of steam sexually – maybe we just needed the release? The physical liberation from so much emotional frustration?

'I miss sex,' I admitted. 'Well, not sex exactly but intimacy. Not that I've had much experience of emotional intimacy. Jamie and I never lay entwined, sharing secrets, giggling as dawn broke.'

'But at least you didn't have to schedule sex,' sighed Lucy. 'That's what Edward and I have to do as kids remove all spontaneity. And then he's so predictable. He presses my nipples like they are some sort of direct dial to my clitoris. All I want is a little tenderness, a feeling of real emotional connection, not this hurried foreplay as if he's checking off a list.'

I blinked away water that was splashing up into my face. 'It's just so difficult to get it all right, isn't it?' I said. 'Men, sex, communication, emotional fulfilment, feeling like enough of a woman to be the person you want to be. Fancying them and liking them as well, while feeling confident that they feel the same about you. I've begun to think that nothing is ever rock-solid long term – no man, no situation – and that the happiest people just accept small pockets of bliss, or even contentment, when they can.'

Lucy shrugged as if to say 'maybe'. After a while, I admitted: 'I've had this terrible twitch beneath my eyes. Just doesn't stop.'

'Nervous tension,' she nodded.

'Sexual frustration more like.'

'No, that makes your teeth fall out in dreams,' she said.

'Yeah,' I confessed, 'I dream about that too.'

Later, in the sauna, I lay back and wailed: 'Oh, what am I going to do? I've no job, no home, no man, I'm pretty much broke – my life is a complete failure.'

'Daisy, you need to get a job,' Lucy said admonishingly. 'You have far too much time on your hands to get even more obsessive and neurotic than you already are.'

I agreed with her. Three years out of work since I married Jamie hadn't given me relaxing time at the drawing board of life as I calmly planned my next move. Boredom and lack of achievement had simply annihilated my sense of self-belief to the point that I was completely poleaxed when it came to thinking about anything I could ever do again. And now I was running out of money. The little nest egg I'd sat on after leaving Jamie and selling our flat was nearly empty. I could just about pay my way with Luce and Jess when we went out to drinks or dinner if I carried on living at Mum's but I couldn't contemplate planning a holiday or buying new clothes, let alone anything as grounding and grown-up as getting a mortgage on a pad of my own. That was why I felt so trapped. I was in stasis, stuck in a situation where there didn't seem to be any potential for growth or change.

I knew I shouldn't have but when I got back to Mum's after the weekend, I couldn't resist sending Julius an email. 'It's not difficult to be successful.' I typed. 'It is difficult to be successful and fulfilled. And success without fulfilment is failure.' I waited for his reply.

# Chapter 5
# Dick Delivery Boys

It was over a month and Julius still had not replied to my email. Nor had the various publishing companies to whom I had sent my imaginatively doctored CV. However, the obsessive checking of my inbox suddenly yielded a punch-the-air result. Miles emailed to say that he had quit Hong Kong and was coming back to London, where he had bought a second-hand bookshop. Even better, he offered me a job.

Okay, so when I waltzed out of university throbbing with my own importance having gained a respectable 2:1 degree in English, it never occurred to me I'd be working in a bookshop. Be nominated for a literary prize, more like. I had such an unshakeable sense of my own destiny that I assumed I'd do something high-ranking and important – something that would mark me out as capable and special. Well, that was then and this was now and while it wasn't that I was aspiration-less, I just felt that the pluck had drained from me. I wanted to find a sense of purpose and of course earn professional acclaim (and with that surely the respect of my father?) but ever since I gave up my career in publishing, I'd lost faith in my future and myself.

While I was relieved that this twist of fate meant that at least I would be employed again – and secretly put it down to my nightly missives to my guardian angels where I wrote out my requests like a Christmas wish list, then tucked them under my pillow – Lucy and Jess greeted the news of Miles's imminent return with condescension. 'Miles is a mixed blessing,' huffed Jess. 'He's good for a mercy jump but you must remember, like all male commitment-phobes past forty, Miles is basically a screwed up, selfish git.'

'Firstly,' I said, sucking the froth off my cappuccino, 'even if I do need a shag, I don't need a man to do it with me out of pity and anyway, I'd never sleep with Miles. It would be like sleeping with my brother, if I had a brother. Secondly, you're just jealous because I'll have a good-looking, single man to go out and play with.'

'That's true,' said Lucy, wistfully. She twiddled her wedding ring. 'Maybe Miles is the man I should have an affair with?'

'You're still thinking about that?' I said, vaguely aghast. I thought she'd gone off the idea. 'Anyway, Miles can't stand needy women,' I carried on. Lucy shot me a look. 'Sorry, I didn't mean it like that but surely if it is your first affair, you're going to crave a lot of attention.'

'Miles would be just the ticket then,' said Jess, rubbing her hands with glee. 'He'll have a lot of tricks up his sleeve, so to speak, having doubtless bedded half of Hong Kong and South East Asia.'

'Oh, that would put me off.' Lucy shook her head. 'I'd find

myself comparing myself with the scores of sluts in his wake, thinking "did she do this better than me?" or "am I doing this right?"'

'I agree,' I giggled. 'Sexy in the sack is men getting the balance right between knowing what they're doing but not turning it into some well-worn porno routine where you sense their irritation if you deviate from their fantasy script. You want to know that your mere presence is enough.'

'God, you two are so unadventurous,' sniffed Jess. 'There's nothing wrong with wish-fulfilment. You've just got to know what you want and ask for it. Simple as that.'

'Do you know,' said Lucy, 'in over ten years of sleeping with Edward, I've never once said to him in bed, "Can you do it like this?"'

Jess nearly choked on her coffee. 'I never had steady Eddie down as a bully.'

'Edward's not a bully, he's just so predictable. I can't communicate with him when we're naked any more.'

'One of the most important aspects of oral sex is knowing how to talk in bed,' I said. 'Asking "how was it for you?" shows a dreary inability to feel your way around the situation.'

Lucy and Jess laughed. 'So speaks Miss Daisy: celibate and hating every second,' joked Jess.

That was about the sum of it. 'No sex is better than downgraded, casual sex,' I said, unconvincingly.

'So why has Miles bought a second-hand bookshop in Pimlico?' asked Lucy. 'It's not very hunter gatherer, is it? I thought he'd come back to bag a wife.'

'Exactly. He thinks owning a second-hand book shop has huge pulling power,' I said. 'Women will fall for his erudite, sensitive side, apparently.'

'Why? Did he take an acting course in Hong Kong?' Jess pulled a face. 'I mean, let's face it, with a serial shagger like

Miles, there's not much touchy-feely, let's snuggle down with a Wordsworth sonnet, is there?'

'Maybe he's grown up,' said Lucy.

'Developed a conscience, more like,' said Jess. 'You'll have to leave your Mum's and live in London now you're going to be a working girl. Do you want to flat share with me while you get yourself sorted out?'

'Thanks, my friend,' I said. 'I can get your place in neat-freak order in no time.'

'But will you be able to stand the steady stream of Jess's conquests as they come and go?' asked Lucy, dryly.

Jess looked a tad put out. But Luce had a point, even if she was being uncharacteristically caustic. 'Well, maybe *I'll* meet someone in the bookshop,' I said, in a bid to diffuse tension. 'Miles has said that I can run the Mind/Body/Spirit section.'

'Save me from the self-help addicts,' said Jess, getting up and blowing me a kiss goodbye. I noticed she didn't acknowledge Lucy as she left.

That night, emailing Miles, my stomach flipped when I saw Julius's name in the inbox:

*D. Believe me, I am not marrying Alice with the same blithe blindness that sends a bungee jumper off a bridge. She is right for me for now because she is not going to challenge me. She is not the diversion that you are. You may believe that you are ready for me but I am not ready for you. The timing is not right. I'm sorry to disappoint you now but I promise you this: when we are old, I shall come for you. I shall buy a house somewhere warm and we shall sit in the sun and tell each other the story of our lives. Make it a good story and a good life. I love you. J. x*

No, I thought, tears streaming down my face, if he loved me, he wouldn't make me wait.

I was so distraught following my email from Julius, that Jess called a girlie summit at Mum's. It was a perfect spring weekend, and while Lucy stroked my back and Jess tickled my feet with a feather, I sat under a magnolia tree and groaned: 'How am I ever going to feel this way about a man again?'

'You thought you loved Jamie but you got over him,' said Jess matter-of-factly.

'No,' I said softly, fingering the waxy petals scattered on the grass, 'I thought I loved Jamie but I know I am in love with Julius.' I sighed. 'It's a completely different feeling. Basically, the difference between being in love with someone and loving someone is the difference between kneeling on the ground and being a midget.'

Jess laughed: 'What about a kneeling midget? What sort of love is that?'

'Obviously, that's the realest thing.'

Lucy stopped soothing my shoulders and sat beside me. 'You are single now, Daisy, and God knows, the minute you get married with kids, I promise you, you'll wish you had spent longer relishing being alone. I listen to my single girlfriends who spend their lives flitting from party to party, sleeping in until lunchtime the following day, jetting off to Europe for impromptu mini-breaks, snogging strangers, power brunching on weekends, reading novels and newspapers by the truckload, able to go to the cinema on a whim and not have to orchestrate a military-style manoeuvre of the babysitter, the kids' supper, the bath-and-bed routine, let alone contemplate the hellish expense of it all and I wonder why they moan about needing to settle down and breed. I'm sick of hearing that their pain is enormous, when all I see is unlimited freedom and endless possibilities for uninterrupted sleep and pure self-indulgence.'

'I've been telling you that for years,' said Jess. 'I never understand the women who come to my surgery and want children with the biological desperation that I feel when I want an emergency loo stop on the motorway.'

'Marriage isn't an answer, it's a riddle,' said Lucy, sadly. 'It's a complete mystery about two people coming together and trying to make it work.'

'Isn't marriage a defiant gesture of optimism?' I said, hopefully.

'After a while marriage is like familiarity,' said Lucy bitterly. 'It breeds children and contempt.'

'Are you that unhappy with Edward?' I asked.

'Not *that* unhappy,' said Lucy, 'It's not like I actively loathe our life together but I don't totally love it either.'

'That's a dangerous no man's land because you get complacent,' cautioned Jess. She shook her head. 'It's the long but not happy marriage, like my parents had, that breaks my heart. Those who feel duty bound to remain handcuffed to a life sentence, serving marital time together, but lonely.'

Lucy and I stared at Jess. She hardly ever talked about her family and although we knew that this was why she ran shy of commitment, I rarely sensed that deep sadness. 'Do you wish your parents had divorced?' I asked, keenly aware that however unhappy Mum and Dad might have been I still wished that they were together because of my selfish bratty inner child.

''Course. I've told you that,' said Jess. 'When Dad died of a heart attack in my early thirties, part of me was relieved. I thought that at least Mum can start to live her own life now, but the saddest thing was that it was too late. She was in her early sixties, yet she considered herself old. She didn't see any other existence for herself because she'd been mentally chained to my father for so long. I'm quite convinced that's why she let her cancer eat her up. She wasn't seventy when she died. All those years of emotional repression didn't amount to anything in the end. What's the point of that kind of marital duty?' Jess looked choked. 'Lucy, don't stay for the kids alone, stay by all means, but stay for you.'

'It's easy for you to say that when you don't have any responsibility,' Lucy said sullenly.

'But I can tell you that when they're old enough to understand, they'll feel your sacrifice as their own,' said Jess. 'Sometimes my guilt is unbearable.'

I felt a stab of shame because I still craved the façade of marital unity and familial stability between my parents. I still wished that while Mum and I were gossiping around the kitchen table, there would be the rustle of the newspaper in the background or a surreptitious snort from Dad. Even though he never gave much input into our lives, it was reassuring that however irritating we found him, he was there.

'There is the other side of it though. When your parents split up and your mother is on her own you feel a heightened sense of responsibility,' I said. 'I long for Mum to meet someone because I want her to be happy.'

Suddenly Mum appeared with a tray of tea and a pile of sludge on a platter. 'Here you are: Tetley's finest and my molasses layer cake. You lot look like you need a shot of sugar – I love you girls dearly but honestly, you're such neurotics. You must learn not to over-analyse and just press on with life.' She put the tray down. 'I'm off to group therapy now. See you later.'

Jess sat bolt upright, outraged. 'I can't believe it, Mrs D. Daisy hasn't got you into therapy, has she?'

'Good grief no,' smiled Mum. 'It is my FOCDA meeting.'

'Fockder?' Lucy enquired gingerly.

'Haven't you heard?' I said. 'It's the latest twelve-step meeting sweeping the Home Counties. Families Of Canine Disorders Anonymous. It attracts only the truly barking. A load of batty toffs sit in damp village halls and share their torment over Blackie, who chews his paws or Fido, who barks incessantly when his owner plays Rachmaninov badly on the piano.'

'And why are you going, Mrs D?' asked Lucy. 'Dougie has a new anxiety condition called Canine Compulsive Disorder,' said my mother gravely. 'It affects two per cent of all dogs, according to a veterinary professor in Indiana.'

'Why, what does he do?'

'He's rubbed his eyebrows off on the coconut matting in the back hall,' said Mum.

'He should learn to press on with life,' I said, 'And you should stop analysing your animals.' Mum waved at Dougie, barking at the kitchen window and dashed down the lawn. 'Poor demented Mum – I mean, mutt,' I said.

I don't know if we hit a sugar high but later, we fell about laughing. A bottle of wine or two and I was tempted to drink-and-dial. 'Don't you dare,' screamed Jess, grabbing the phone. 'You must not contact Julius again. He'll think you're stalking him.'

'Communicating is not stalking,' I reasoned. 'Anyway, I'm not ringing Julius, I'm ringing Miles. He's coming to lunch tomorrow.'

'Great,' beamed Lucy, 'my flirting is awfully rusty.'

Miles, Lucy, Jess and I were sitting in the garden drinking after an epic Sunday lunch. The lawn was awash with crumpled Sunday supplements and empty bottles of plonk.

When I went inside for a tray of coffee, Lucy followed and collared me. 'I'd forgotten that Miles is so goddamn sexy,' she said, breathlessly. 'Even hung-over, he's completely gorgeous.'

I stared at him from the kitchen window. He had been regaling us with anecdotes of his conquest the night before and suddenly Jess threw back her head in hysterical glee – no doubt at the eye-wateringly awful, tawdry detail.

Lucy was right. For a fleeting moment, when I first saw Miles grinning at the door, I considered him for myself. No doubt about it, he was one hell of a catch and while I fancied him, I also knew that the frisson of physical attraction breathed life into our friendship. That the 'will we, won't we?' possibility loitered in the ether, gave our alliance an enduring, edgy quality. While it was fun to fantasise about getting down and dirty with Miles, the rational part of me knew that it would never work between us. What did work was being best mates with a guy I found attractive – after all, what male–female friendship is ever one hundred per cent, bone-dry platonic?

Lucy put her hands to her flushed cheeks. 'Do you think Miles could find me attractive?'

'Well, he was harping on about wanting to bang a yummy mummy,' I said. 'Look at you, Lucy. You're beautiful with a stunning figure. You've got exactly the sort of bullet body that Miles goes for. Why wouldn't he want you?'

Lucy bit her lip. 'Oh Jess, you've no idea how years of married going-through-the-motions sex with a man who doesn't even notice if you've cut your hair, let alone had a bikini wax, erodes your self-esteem. I look at Miles, who's so full of life and vigour, and I feel stale and shy and boring in comparison.'

'But is the answer to have an affair? Do you really think that cheating on Edward will make you feel better about yourself? Yes, you may get away with it and Edward may never know but you'll know. How will you live with it up here?' I asked, gently tapping her forehead. 'Is there really no way you and Edward can re-ignite things?'

Lucy slumped into a chair by the kitchen table. 'Daisy, you know as well as I do that there is no greater loneliness than being in a marriage with someone who can no longer fulfil you.'

I nodded. 'I do,' I said. 'The worst is when you wake up, look at the man lying next to you, and realise that you have outgrown him. When your dreams and aspirations are no longer compatible, it is like sleeping with a sibling. The key is to chose a partner with whom you can develop at a similar rate.'

'When I got engaged to Edward, I felt as if I had won some sort of life competition. Now, I know to my cost that the point is not winning, it is knowing and being known. Edward doesn't begin to know who I am any more.'

'But do you know him? Perhaps he's as lonely and unfulfilled as you.'

'How can you say that, when you left Jamie?' said Lucy, getting huffy. 'You know what it's like not to be able to reach the man you married.'

'I do,' I said softly. 'Jamie had this brick wall protecting his emotions which I tried to sandblast down with probing affection but I just exhausted myself and he remained as blocked off as ever. All I am saying, Luce, is that you know when a relationship is truly over. You reach this ghostly dead zone, with its permanent chill, where you can't raise any passion and you kill each other with phoney politeness. It's all: "Do you want to use the bathroom first?" "No, really, it's okay, after you." As soon as you find yourself putting a towel around you when they catch you naked, you know it's finished. I'm just not convinced that you and Edward are there yet.'

'You just don't want me to sleep with Miles,' laughed Lucy.

'You're probably right. More, I don't want you to get hurt. Miles is still into casual encounters. He's forever gorging on McSex, the fast-food coupling that leaves you feeling empty and slightly nauseous.'

Lucy got up and peered through the window at Miles, who was stretched out across the grass, his shirt buttons undone. 'Oh, but a bit of a binge on something that's bad for you can hit the spot sometimes. Can't it?'

Although it was some time before I was to start work in Miles's bookshop, I frantically researched books for the Mind/Body/Spirit section that I was going to run. I had moved some of my stuff into Jess's spare room. It could have been a drunken disaster us living together semi-permanently, but instead of us going out and having lots of giggly girlie nights, I did hours of soul surfing; getting spiritual on the web. Jess couldn't believe it the first time she came home from work and I was still hunched over my laptop. Despite her best efforts, I refused a trip to the local wine bar. 'No thanks. I prefer to expand my consciousness, not my waistline, tonight,' I said. 'I'll get high on happy thoughts instead.'

'Your brain is already addled by all that Californian crap,' she said, lighting a fag.

I batted the smoke away. 'Actually, I've just been reading about Sattva: the power of beingness. You should try to access some sattvic strength. It's all about the inner integrity that let Buddha sit under the Bodhi tree until he became enlightened. It's the same sort of power you feel in cathedrals and in forests.'

'And in looney bins?' she retorted.

Suddenly, the doorbell rang. It was Lucy. All my sattvic

calm drained away and I felt a flood of panic. Lucy looked like a gargoyle; her face was completely distorted with pain. Mascara streaked her cheeks and her usually sleek hair appeared to have chunks hacked out of it. Before we could speak, she threw herself on the floor and coiled up in the foetal position. Rocking back and forth, she emitted a guttural roar of agony.

'I'll call an ambulance,' said Jess. 'Stay calm, keep breathing. You've probably got a burst appendix.'

Lucy started beating the carpet with her fists. 'I wish I bloody had.' I gently took her hand. Jess poured her a brandy. When Lucy's manic sobbing had subsided, she shouted: 'The bastard! The complete, cowardly, fucking shit.'

'Who? Miles?' I said, thinking: 'Here we go. He did 'n' dumped her.'

'Not Miles. Edward.' Lucy flopped forwards and started grabbing at her hair, trying to pull it from her head.

Jess eased her arms away. 'Lucy, whatever is it? Here, sip some brandy and tell us what has happened.'

Lucy took a swig, then a deep, steadying breath and began: 'It was just past eight. Edward always leaves the house at six to be in the office when the markets open. Sometimes he rings while the girls are eating breakfast to say hello to them, but more often to bark some errand for me to run. I'd just come out of the shower and I picked up the phone and said: "Hi, darling, what do you want?" and there was this strange pause. Then a woman's voice said: "Is this Mrs Primfold?" She sounded decent and above board, so I assumed it was one of the mothers on the school run that I hadn't met yet. Possibly a new mother looking to join our run. So I said cheerily, "Yes, this is Lucy Primfold, how can I help you?" I wasn't really concentrating, as I was sitting on the edge of my bed, still in my towel, rubbing in hand cream that I found on my bedside table. Then this voice said: "I'm really sorry to call you like this," and I suddenly got this ghastly feeling in the pit of my stomach. It's so strange how our instincts prepare us a second before the body blow. I knew then that this wasn't a stressed mother looking for a favour. So I said: "Who is this?" and again these was this long pause. My heart was racing. Eventually, she said, "My name is Susie and Edward and I have been seeing each other for two years." "Seeing each other?" I asked lamely and she simply said: "We love each other. Look, I'm sorry to say this but it's time to let him go."'

Lucy began to sob again. 'She's got a cheek,' I said.

'At first I didn't believe her,' said Lucy, choked. 'I sat on the bed with the phone in my hand, vaguely aware the girls were playing on the landing but there was this awful feeling of "Please, no! This can't be happening to *me*." It was like a moment out of a film and even though you've seen it a thousand times, you never in your wildest dreams think it'll happen to you. I rang Edward at work and said "Who is Susie?" and there was this awful scared silence and I knew instantly it was true. I just put down the phone, got dressed and took the children to school. I was on automatic pilot. I don't remember one thing about the drive or what I said to the girls. I could have been high on drugs I was so out of it.'

'That's when your guardian angel steps in and protects you,' I said.

'Well, why didn't her guardian angel step in and stop Edward having an affair?' asked Jess sarcastically.

'Edward has been unfaithful to *me,*' hollered Lucy. 'Can you believe it? My husband has been having his end away for two years. Our marriage is a sham.' She downed another brandy in one. 'I've wasted all this time being faithful while Edward was cheating on me. I look and feel an utter, ugly fool.'

'He's the fool,' I said, quietly. I took Lucy in my arms and she fell against me, weeping. After a while, she pulled away. 'Do you know what really hurts?' she said, in a little voice which broke my heart. 'That Edward had his affair, while I only fantasised about having one.'

'Lucy, you are far too decent to betray anyone, let alone the father of your children,' I said, tears welling up. 'It was just a mental diversion.'

'It's not only that I gave up my career, took on the mantle of trophy wife, then morphed into a loving mother or that I ran a perfect home and that I was always there, supporting him,' said Lucy, digging her fingers into her eye sockets, 'it's that deep down, I . . . I bloody trusted him.'

Jess and I nodded, not knowing what to say. Lucy gave a twisted laugh. 'When I got back from the school run, I went into the house and it was as if our home was in shock too. It was silent and tense and I felt possessed. Do you know what I did? I grabbed a carving knife and went into the drawing room and slashed all Edward's family's beloved Old Master paintings. You know why? Because when he gets home tonight, I want him to feel in as much pain as I do.'

Jess clapped. 'Good for you. How did it feel?'

'When I was dragging the knife through the canvas, it felt incredible,' said Lucy. 'The ripping noise was fantastic. It was the most rebellious thing I've ever done in my life.' She slumped back. 'Oh God, they're worth a freaking fortune. What am I going to do?'

'They'll be insured,' I said.

'From robbers not wives-turned-maniacs,' she said. She let out a tortured sob. 'How am I going to get through this?'

'Lucy,' said Jess softly, 'you've spent so much time being the woman behind the man, try being the woman behind the woman and see what happens.'

'You're strong, Luce,' I agreed. 'You'll survive. What I don't understand is why that bitch had to phone you in the first place?'

'It gets worse.' Lucy bit her lip. 'Edward's lover told me that he bought her a flat eighteen months ago. Half the time he's not at work but is semi-living with her. Today was the day that he promised her that he was moving in with her for good.'

I knew from experience that Lucy would wake unfeasibly early because unhappiness, like loneliness, pushes its jagged edges through sleep and rouses you when you most want to ignore it. I had been exactly where Lucy was now – after leaving Jamie and after my abortion with Troy's child – lying in an alien bed in a friend's spare room (usually Jess's), eyes so swollen from crying you could hardly open them, body aching from lack of sleep, mind whirring into self-punishing over-drive, heart pounding with fear yet broken just the same. It was before six when I crept in from the sitting room where I had been sleeping on the sofa, with a cup of tea. Just as I suspected, Lucy was awake, staring at the ceiling and the room was choked with despair.

I got into bed beside her and handed her the sweet tea. She sat up, took a sip and said: 'I'm forty years old and I've never let myself go. I've looked after my skin, my hair and my figure. Edward has never seen me with a greasy fringe, dark roots, an unruly bikini line or bulging blackheads. For Christ's sake, I exfoliate my T-zone and body brush every single day. If I'd let my standards slip, if my husband had ever seen me with cracked heels or cellulite, if he'd ever commented on a few strands of non-bleached moustache, or smelt a hint of BO, maybe I could understand. But to betray me when all I've ever done is my best for him, when all I've ever done is to love him and look after our children, is unbearable.'

I threw some soggy tissues into the bin and handed Lucy a fresh wad. She turned to me, her face streaked with tears. 'I didn't deserve this.'

'No,' I whispered. 'You didn't.'

'You know what really frightens me, Daise?' I shook my head. 'That I don't think I have the strength to fight for him nor the courage to shoulder the pain now that I have lost him.'

'I don't think that you've lost him,' I said. 'He's clearly lost the plot but if you want to, you'll sort it out.'

'What, with Edward buying a flat behind my back and telling some chick he loves her and is moving in with her? I don't think so.' Lucy sank back against the pillows. 'I'm so ashamed,' she sighed. 'What am I going to tell my parents? My children? My friends? The worst thing is that I haven't done anything wrong and yet I feel mortified because of the slur on our family. On *my* life.' She started beating the duvet with her fists. 'Don't these bastard men get it? By sticking it elsewhere, they don't just betray us they do something far, far worse.' Sobbing, her face puce with pain, Lucy started screaming: 'They make us doubt ourselves. When your husband cheats on you, you can no longer trust your own judgement. The man, the marriage, the make-believe-happily-ever-after is all shot to pieces, just so he can feel like a sex god getting his end away in his lunch hour.'

The anger seemed to drain from Lucy as she said: 'It's not just the lies and deceit that really hurts or even the actual sex. It's the fact that he lay entwined with another woman and woke up with her. Letting someone see you sleep is far more personal than seeing them awake, no matter what you get up to, because then they see you how you really are in life: vulnerable and alone.' Lucy's body convulsed with grief.

'How am I going to get through this? I've never felt lonelier or more scared.'

'When I left Jamie, I was petrified of life on my own,' I said softly, stoking Lucy's arm while she quietly wept beside me. 'The only thing you can do is to get away and think. For me, living with Mum was the final insult to my ego but somehow, through the maelstrom of emotion, there would be milliseconds of peace when I felt at one with myself. Over time those milliseconds turn to minutes and minutes to odd hours and then suddenly you find you're actually living a better life for yourself than before, regardless of the circumstances, because there is a clarity and hard won self-respect.'

Lucy blew her nose. 'I want to be as brave as you've been, Daisy. I want that better life. To feel okay inside.'

'I know,' I said. 'We all deserve nothing less.'

It had been just over three weeks since Lucy discovered that Edward was having an affair and once she had ferried her children to her parents where they would feel safe and adored, as Luce was keen to shield them from what was happening, she more or less camped out with me at Jess's. We spent hours dissecting her plight, dusting down her pain and allowing her anger to surge.

Just as she was rallying, I fell flat on my face, emotionally speaking, when I saw the latest copy of *Hello!*. Julius and Alice's wedding was plastered across five pages as it was deemed the society wedding of the year. The saddest thing was that, as I obsessively pored over every millimetre of every page, I knew that even if I had been invited, I would have had nothing to wear. All the women sported those wide-brimmed hats that cost a small fortune, and wore family jewellery that had been passed down through generations. The massive three-strand pearl choker that had been

Granny's, the socking engagement rings that had been their great-grandmother-in-law's, the jaunty teardrop diamond earrings that had been Mummy's aunt's. The guests weren't just rich Sloanes they were a mix of Euro aristos and the private-jet set. I tried to tell myself that it would never have worked if Julius had married me; can you imagine how tired and scruffy my parents would have looked, like a couple of old badgers next to these smooth, sleek seals, but of course I was devastated. As I stared at Alice, dainty in Empire-line ivory duchess satin, with a glittering tiara that must have weighed a ton, I tried to console myself that her victory was Pyrrhic because couldn't you tell from Julius's tight smile that he didn't love her? But inside I felt the well-worn beat of failure. Let's face it; she had won.

When the absurdity of life hit – that here we were, me and Lucy, weeping and single at fortyish, as opposed to being happily married and settled – we would collapse in fits of giggles. It was like being back in our flat sharing days of our early twenties, especially as Jess didn't see our presence as a barrier to bringing the odd lover home. One evening, Lucy and I returned from the cinema to find a naked man making toast in the kitchen. Without uttering a word, he threw a tea towel over his manhood and winked at us as he took a tray of buttered buns and tea back into Jess's room. I turned to Lucy and said: 'That'll be Jess's dick delivery boy.'

'I'm beginning to understand Jess's penchant for casual sex,' said Lucy, re-filling the kettle. 'Did you see how buffed he was?' She imitated his cheesy wink and we doubled up. 'Why are we bothering to try to have fulfilling relationships when we could get shagged when we need it and spend the rest of the time luxuriating in the bed alone?'

'You know as well as I do that we don't have the single-mindedness to pull it off,' I said. 'I've tried casual sexual relationships and they were never quite as casual or sexual as they should have been.'

'But the more you love someone, the more you open yourself up to pain when they betray you,' said Lucy, bitterly.

'Here, let's see what the Universal wisdom has to say.' I grabbed my copy of *Dating Dharma*, opened a random page and read out: '"It only takes a minute to get a crush on someone. An hour to like them. A day to love them but a lifetime to forget them."'

'Oh, great!' said Lucy. 'I've only got a lifetime's misery ahead.'

'Hang on, hang on,' I said. 'That can't have been the real message. I wasn't fully focused.' I clutched the book to my chest and closed my eyes. When I opened them, I flicked through the book and read: '"It's true that we don't know what we've got until we lose it but it's also true that we don't know what we've been missing until it arrives." There!' I said triumphantly. 'Keep positive because who knows what lies ahead?'

The next day I was due to have lunch with my father at Thai Temptations before meeting Lucy and Miles, as Lucy had asked us both to accompany her home so she could collect some clothes before Edward returned from work.

Dad was sitting in his booth with a science book open in front of him, spooning greasy noodles into his mouth. A dribble of soy sauce ran down his chin. He looked old suddenly, or at least fallible, and I felt myself bristle. I wanted him to be strong and supportive – there for me. Suddenly, I was sick of my parents looking like they needed a free pass to the nearest mental asylum. Why couldn't he have been the sort of father crisply dressed in a city suit with a copy of the *Evening Standard* tucked under his arm, who you knew had a fat pension amassing in some private account and who fully intended to spend his retirement travelling the world in high style? Unlike my father who looked one step up from a homeless person and acted like it. Like most academics, he considered clothes an irrelevance. After all, it's what's going on upstairs that counts, isn't it? Who cares if your tie is soup stained or your cuffs are frayed, if your brilliant brain is pulsing with facts and finely calibrated figures? Dad still wears the discount Kickers he bought from Kickback, a seconds store on Wandsworth Bridge Road nearly thirty years ago. Their rubber-rutted soles are worn down to paper but educated, university types seem addicted to shoes that squelch as opposed to snap and echo through academic stone corridors of power. Bizarrely for an Englishman, Dad is fond of the preppy look – more New England than Home Counties – and so he was wearing a long-sleeved cotton polo neck and chinos darned in various places. His watch was a staggeringly awful black plastic number with a smattering of diamanté on the face; a gift from some scientific attaché from South Korea. Do you think these guys are having a laugh? Do they know that the only specimen of English gentleman likely to wear their tat is a scientist who firmly believes it's gauche to care?

I rushed up, 'Dad, sorry I'm late.'

'I hope you don't mind, I started,' he said, without seeming to acknowledge me. 'Did you know that they've put the parking meter prices up? I've got the meter filled until 1.40pm but that cost me nearly six pounds. It's obscene.'

Yeah, six pounds for the meter and almost eight quid a head for this muck and you're really shelling out, I thought. What it must be to feel utterly spoilt by Daddy? I sank into the booth opposite him. 'Osmosis is fascinating,' continued Dad. 'Did you know that when a cell splits . . .'

Why do we do this? I thought. What is the point in running

through this charade when we never connect on any level that means anything to either of us? I stood up. 'I'm sorry. I can't do this any more.'

He looked up, incredulous. Finally, I thought, I've shocked him into some sort of feeling-induced reaction. 'But Daisy,' he said. 'You can't go. I've already paid for your meal.' He stared at me beseechingly. 'It is £7.99 a head.' He looked genuinely hurt (yes, a wasted tenner, that's bound to sting), so I slumped back into my seat. I put my head in my hands, not sure whether to laugh or cry. When I looked back he had actually put his fork down and was viewing me, not with particular concern or alarm, more with the detachment of the scientist, watching and waiting to see what colour the litmus paper will turn.

'Dad,' I sighed, 'I . . . I . . . just feel that you don't know who I am any more. I'm not sure what purpose these lunches really serve?'

'Purpose? Purpose?' he repeated pensively, as if filtering and de-coding everything for extra meaning. 'Does everything have to have a purpose? In science not everything has a purpose as in "What's the point of it?" When somebody asked Michael Faraday . . .' catching my blank expression, he filled me in, 'he was the inventor of electricity, Daisy. Anyway, when someone asked Faraday "What's the point of electricity?" he answered "What's the point of a new born child?"' He gave a warm chuckle of delight. 'But when Gladstone asked Faraday "What's the point of electricity?" Faraday said "You can tax it!"' Tickled pink, Dad was guffawing with laughter and against myself, I felt myself soften.

'Dad, you once said to me, "The difference between you and me, Daisy, is that you're interested in people and I'm not." The problem is that I don't feel that you're particularly interested in me because I'm a person. I don't feel,' I said, looking straight at him, 'that we have a connection.'

'You're quite right,' he said proudly. 'I'm not interested in people.' He grinned as if he'd just said: 'Forget professional validation and critical acclaim – it's my family that means everything to me!'

'But how do you have a connection with people if you don't like them?' I asked.

'I have a connection with what they do. I'm interested in lawyers, in artists, in painters . . .'

'But I don't have a great job, so what about me? How can you connect with me?' I said, aware that I sounded, as ever, painfully petulant. Daisy – nearly middle-aged and still it's all me, me and more me.

Dad took a sip of water – tap, naturally – and said: 'I admire you Daisy, because you always try to connect with people even if it means getting hurt.' He continued speaking steadily, in his usual measured way. 'Ever since your mother and I, well, we . . . we, you know . . .'

'Divorced?' I chirped helpfully.

'Yes, since we divorced, I've shied away from that kind of connection. I find books and theories safer, but you're a great risk-taker whatever the consequences. You keep searching, as love or that sort of connection clearly means something to you. That, my dear, is to be applauded.'

Afterwards, as I walked to the tube, I felt unusually buoyant. So what if my father wasn't a wealthy pin-striped slicker with an animal print Hermès tie and Italian loafers? It didn't matter that he didn't ply me with compliments or dole out cheques on demand. Like my mother, in his batty, offbeat way, he was able to let me know that he cared. Isn't that what that sort of love connection is all about?

I met Miles and Lucy at the top of her road at 4pm. 'How was lunch?' asked Lucy.

'Better than expected,' I said. 'For once Dad tried and so did I.'

As we walked up the pavement, we saw a pretty blonde woman with a floaty floral top sitting on the front doorstep. Lucy froze. 'Oh my God. It's her. I just know it is. She looks exactly like she sounds.'

'Who?' asked Miles.

'Edward's mistress,' hissed Lucy, adding loudly. 'The bitch who's been banging my husband.'

Suddenly Miles dropped his bag and ran up the steps of Lucy's house. 'Susie, what on earth are you doing here?'

'Susie?' I asked, incredulous. 'Oh, so you've slept with her too?'

'Hardly,' he said. 'You remember Susie? She's my step-sister.'

# Chapter 6
# Married Singles

Lucy swept passed Susie with aplomb. I marvelled at her discipline: she did not howl out her anger, hurl obscenities in her rival's face, grab Susie's beautiful soft curly hair and yank hard as I undoubtedly would have done, nor did she succumb to any behaviour that might undermine her public façade of control. She simply closed the front door behind her, neatly underlining her territorial rights and leaving her husband's mistress, Miles and me standing awkwardly outside. Susie slumped down, hugged her knees and wept. Miles knelt beside her. Torn, I sat a few steps beneath them. Susie told her stepbrother that she had had no idea that Edward's marriage was intact. He'd told her when they met that he was separated and that his marriage was over in all but name. Oh, and that he and Lucy never had sex. He'd also said that it was Lucy who wouldn't give him a divorce out of spite. I listened in stunned silence as Susie said that Edward had promised to leave Lucy and move in with her the day she rang Lucy. She only rang as a desperate last resort because she thought that the marriage was finished anyway, and this might be reason enough for Lucy to agree to a divorce. But once Edward knew that Lucy knew, he went nuclear and stopped taking Susie's calls. Now, he wanted her to leave the flat where she'd been living as he was going to sell it.

I put my head in my hands. It was a depressingly familiar echo of my own experience with Troy Powers. Okay, so Troy wasn't married but he went all out to spin me round and make me dizzy with delight but then he never called, and when I fell pregnant, it felt like he hurled a bucket of icy water in my face. Edward had promised Susie the world and then reneged when she called him on it. Why did men always start unravelling like this? It was as if most of the male species exist with two opposing forces at play which are magnetically repelled. One minute they are the respectable husband and dosh-earner, lovingly making eggy bread for their kids, tenderly wiping an eyelash off their tired wife's cheek and chastely kissing her goodbye, the next they have loosened their tie and are banging some hot mama against the boot of their car as they whisper their dirtiest desires in her willing ear. Just as they can look at you as if you are the only woman in the world to light their fire in the morning, but give them unwelcome news that afternoon and they blank you as if they've never seen you before in their life. Why is it that most married men develop emotional autism once the rot of domesticity sets in? It's as if however successful they feel professionally, personally they go to pieces if there isn't some sex kitten boosting their ego flagging from the demands of family life. How does a wife and mother keep her man if she does the unthinkable and puts her children first?

As much as my loyalties lay with Lucy – imploding with the thrust of Edward's betrayal – I felt for Susie. It wasn't just that she was Miles's step-sibling; I could see that she was one of us. She was pretty in that easy, uncomplicated way with a fresh complexion and an effortlessly slim figure. There was nothing contrived about her. She wasn't overly made up or trying too hard. She hadn't set out to destroy a family, she wasn't some scheming bitch; she had merely tried to bag herself a decent bloke, just like the rest of us. That's what got me about the duplicity of a married man like Edward. He didn't stop to think that he wasn't merely cheating on his wife, he was also destroying some single girl's chances of getting love right first time. Susie must have pinned so many romantic hopes on Edward when he started pursuing her, and now she was left as humiliated as Lucy. She must have told her friends, and her family even, that she was seeing this great guy and perhaps they had all joked and secretly prayed that he was The One. Maybe she had even tried writing her potential married name, Susie Primfold, on the back of an envelope for size, or rolled possible children's names around her tongue. She might have planned a cosy Christmas with him or fantasised about the holidays they would have or the home they would make together. Who knows what dreams we weave when love looms on the horizon but now, thanks to Edward, the future for Lucy and Susie looked equally bleak.

I got up and rang the doorbell. Lucy answered cautiously via the intercom. 'It's me. Daise. Are you okay? Can I come in?'

'I just need to be by myself right now,' she said, unable to conceal that she had been crying.

Just as my bile was rising further towards Edward, he walked towards us. I couldn't believe he actually had the gall to be sauntering down the street. Suave in a bespoke suit, his shoes impossibly shiny, he moved up the pavement with the cool assurance of a man apparently untroubled by life.

Miles lurched forward and ploughed his fist into Edward's face. I let out a yelp of delight and clapped my hands. Edward seemed to stagger backwards in slow motion, and the spray of blood across the pavement was impressive. Susie started shouting 'No, Miles, no!' while Edward eyed her with unconcealed dislike. Secretly, I'd always considered Edward a tosser but in that moment, I actively loathed him.

As Edward held his handkerchief to his nose in a bid to regain his composure, a couple walking down the opposite pavement stopped to stare. Miles was right up in Edward's face, shouting: 'She's not some slapper you fuck and chuck. Susie is my sister.'

'Isn't every woman some man's daughter or sister?' said Edward, with disdain. 'Your sister is a fully consenting adult. I didn't have to drag her into bed.'

'No, but you could have told her the truth,' I screamed. 'She wouldn't have been so hot to trot if she'd known you were actually married, would she?' I grabbed his hand. 'Easier to spin when you don't wear a ring, isn't it?'

Edward pushed me aside and tried to get up his front steps, but Miles grabbed him back. 'You've got responsibilities, mate,' he said. 'Be a man for once.' I was vaguely aware that the couple across the road were coming towards us, and that they seemed familiar. Hadn't I seen that sickeningly skinny blonde somewhere before?

Suddenly, I wanted to rewind the last ten minutes and let life play any other scenario in the world than this. The man crossing the road was Julius. I watched as Alice trotted to keep up. Time seemed to stall as Julius called out: 'Daisy. Is everything all right?'

I fought the urge to say: 'Everything is relative. It was bad but bearable until you showed up.'

Fate could not have contrived a worse situation for me to run into Julius. All those hours I had wasted fantasising about bumping into him in some smart restaurant, beautified and blow-dried, a head-turning toy boy in tow, were shot to pieces. Instead of being overly worried that Miles was about to kick Edward to mulch, all I could obsess about was my hair. Too lazy to wash it that morning, I had scraped it on top of my head in what could hardly be considered an elegant chignon – more like a straggly, greasy bun.

Alice, standing proprietorially close to Julius, was clearly a three blow-dry a week babe. Not only did her expensive blonde hair tumble to her tiny shoulders, her breasts were impossibly perky through her flimsy white kaftan-style top. Her physical perfection made me feel stocky and ungainly – ugly even – and I hated myself for my rampant self-doubt. Not even my impassioned and overblown 'character', which usually gave me the edge over brain dead, emotionally botoxed women, could save me now. It was woefully obvious why Julius had chosen Alice over me. She was younger, richer, prettier, thinner, better bred, more malleable and less mouthy, so what guy in their right mind would plump for a bullish bright spark when he could have non-questioning, adoring calm? When Alice tilted her chin and gave Julius a smile as if to say, 'Can we go now?' I had a strong feeling that he would always be unfaithful to her and that she would let him roam free. His marital pledge bought her silence and a long leash; that was their unspoken deal. For the first time, I could see that maybe it would never work between Julius and me because there would always be too much I would want to say.

Julius's mobile phone rang. As he answered the phone, I turned to Miles and whispered: 'Pretend you are my boyfriend.' I knew it was immature, but I just couldn't help myself. His brow furrowed, so I hissed: 'Don't ask, just do it.'

While Julius turned aside to have a business conversation, words like 'undercut', 'immediate acquisition', and 'sweat equity', floating through the air, Miles introduced himself to Alice.

Julius snapped his phone shut as Miles put his arm around me and said: 'I'm putting my sister into a cab and then I'm taking you, gorgeous girl, out to dinner.'

He kissed me briefly on the lips and I caught Susie's shell-shocked expression as if to say 'What the hell's going on now?'

As Miles frogmarched poor bewildered Susie down the road, Julius looked at me and asked: 'Who is he?'

'Miles Kingly,' I said.

'I mean,' Julius said sharply, 'who is he to you?'

I looked at Alice, standing by patiently, her face as devoid of feeling as if we were waging the merits of organic versus farmed smoked salmon. Didn't she think it odd that her husband was this rattled by some girl in the street; did she even care?

'Miles is someone who believes in me,' I said.

'Out of blind stupidity or is that an informed opinion?' Julius raised an eyebrow.

I hated to admit it, but he was good. Julius never missed a beat and always made me laugh. Our eyes locked in combative delight and I could have sworn that as we stared at each other, we were sending the same psychic email: 'Why are you doing this to me?'

I felt an arm creeping around my waist and almost jumped like a jack-in-the-box before I twigged that it was Miles in full-on boyfriend mode. He nuzzled my neck and I let the weight of my body sink against him. I hadn't realised how much I was still plagued by the side-effects of divorce: being single, I was ravenous for physical affection. Although, with him standing there, I had never been more keenly aware that Julius was the only man with whom I would ever have this indelible soul factor connection, perhaps a sizzling no-strings siesta with macho Miles would boost my *prana*, wouldn't it? And if I energised my sexual chakras, might I feel more complete and better able to cope? Finally firing on all cylinders again?

I said goodbye to Julius and as Miles took my hand, I squeezed it. 'Okay, the charade's over,' he said, pulling away when we were out of sight and earshot.

I turned and kissed him lightly on the lips. 'Actually, this is for real.'

Miles didn't relent to a full snog but we both felt the pluck of desire. When we pulled away, we stood staring quizzically at each other as if to say: 'Are you sure you're up for this?' Before I could respond, he stuck his arm out and waved down a passing cab.

In the taxi, I was fizzing like a lit sparkler. Unnervingly, Miles kept his distance in the corner of the cab, his long sinewy legs thrust forwards. He kept flicking back his fringe and throwing me searching looks. It felt as if there was an electric fence between us and that any physical contact could spell disaster. Passion had never seemed more terrifying because it would inevitably destroy certain boundaries in our friendship and while part of me was up for that, I feared it just as much.

I knew that Miles's reputation as a serial shagger meant that I was signing up for a purely physical partnering. Even with a fuck buddy like Miles, an orgasm with a one-night stand was somewhere between a sneeze and a snooze, so why would I settle for a quickie when I craved endless galaxies exploding? The body has its limits, the brain has none, and as most of good sex is in the head, I needed to be in love for seismic connection. I loved Miles as one of my oldest friends and had always found him hunky but curiously had never envisaged going to bed with him myself. Perhaps I was secretly scared that he would find me lacking or that he would be unable to bypass the history of our friendship in order to lose his inhibitions with me. Then I realised that that was a typically girlie reaction – men can bypass anything for full-on shagging. It's only women who let redundant thoughts get in the way.

'Do you think this is a mistake?' I asked, cutting through the radioactive silence that permeated the taxi.

'How can it be a mistake?' he said. 'Don't you know that men pretty much evaluate everything that happens in the world, from stock market fluctuations to shifts in continental drift, according to whether or not it will lead to us having sexual intercourse?'

'So when they say that men do most of their thinking by their "little brain" instead of their "big brain", it's ridiculous because men don't have a "big brain", do they?' I said.

Miles laughed. 'You got it. Just as women crave flirtation, we would rather fast forward. Chicks want to ignite a shivering spark of electricity whereas any bloke would rather plug directly into the socket.'

'So how does a woman ever seduce a man without offering herself up on a plate?'

'Plate offerings are good,' said Miles, stroking his thigh, 'but even better is that crucial word . . . maybe.'

'Maybe?'

'Yes, you let him know that you are interested but not easy.

"*Maybe* we should have a drink tomorrow, *maybe* we should see your place?" There is enough "yes" in "maybe" to keep a guy from feeling rejected but enough "no" to keep him on his toes.'

I knocked on the glass partition of the cab and called out: 'Can you pull over, please.' Miles's face fell. 'Maybe,' I said, as I got out of the taxi, 'we should do this another time.' I raised an eyebrow as I shut the door behind me.

Miles mouthed 'prick tease!' as the taxi moved off. Standing on the pavement, I felt an instant kick of regret. Typical of my overblown analysis, I had just talked myself out of a night I was bound never to forget. Why did I always do this? It was as if the feral part of me hankered for a thrill but my mind automatically overrode spontaneous fun. Unlike men, I was ruled by my bloody boring 'big brain'. Was I always going to go through life with my fingers curled around the banister, fighting the instinct to break free?

Later that night at Jess's flat, Lucy, Jess and I sat on the sofa, nursing a bottle of wine. Earlier, Lucy had put the girls to bed, got a babysitter and legged it over to Jess's for a thorough post-mortem. 'Can you believe it, Edward has an affair and he tells me that *I* should see a therapist?' Lucy said indignantly. 'As if I need to be shrink-wrapped!'

'If anyone needs help, it's him,' snorted Jess.

'Exactly,' Lucy drained her glass. 'Edward once told me he'd rather be impotent than bald. Imagine a man who would rather go without sex than hair!'

'Hair is a badge of masculinity.' Jess explained. 'It's all about image to them. Men are far more wound up about their sexual identity than we are.'

'I don't know,' I said, pouring myself some wine. 'I'm pretty screwed up about mine.' They looked at me, surprised. 'I just turned down hot sex with Miles.'

My mobile bleeped. I had a text. 'It must be Miles,' I said, secretly chuffed.

'Well go on,' urged Lucy. 'What does it say?'

I opened the text message and let out a shriek. 'Yes! It worked!'

'What did?'

'Making Julius jealous. This text isn't from Miles. It's from Julius. He wants to see me.'

Spending the weekend with my mother before meeting up with Julius was a mistake because there are times in life when you don't want to be intimately observed. It was obvious that Mum would catch me out because she was always on to me before I had time to check in with myself. She knew my fragile places and although it was not intentional, she wasn't always tender with them.

We were driving home from a dog show with Donald and Dougie and her new puppy, Dandelion, in the back. Mum kept turning round to stare at Dandy, as she'd already nicknamed him, asleep on the back seat. 'Look at that little angel!' she urged. 'Oh, Daisy, do look. Isn't he adorable?'

Nodding was easier than admitting that while I thought he was sweet, he didn't turn me to treacle. Mum, sensing my ambivalence, got quite cross. 'Look, I know you had that little, urm, mistake . . .' she said awkwardly.

'Abortion?' I cut in.

'Well, yes, that, well yes. You know. But you were simply a victim of circumstance then, so that aside, don't you want children?'

'Yes. Of course, I do,' I said.

'I sometimes wonder,' she continued, 'I mean, it's not as if you ever show any maternal instinct.'

'Firstly, I said I wanted a baby, not a puking, pooping

puppy, and secondly, just because I don't do back flips over your stunted little logs of fur, it doesn't mean that I don't want a real family of my own.'

'Then what are you waiting for?' asked Mum, exasperated. 'I would have loved to have had another child but after you, well, you know we tried, but it obviously wasn't mean to be. But most women approaching forty are frantic for a partner, or failing that, some decent seed.' She paused, then continued, 'At your age, do you think you can afford to be picky?'

'Thanks for reminding me, Mum,' I said flatly. I hadn't allowed my raw yearning to surface since I left Jamie but suddenly I found I was freefalling with despair. Hot tears trickled down my cheeks. I was one of the many women of my generation who had never considered the possibility of *not* having a baby and yet, here I was, hot-footing it to my fifth decade, partner-less, childless, homeless, career-less, pension-less and with pretty much less of everything that I had anticipated I would have by now.

My problem was that while I had an insistent longing for a child, it wasn't the sort of deafening clarion call that consumed me. Even after my possible last chance for motherhood with Troy, I wanted the man and *then* the baby (preferably in that order), not a baby at all costs, or I would have kept Troy's. I knew that there were women of my generation – Jess, for example – who considered it demeaning to keep harping on about wanting a boyfriend like a moony teenager, and who, in the face of an absence of a willing cock, would simply shrug her shoulders and adopt. Or in a cold, corporate-type transaction, would pay a sperm donor. But I didn't want to do any of it on my own; the idea of single motherhood was far, far worse than simply being single and alone.

Mum was right about one thing though: I wasn't getting real about how stuck I was. But at what point do we finally accept that our dreams are just that – dreams – and press on with hard-edged reality? 'What are you waiting for?' repeated Mum, softly.

I wanted to scream: 'Julius! I am waiting for the only man who has the ability to turn me inside out, the only man whom I felt I loved before I even met.' I couldn't tell my mother that the imprint of Julius, who was married to someone else, was still embedded on my psyche, could I?

I stared out of the window at the fields flashing by. When we got home, I put on my faded flannel pyjamas, filled a hot water bottle, went to bed and sobbed. The grief that spilled out across the pillows was almost a relief because it explained why I felt like an outsider in my own world. As if part of me was never present – yet how could I function when so much of me was numb with disappointment? Would I ever get over the fact that my marriage failed? It was a shock to discover how much pain I was still in. But the truth was that I wasn't just mourning Jamie and the life we never had together. I was in turmoil over Julius and the life we would never have.

Three days later, I met Julius for dinner. We sat in a minimalist sushi bar, full of sleek, figure-conscious types, and the way he ordered for me, knowing what delicacies I would enjoy – the lobster cerviche and the scallop tempura – made me see everything with sudden clarity. Being with Julius felt like coming home but I couldn't run from the truth a moment longer. It was like we were in a bubble of perfection but it wasn't real. I didn't want the certainty of the present time, however dreamy. I wanted the unknown of a future together. 'I can't do this any more,' I said, sighing.

'What?' he said.

I gestured towards him. 'This.'

'This?' he questioned, laughing. 'How can there be any "this" when you have a boyfriend?'

I looked at him blankly. 'Miles?' he prompted.

'Miles is irrelevant to "this". Just as Alice is. You know that.'

He smiled at me.

'Don't look at me like that,' I said. 'It's not fair.' I cleared my throat. 'You know, we fall in love for the major reasons but they manifest themselves in the minor things. Pretty soon, you can't tell if you love the quirks because they're his, or you love a man because of the quirks. All I know is that I love you, Julius. I love you because you drive sitting bolt upright and you lean forwards when you over-take. I love you because of your impeccable manners. I love you because you loathe coriander and because you adore the scent of gardenias. I love you because we share a sense of the absurd and because you are the most attractive man when you laugh caught off guard. I love you because you are secretive and passionate about your butterflies and because breeding them must be the most tender hobby in the world. I love you because despite your vast wealth you're unmaterialistic because to you it's the priceless things that matter; the dew on morning grass, a delicious cup of coffee at a pavement café in the afternoon sun and yet you have one of the most valuable *objets d'art* in the world, a Fabergé egg, sitting on your bedside table. I love you because you never bore me and because you always make me feel that any time we have together isn't enough. I love you because you are you, but I can't go on like "this" because not being with you is tearing me apart.'

I sat back and watched as Julius meticulously folded his napkin into a perfect square. When he looked up at me, he said: 'I didn't think that amount of love was possible until I met you.'

'Well, it is,' I said. 'You just have to have the courage to receive it.'

'It's not that simple.'

'It doesn't have to be this complicated either.' I stood up. 'Why does it feel like I'm the only one getting hurt?'

'Don't think that just because I don't have the answer I'm not searching for it,' said Julius.

'Goodbye, my darling one,' I said, not wanting to leave but willing myself to.

'Don't go,' he implored.

'No,' I said, impatiently. 'If you love me, let me go.'

He grabbed my hand. 'First, hear what I have to say.'

I sat back down and leaned towards him, tapping my fingers nervously on the table. 'So? What is it?'

Julius drew back his shoulders and took a deep breath. 'Alice is pregnant.' Each word felt like a hammer blow to my body. I stared at him, stunned. 'Alice is four months pregnant. She's having my baby,' he repeated, his eyes locking with mine.

Inside I began chanting: 'I must not cry, I must not cry,' yet the shock was so intense, I could feel tears welling from my very core. I kicked myself for not having left ten minutes earlier because then, at least, I would have walked away on high ground. Now he had pulled the earth from beneath my feet and it was all I could do not to buckle. Part of me considered that he must really hate me or why would he torture me with this information when earlier I had confessed how much I loved him?

'She was up the duff when you married her?' I said, aware that my lips and legs were trembling.

'Elegantly put, but yes,' smiled Julius. 'It was a happy accident. I've told you, I would have married her anyway.'

I realised that it was pointless trying to be brave or pretend that I was pleased for him because I was completely broken by this. I lowered my head and watched the tears roll into my miso soup. Before long, my crying had developed into full-on, runny snot sobbing. 'Don't mind me,' I gasped. 'I'm just having a breakdown.'

I knew that usually Julius would have recoiled from such an emotive scene yet what did I care now? I was completely taken aback when he looked at me tenderly and said: 'No, you're not. *We're* having a breakthrough.'

'Yes, you and Alice,' I said, bitterly. 'Not me.'

'No,' said Julius, 'let me explain. Finding out that Alice is having my child has changed everything.'

'You said it,' I sighed.

'You don't understand.' Julius was almost laughing. 'Knowing that Alice is having my baby these past months has made me realise how much I love you.'

I looked at him through a haze of salty tears and smudged mascara.

'Actually, I think *you're* having the breakdown,' I said. 'You've gone crazy.'

Julius shrugged. 'Becoming a father does funny things to you but when Alice told me she was pregnant, I was aware of only one feeling: of wishing I was having the baby with you. I tried to ignore it but it won't go away.'

My heart seemed to rupture. 'Oh Julius, that's the sweetest thing you've ever said to me but it's too late.' I said. Not for the first time, he handed me his handkerchief. It felt cool and expensive as I held it to my face.

'It's never too late,' he said.

I tried to stem the flow of my tears but it was useless. 'Why is this happening to me?' I said, pressing against my pounding forehead. 'Why is our timing always out of kilter? You can't abandon Alice now. It's completely hopeless. We'll never be together.'

'You're right. I can't divorce Alice but I still want to have another baby with you.'

'Are you completely insane?'

'Not at all. From the minute Alice told me the news, I've thought of nothing else. I want you to be the mother of a child of mine because what we have is so special, Daisy. Sure, things are messy but it's never been conventional between us. I love you more than anyone because you're the only one who understands me.' He paused. 'I love you, Daisy Dooley, because you eat porridge and puddings with a teaspoon. I love you because you adore green olives but you loathe black. I love you because you feel everything, all the time and because you have to tell everyone, all the time, how you are feeling. I love you because you are the craziest girl I have ever met – because you are you and because you get me.'

I was crying so much, laughing in parts, that I wondered if the restaurant would be calling psychiatric backup at any minute. 'Oh, Julius,' I said. I held my hand against my chest as if I feared my heart might rupture.

'I know that you'll be a great mother,' Julius said 'because you were brought up to believe that you could do anything in life whereas I was made to feel that nothing I could do would ever be enough.'

'Don't you think I haven't prayed that one day we would have a child together?' I said. 'But not like this. I didn't dream of being a single mother, while you and Alice played happy families down the road.' Almost hyperventilating, I tried to steady my breath.

'I thought you loved me,' said Julius, crest-fallen.

'I do but I can't have a child under these circumstances.'

'You'll want for nothing,' he said. 'You'll have everything.'

I looked at him. 'No, Julius, I'll have nothing because I won't have you.'

*

I left Julius, my equilibrium shattered. My head was in such turmoil that I decided to walk back to Jess's Battersea flat. The night air felt cool against my puffy, tear-scorched face. Any gust of wind was a relief.

As I walked down Embankment, I thought of Virginia Woolf, who wrote of Turgenev's fiction that the meaning of what he said went on long after the sound had stopped. Regardless of the decision I made, Julius's offer would stay with me for ever because it was life changing. If I did not choose to have his child, would I ever have a child with anyone else? Would I end up alone, pregnant with regret? If I did agree to let him father my baby, would I be signing up for a lifetime's heartbreak, similarly underpinned by regret? It was typical that in his Master of the Universe style, Julius saw nothing as beyond his reach. Just married a society beauty who's pregnant? Why should that be any kind of barrier to having another child out of wedlock with your first and true love?

I sat down on a bench and stared at the reflection of the lights bouncing on the water. Grief seemed inevitable because this was an emotionally charged, complicated situation. Why couldn't I play my life safe like everyone else? It would have been so much easier if I could have stayed married to Jamie, had a couple of Prattlocks and built a life on safe, solid rock, instead of running on porous pipe dreams.

'Daisy?' I felt a hand brush against my shoulder and jumped. I turned around to see Susie standing behind me. She gestured to the bench: 'May I?' I nodded. She sat down.

'How are you?' I asked.

'I've been better,' she said.

'Me too.'

We sat in amiable silence before she said: 'I moved into a new flat last week.'

'God, I'm so sorry about Edward.'

'Yes,' she sighed. 'But I think in the long run, it was for the best.'

'Did you think Edward was going to marry you?'

'I suppose I did,' she said. 'I mean, when he put my name on the deeds of the flat, I thought that was a real commitment. I knew if we ended up together there would always be the spectre of the ex-wife and kids and while that wasn't what I'd dreamed of, what situation is these days?' I let out a hollow laugh. 'I used to think I wanted to get married more than anything,' continued Susie. 'But Edward's deceit has changed that. For some people, marriage means "You're mine now." That can be the beginning of the failure of a relationship. Psychologically, something happens when a man says: "You're my wife now. You can't do this or that." It's about ownership. That freedom of two people loving each other and wanting to be together – and being able to leave if anything is wrong – is gone. Ideally, I'd like to have a child in a committed relationship but I don't crave the ring and the register office any more. Maybe something good has come out of this because I've moved on from that.'

Susie seemed so wise and centred that I couldn't help blurting out everything that happened during my dinner with Julius. After she had digested it, she said: 'It's tempting because you love him and I suspect part of you is drawn to the romance of the unconventional but it sounds to me like you want the man more than the baby and that's not what's on offer here.' I swallowed hard. Susie had nailed it. 'You'd always be connected to him through a child but it would be a mistake to think that he's indirectly dangling the carrot of commitment in front of you because he isn't, any more than Edward was to me when he bought that flat. I suspect that he doesn't want to lose you from his life but he isn't brave enough to wholeheartedly claim you either.'

'You're right,' I nodded, fighting tears. 'I needed to hear this. Thank you.'

She hugged me tight. 'Ditch the man-child, then everything becomes clear.'

'I'm so tired,' I said, pulling away.

Susie studied her watch. 'Christ, yes, it is late.'

'No, tired of having to save myself because I've realised that maybe the guy on the white charger ain't gonna show.'

Although I knew that I had made the right decision not to have a child with Julius, it was torture trying to get him out of my head. I was like a junkie; my thoughts about him exploded in spasms of need and desire. As I had read that the underlying suffering of all addiction is self-centredness, I decided to focus on someone else who was trying to navigate the moral speed bumps of life. I went to visit Lucy, who had taken her daughters to stay with her parents in Dorset for the beginning of the summer holidays. While her girls frolicked on the beach with their grandparents, Lucy and I lay morosely in the garden.

'Do you know what Edward said when I challenged him about his affair with Susie?' said Lucy, applying sun block to her face. 'When I said, "Why Susie?" he said, "There wasn't anything that special about her but she listened and she was interested in me. That made *me* feel special." I was so furious I said, "Yes, Edward, we all want to feel like we matter to somebody."'

'I think Edward is quite wrong about Susie. You may not want to hear this Luce, but Susie is kind and perceptive. She deserved far better than Edward, just as you did. Anyway, you know it's over between them?'

Lucy nodded. 'Yes. Susie wrote me the most decent letter apologising and explaining that she had no idea that Edward's marriage was intact when she slept with him.'

'What are you going to do?' I re-filled our glasses with chilled rosé.

'I'm going back to him,' said Lucy, twiddling her wedding ring.

I felt a jolt of outrage. 'Why?' I cried out plaintively.

'Because I haven't got the strength or the courage to start all over again. Plus, I have two little girls who need their father.'

I managed to remain silent while Lucy continued: 'I've spent the last weeks combing through the ashes of our marriage, wondering if there was anything to salvage. I realised that the idea of marriage to Edward didn't repel me. Edward and I had a long talk last weekend,' said Lucy. 'I tried to practise empathetic listening, to see if I could understand him.' She groaned. 'God, it was torture. Half the time I wanted to reach out and throttle him.'

'It's like the Buddhist principle which is to ask yourself before you say anything, "Is it kind? Is it true? Is it useful?"' I laughed: 'Sure, it's a good idea but if I applied that, I'd never be able to speak again.'

Lucy giggled and rolled on to her side. 'The weirdest thing was that I had no idea that I made Edward feel inadequate. I was far too busy feeling inferior myself.'

'Yup, it's a mistake to buy into the super-masculine myth,' I said, thinking of Julius. 'Up close, men are just as screwed up and complex as we are.'

'Edward said that when a man feels lousy, he thinks his partner purposely tries to make him feel bad,' explained Lucy. 'For example, if we say, "You cut yourself shaving", it's as if we've said, "What's wrong with you? You're such a loser. A real man would know how to shave."'

'So when are you returning to the fragile male ego, the tiny hairs in the sink, the piles of coins and crumpled receipts?' I asked, smiling.

'Soon. I'm only here because I've got to be somewhere. The problem is that it's taking me so long to get past my rage.'

'Give yourself time. Buddhists say that the longest journey you will make in your life is dropping from your head to your heart. For this to work you've got to stop thinking about what Edward did and concentrate on feeling forgiveness and rebuilding trust.'

'I don't have many expectations now,' said Lucy, emptily. 'I've finally resigned myself to the fact that life-long marriage means shared disappointment, boredom and endless bloody compromise.'

'That's not marriage, that's settling,' I said.

'But you didn't settle and you're still on your own,' said Lucy. 'Is that any better?'

'Infinitely,' I said, half-believing it myself. 'Because I still live in hope that I won't be alone for ever.'

## Chapter 7
# Mr Knightly-in-shining-armour?

As Miles had postponed the opening of his bookshop due to the discovery of woodworm in the bookshelves, I had a week to myself before I began work in the Mind/Body/Spirit section. I went to visit my mother, a hefty sack of self-help books in tow. On the train, I got busy with the highlighter pen. 'If you feel incomplete, you alone must fill yourself with love in all your empty shattered spaces.' It was true my heart was like Miles's shelves, gnawed and splintered with emotional woodworm. I read on: 'The difference between a little life and a big life is trust. Trust is the midwife of a big life. People only choose little lives because they don't trust and they want to control.' That's the most difficult thing in life, I thought, getting the balance right between not giving up on your dreams, yet having enough faith in their fruition to let them go.

Mum, who was waiting for me at the station, ran forwards to greet me, waving exuberantly. She had clearly come straight from the hairdresser's as her hair was backcombed to a gravity-defying height. She seemed giddy with pleasure as she hugged me tight and her erratic concentration on the way home made her driving dangerously cavalier. As she swung into the drive, narrowly missing the gate posts, she drew the car to a juddering halt before she let out a strange bone-shaking cry. 'Oh, Daisy, I've got something so wonderful to tell you,' she said, holding her head as if in disbelief. 'I never thought this day would come but it has.'

I raised an enquiring eyebrow. 'What is it? I've got a long-lost brother? You've won the lottery? You and Dad are getting back together?'

'No, no,' she snorted, 'it's far better than that.'

She closed her eyes and inhaled deeply, as if to prolong the magic of the moment. Then, she threw her arms in the air and exclaimed: 'I'm in love!'

'Oh God,' I said, getting out of the car. 'You haven't gone and bought another puppy, have you?'

Mum followed me into the house. 'Not with a dog, Daisy. With a man! A flesh-and-blood-proper-penis-sporting man!'

As I stared at my mother, her cheeks flushed, I felt like a stranger in my own world. Nothing seemed familiar any more. Each day seemed to bring new revelations which unearthed me. Selfishly, I had envisaged a cosy weekend alone together. We'd sit around the kitchen table and she'd listen patiently as I questioned whether I would ever meet any bloke whom I loved as much as Julius again. Mum would soothe and bolster, expressing her concern with homemade soup and her stellar choc chip cake, and bring me morning tea in bed. She would have put a posy of fresh flowers from the garden on my bedside table – some blowsy scented roses

– along with glossy mags to relax me. After dragging me out on long walks, I'd go back to London nourished in every sense. So the last thing I had envisaged was dissecting my mother's blossoming love life around the Aga. I didn't know how to react as she made the coffee, eagerly filling me in. It wasn't that I wasn't thrilled for her: I was. But what I found myself asking was whether I was grown-up enough and generous enough to want her happiness more than my own? I mean, the last thing I ever expected was to feel jealous of my mum because she had a man and I didn't.

It turned out that she met Archibald Fleming at a dog show. A gentleman farmer, he breeds rare sheep. Archie's wife died five years ago and he has two grown-up daughters who, naturally, are happily married and cheerfully breeding, unlike poor Mum's loser daughter. Archie's mangy old sheep dog, Rusty, almost decapitated Dougie, which is how Mum and he met. Mum ran forwards, hurling red-hot expletives and her handbag at Rusty, who had Dougie dangling from his jaws. Archie skilfully extracted Dougie and handed the traumatised, slobber-coated dachshund back to her, then suggested a drink by way of apology. That was it: late-life love was sealed over the man-sized marrows and gnarled gourds in the tea-tent.

'It's not a sizzling sex thing,' said Mum, 'Although he has lovely soft lips and impressively clean fingernails for a man who lives on a farm.'

'Please, euch, no details,' I interrupted.

Mum waved her hand dismissively. 'What I wanted to say, darling, is that I had one of the most wonderful moments in my entire life with Archie. He came over last week when I was mucking out the kennels. When I stood up to ease my back, he put his arm around me. It wasn't passionate but it felt so wonderful to lean against a man and let him take the weight of me. He whispered: "You don't have to do it all on your own, any more, Diana," and I thought I was going to break down and cry.'

You and me both, I thought.

'Oh Daisy, I do pray that you find something similar because as Archibald Fleming held me, I realised that all these years of holding it together on my own have been such a terrible strain.' Mum burst into tears and I hugged her.

'Oh Mum,' I said, 'I'm so happy for you. I really am.'

Mum was such a trouper when I was growing up, so hearty and hail-fellow-well-met; organising wonderful seaside holidays and making the cold, unyielding countryside seem vibrant and fun that I had had no idea until now that she had nursed a violent longing for something other than safe, domestic routine. Her secret, which she hid unnervingly well, was that she prayed that there was more to her life than this. In a macabre way, the discovery that Dad had been having an affair unleashed her. Now she, too, could hold out for a chaotic passion that would enable her to redefine herself and turn her neat, contained world into something glorious and messy.

'It's so wonderful with Archie because he actually listens to what I say to him,' Mum said, as we walked the dogs by the river. 'I'm unaccustomed to being with a man who takes this much notice of me and is interested in what I'm feeling. I almost died of shock when we were driving home from the animal suppliers the other day and Archie turned to me and said: "Diana, what are you thinking?"'

'I had no idea that you were so unhappy with Dad,' I said.

'A happy marriage where knowing the truth would break your heart is a tricky kind of happiness to sustain,' she said.

'Oh no,' I sighed, instantly depressed. 'I hope you didn't stay just for me.'

'No,' said Mum, smiling. 'It was more complex than that.' She sat down and patted the grass beside her. 'Listen, Daisy. This is important. In our twenties and thirties, we search for ourselves and if we're lucky, we find our niche in roles that bring out our best; mother, career woman, wife, etc.'

'That makes me unlucky,' I interrupted, 'because I'm still searching.'

'No, actually, you're at an advantage,' said Mum. 'Because when these roles reach maturity in our forties and fifties, children leave, careers shift and marriages end – we feel lost, scared and unsure. We wonder "Was what I left behind the best expression of myself?" You have a chance now to discover how you can best fulfil yourself and live a vivid life that's true to who you really are.'

'What was your best expression of yourself?' I asked.

She pulled me to her: 'You, silly.'

'Phew,' I giggled. 'For a moment I thought you were going to say all those prize dachshunds you bred.'

She looked at me. 'You have no idea how proud I am of you, do you?'

Choked, I lowered my head. 'How can you be? I've messed up everything.'

'Don't give up on yourself because if Archibald Fleming can see the point of me when I'm sagging and sixty-odd, there is a wonderful man out there waiting to claim you.'

When we got back from the walk and I saw a strange van in the yard, I felt a twang of anxiety. I knew Archie must be in the house and that it was clearly serious between him and Mum or she'd never have given him a key. Suddenly, I felt worried for her. What if Archie was some sort of cad on the make, out to flatter gullible female old fools? But the minute I saw him, any misgivings melted. Although he didn't look dissimilar from Dad, in that he has that grey-haired, patrician look, he appeared softer and kinder than my father. Maybe he has less to prove, unlike Dad, still furiously toiling over his Bunsen burner determined to achieve a scientific breakthrough that would make his name.

Archie had made a tray of Pimm's complete with mint, apple slices and lemon wedges – something Dad would never have bothered with – and as we sat in the garden enjoying the early evening light flood across the lawn, I thought how he pitched it just right. He wasn't overly familiar; he was justifiably cautious but he seemed genuinely keen to impress me and impress upon me that he was genuine about Mum. Something about him touched me because when he asked me what I did and I told him about the bookshop, he wasn't patronising as Dad would have been. He didn't try to belittle me. He said: 'The marvellous thing about opportunities that drop straight in your lap is that they are yours to do what you want with.' Later, he looked fondly towards Mum and said: 'You must be very proud of Daisy, Diana?' and he meant it. He wasn't trying to suck up. He made me feel that if he could see my potential before I saw it myself, then another man could. As he chatted away and I saw Mum watch him, enchanted, I felt immense gratitude on both our counts. I already knew that I would always have a soft spot for Archie because he believed in us.

When I returned to London my belief in the redemptive power of love soared. I saw working in Miles's bookshop as a perfect opportunity to re-ignite my career and possibly meet new men. It wasn't until I had spent the first week manning the till that I realised Miles and I were reading off the same transparent sheet. Every woman with a pulse and (preferably) a push-up bra who browsed the aisles was considered instant eye 'n' arm candy. What got me was how many returned the following day, all google-eyed and giggly. Miles remained unperturbed when I challenged him. 'Daisy, don't you know that for men, having sex with the same woman, no matter how good it is, gets lame?'

'But doesn't waking up with a different head of hair or worse, a set of tacky hair extensions on your pillow get just as trying after a while?'

'That's why I always try to get them to leave before I go to sleep,' laughed Miles. 'It would be hell to wake up to their bleary faces and their make-up smeared across my pillowcases.'

'Don't you want to fall in love?' I asked.

'I'm not sure I believe in love,' he shrugged.

'You're so cynical it must be terminal,' I said.

'And you're so gullible it must be painful,' he countered.

'Not at all. Falling in love is simply a consuming desire to share the very marrow of another human being in the hope that life will become profound and everything will fall into place.'

Miles guffawed. 'You're a true crack-pot Daisy.'

'Actually, I'm going to find true love,' I said. 'Just you wait and see.'

Every day I picked at random a soul-stirring sentence from the plethora of self-help books on my shelves, wrote it in coloured chalk on a tiny blackboard and stuck it in the window of the shop. It thrilled me to see customers standing outside reading and absorbing its meaning, not least because it made me feel less alien and alone. Anyone who stopped for an inspirational nugget was clearly searching for something too, weren't they?

'If you feel held and supported by life, you can let go and allow the unexpected to happen.' I thought yesterday's bon mots were particular gems because I was beginning to realise that the more frightened we are, the less we trust life, so the more we grab on to unsuitable props and crutches. My God, dodgy men with dire agendas had certainly been the pot-holes to trip me up in my thirties when foolishly I was most convinced that my foothold was secure. Deluded? Certainly. In denial? Not any more.

Miles manned the espresso machine as I cleaned the blackboard and wrote the meaningful missive of the day. 'Leaving a bad relationship is like having cosmic diarrhoea. Elimination hurts but once the poison is out, you will feel much better.'

Miles repeated the sentence, his voice dripping with sarcasm. 'The idea is to draw customers in, not frighten them off,' he said. 'I want them to think we have sane humans working here, not unstable self-help zealots.'

'Let's face it,' I laughed, 'the only reason you don't enter into proper relationships is because you are too afraid of the pain they would cause if they ended. One-night stands are for scaredy-cats because they don't pose an emotional risk.'

'Emotion is over-rated,' said Miles. 'Look how mad you are and you're the most emotionally open person I know. Your feelings are always hanging out as if they've forgotten to sew you up after open heart surgery.'

'Miles,' I said, poking him with my chalk, 'I'll just conclude this happy little chat with tomorrow's spiritual saying which is: "People who study others are wise. People who study themselves are enlightened."' Miles put his hands to his ears and let out a frustrated roar. Laughing, I ran to the window to put the blackboard up, while Miles went to check some stock.

Spending time with Miles, even if he was the unevolved yin to my analytical yang was comforting because although we never stopped teasing each other, at the bedrock of our friendship lay solid affection. Being with him, the less I mourned the lack of a relationship. It was liberating to watch couples browse books together and not feel the sting of envy. Okay, so sometimes I got a teensy stab, like the Saturday afternoon I was frothing some milk for a cappuccino – Miles had spent a fortune on Alpha Male gadgets for the coffee bar which required a degree in something highly left brain and technical – when a man ushered in a pretty girl. Instantly, I recognised that they were in morning-after mode. Why do so many lovers bumble along to bookshops after they've slept together? Do they envisage cosy afternoons curled reading before relationship rot sets in? While the man stroked the girl's neck as she perused the bestsellers, I got a surge of horror. It was Troy Powers.

When Troy saw me he nervously flicked his fringe and his eyes darted back and forth. It should have been gratifying to see the power leak from him but strangely, when my moment came, I didn't have the heart to humiliate him. I could almost hear him say, 'Please, for God's sake Daisy, don't make a scene.' He was terrified of what I might reveal in front of the lithe blonde standing by his side, her fingers curled around his. But what would be the point of warning her off when her face was lit from within over the night they had just shared? She had that slightly drained – that is, shagged senseless – tired but buoyed look. Just because Troy had done the dirty on me didn't mean that I had the right to scupper their shot at happiness, did it? That would only drain my piggy bank of karma and make me look bitter and small.

Troy stared at me, his expression fixed, waiting for the verbal detonation, while the girl had that benign air of expectancy as if we were about to be politely introduced. I said sweetly: 'Let me know if I can help you with anything.' I pointed to the Mind/Body/Spirit section and said: 'We've got the new bestseller from the States on self-actualisation over there. It's all about becoming the best you can be.' I smiled, monitoring the concern in his eyes and her slight look of surprise before I swiftly retreated out to the back. I watched on the CCTV camera in the stockroom as a relieved Troy quickly ushered his lover out.

As I sat on a box of books, I was intrigued that my anger had not flared. The more I thought of how Troy had treated me, the emptier I felt. I didn't feel anything as strong and urgent as hatred, I was simply aware of a temperate void. Where does dead anger go to when it expires, I thought? After all those bruised, painful hours I had lain on my bed, hot with shame and temper, it was liberating to realise that I no longer had any need to keep fighting, because the battle within had been won. It was as if a tiny elastic band of tension had snapped inside me and I was free.

In order to celebrate this, I persuaded Jess to join me on a weekend jolly to a fancy hotel in Bath. Miles had given me a bonus for stocking so many self-help bestsellers in the shop and I decided to splurge it on our girlie spa break. Jess had been working non-stop at the surgery and as I had hadn't seen her properly for what had seemed like months, even though we were still flat sharing, I was looking forward to a gossipy getaway. We had arranged to meet at Paddington train station on Friday afternoon and as I kept staring at the clock, I worried that Jess was running late. When my mobile rang and I saw her number, I said: 'Thank goodness. For an awful moment I thought you weren't coming.' There was a pause. 'Where are you?' I said. 'The train leaves in seven minutes.'

'I'm so sorry, Daisy. I can't make it. One of the doctors has called in sick and I've got to be on call this weekend.'

Felled by disappointment, I slumped down on my bag, shoulders hunched. 'Typical,' I said. 'My new beginning is buggered before it's even begun.'

'Why don't you go on your own?' urged Jess.

'I don't want to go to a hotel on my own which is going to be full of loved-up couples snogging in the spa.'

I watched from the platform as people piled on to the Bath train and then I got up and boarded it. Tucked in a window seat, blindly staring at the view, I had a real feeling of achievement. I didn't have that spoilt, childish whine of entitlement about life any more – that it owed me because early on in my dreams I had promised myself that my life would encompass A, B and C. For the first time in adulthood, probably, I felt at one with the concept of being alone. I didn't feel lonely, I felt at home within myself. What on earth had I been thinking earlier – denying myself a luxury that I had worked hard for, all for the sake of not being alone? Of course I wanted to find love but if it didn't happen, I would accept it. I had read that this was called Radical Acceptance; a willingness to recognise and tolerate what is, rather than fight or judge what isn't. It enables you to live with existential disappointment and move on.

Seeing the light warm up the honey-coloured Bath stone and taking in the majestic sweep of the architecture lifted my spirits. I kept closing my eyes and opening within to see if I really was doing okay or if I was in denial but as far as I could tell, I still felt pretty accepting. Even when I was shown my hotel room and rushed to the window to scan the romantic view of the city, I did not feel incomplete without a partner. I looked at the four-poster bed and for the first time since my divorce, it did not occur to me to feel less of a woman or more of a failure because I wouldn't be sharing it. I didn't look at the plump pillows and inviting linen sheets and yearn to destroy them in the name of a damn good time. Actually, I couldn't wait to slip inside without ruffling the covers and enjoy the comfort in neat solitary peace.

The following afternoon, I was preparing to visit the spa when I realised that I had forgotten to pack my swimming costume. I walked across the courtyard to the indoor swimming pool and asked the staff if I could borrow one. When they offered me the only one they could find – a monstrous fifties-style lurid pink spotted number complete with ra-ra skirt – I almost laughed out loud. I considered jettisoning the idea of a swim altogether but the pool beckoned, still and empty, so who would see me trussed up like Ma Larkin, anyway? As I was going for a massage afterwards and didn't want wet hair, I scrunched my hair on top of my head with a dachshund clip – the best stocking filler from Christmas last year – and furtively entered the water.

It was liberating to have the pool to myself and I revelled in slowly moving up and down. Suddenly, I heard a surge of water and the urgent splash of bubbles. I looked around and a man had entered the Jacuzzi near the pool. He was sitting back, surveying me. Crikey, he hadn't seen me get in, had he? How could I get out now and waddle past him looking like a spotted duck? From what I could tell, without openly peering, he was quite a dish. Pretending not to have seen him, I continued my sedate laps up and down, as he sat there. My skin was wrinkling fast but I refused to give in by getting out. Eventually, I heard the Jacuzzi silence and he dived into the pool. When he came up for air near me, I clocked that he was tall, lithe and had enviable thick dark hair. He swam straight up. 'I've been admiring you,' he said. 'You've got great style.'

I clasped my hands across my chest and tugged at the suit. 'You must be joking? This isn't mine. The hotel lent it to me.'

'Not the suit. The way you swim. You can tell you're comfortable in your own skin.'

'If not my borrowed suit,' I laughed.

'It's certainly interesting armour,' he said, cocking his head. He ran his fingers through his hair. 'Max Knightly,' he smiled.

'Hi,' I said. 'I'm Daisy.'

As he looked at me with delight I thought No, no, no! Life doesn't happen like this. You don't realise that you're okay on your own one minute and meet a man like Max Knightly the next. Do you?

My face was red from the heat of the pool, beads of sweat were sticking to my hairline and my fingertips resembled death-white wrinkled prunes but so what? Okay, so Max was cute, but the chances were that he had an even hotter cutie waiting back home, so why should I flatter him with the slightest hint of artifice? I may not have had the glow of youth (only the hormonal gleam of heavy sweat) nor the toned tummy of my twenties, but in my mind I suddenly had so much more. I felt Consciously Female, which according to the latest life literature means that for the first time I was experiencing a high level of intimacy with myself. Finally, I felt secure with the woman I had become, so didn't have to pretend I was something or someone I wasn't.

Avoiding the laughably lame, do you come here often? Max plumped for: 'Who are you here with?'

When I told him I was on my own, he seemed surprised. 'I can't believe you're not taking advantage of the sexy hotel rooms,' he said.

'I am,' I replied, adding: 'Alone.' When he raised an

eyebrow, I said: 'Not like that. Don't you know that for anyone over thirty-five, uninterrupted sleep is the new sex?'

'So you've got kids?'

'Nope. You?'

He shook his head. When I asked why he was staying at the hotel, he told me that he lived around the corner and was a member of the spa.

'What are you doing later?' he asked.

'Having a massage,' was my blunt reply.

'And after that?'

'Enjoying room service in my dressing-gown.'

'Do you want to join me for dinner?'

'That's very kind but I can't be bothered to wash my hair.'

Max smiled, curious, but I wasn't trying to play games. I was just too lazy – or blasé – to be anything other than honest. 'It'll be all oily from the aromatherapy,' I explained.

'My flat is five minutes' walk away,' he said. 'You can wear a hat. Greasy is good.'

'And no make-up?'

'Even better.'

Warming to his direct approach, I said: 'Do you often pick up strange women in swimming pools?'

'Do you often talk to strange men?'

'Do you always answer a question with a question?'

He grinned. 'Do you?'

We giggled. We were leaning against the side of the pool, our arms crossed on the edge and as I looked at the droplets of water on his forearms, I had a sudden frisson being so physically close to an unknown, attractive man. 'Why do we always tell strangers too much too soon?' I asked wistfully. 'We think it's safe,' I continued, 'but then we scare ourselves because we've revealed our hand to someone insignificant.'

'*Insignificant*?' he repeated, before adding: 'But you haven't told me anything.'

'Let's keep it like that,' I said, moving away to the steps of the pool.

'Why?' he called after me, 'I can't imagine that you have much to hide.'

I stood on the top step of the pool, looking an utter fool in my be-skirted, fifties swimming costume and said: 'Oh, we all have something to hide. Don't we?'

'As far as I can tell you're only hiding a great figure under that saggy sack.'

He came up the steps behind me as I was wrapping a towel around my waist. He grabbed a towel too and there was something strangely intimate to be towelling down next to a stranger whom I couldn't help noticing had good strong legs; muscular yet finely shaped. Not a hint of yucky bulbous calf. He was buffed but it wasn't really that which caught my attention; more it was my reaction to him. Why was my over-familiarity verging on plain rude?

'Will I see you later?' he asked.

'No.' I looked up coyly. 'But I enjoyed our brief encounter.'

'I see,' said Max, running his hand through his damp glossy hair. 'You think you're getting rid of me as easily as that?'

'I must go, I'll be late for my massage,' I said. I walked into the women's changing room and shut the door.

I was preparing to check out of the hotel the following morning when the niggle that Max hadn't contacted me developed into a full-blown kick of disappointment. True, I'd fallen asleep immediately after my massage the night before but there was a part of me, a heightened sensitivity even through my drifting dreams, that was waiting for the phone to ring. He had been so cock-sure when we met in the spa that it had never occurred to me that he wouldn't pursue me and as much as I tried to pretend to myself that I wasn't interested in him, there was still that lonely feminine side of me that craved attention. I paid the bill and was turning to leave when the woman at the front desk handed me an envelope. My heart did a mini roll of excitement. Waiting for the taxi to take me to the station, I opened the envelope. Inside was Max Knightly's business card. He had circled his email address, while on the back he had written: 'Let an insignificant stranger buy you lunch.'

I could barely wait to get home and tell Lucy and Jess, let alone get online. The next evening, I called a summit at the bookshop after it closed for the evening. Lucy came with plonk and Jess bought Chinese takeaway and we sat on the comfy chairs by the cappuccino bar, eating straight from the containers. 'The great thing about meeting a man in a swimming pool is that you don't have to worry about him seeing you naked,' said Jess. 'He's already got the general idea.'

'What, you mean he's seen my cellulite and still isn't put off?' I poked Jess with a chopstick.

'What cellulite?' she joked.

'Well at least you don't have to fork out for a blow-dry,' said Lucy. 'If he fancies you with soaking hair, that's a bonus. I always found it such a telling moment in a relationship when you could no longer be bothered to have a blow-dry before you met up.'

'Yeah, men never seem to notice the beginning of the end – the slippery slope down the increasingly greasy hair follicles,' I said. 'Can't they tell that we go from perfectly coiffed and effortlessly sexy to suddenly flyaway or straggly?'

'Love is blind,' said Jess. 'But ends up needing bifocals to spot the split ends.' We laughed.

'Would Max be worth a blow-dry?' asked Lucy.

'Deffo.' I said. 'Though I suspect he may be younger than me. He has that cocky, uncomplicated air of youth.'

'He's in his teens?' Jess snorted.

'No, early thirties is my guess.'

'Lucky you,' said Lucy. 'A younger man is the ultimate fashion accessory for the Born-Again Single these days.'

'You don't think that a younger man asking an older woman out is merely a form of charity?'

'Who cares?' said Jess. 'Let him refresh the parts that older guys can't reach.'

Jess re-filled our glasses before launching into a monologue: 'Listen up. There are three kinds of women.' She tapped her glass with a chopstick. 'The first is the woman who wants to be taken care of. The second is the woman who wants to be in charge. The third is the smart new kind; the woman who wants to shape the guy who's going to take care of her.'

Suddenly we heard a crash from the stockroom and Miles lurched forwards into the room. 'I'm sorry, but I can't take this any longer,' he roared. 'You women are so manipulative. "Shaping men?" urgh.'

'Where did you spring from? I thought you'd left early?' I said.

'No. Been spying on you witches to see if I could learn anything.' He helped himself to a generous swig of wine. 'But you three would get an Olympic gold if manbaiting were a recognised sport.'

'Actually,' said Jess,'if you had been listening properly you would have learned that it's not manipulative to pick a man to shape. It's flattering because we pick intelligent, promising, young guys.'

'Which is why no one has picked you,' I added.

'I thought all you chicks lusted after Alpha Males?' said

Miles, sitting dangerously close to Lucy. 'Men who can be moulded sound boringly beta to me.'

'I agree,' said Lucy. 'Males are either Masters of the Universe or nurturers. No man is ever both.'

'Unless he's on his third marriage,' added Jess.

'I want an Alpha Male because they are not so threatened by a woman's success, so they don't set out to destroy you if are a match for them,' I said.

'Hark at the reborn career girl!' teased Miles. 'Anyway, a man doesn't automatically feel emasculated by a woman's success; it's when the woman in his life is disappointed in him that he feels emasculation.'

Miles put his arm around Lucy. 'So how are things with you? Are you ready to move on from your errant husband and get hot 'n' heavy with me?'

Lucy giggled nervously: 'If only you'd asked me a week ago.' She cleared her throat. 'Actually, I've got something to tell you all. I, erm, I moved back in with Edward last week. Or rather, Edward moved back in with me.'

Disappointed, when I heard this I couldn't get over the feeling that she was settling when she could do so much better for herself.

Jess blurted out: 'No! Why?! Oh Lucy, why?'

Lucy looked at her coldly: 'Until you've walked in my shoes, Jess, don't you dare judge me.' She gave a defensive shrug and before we could stop her, got up and left.

I wanted my lunch date with Max Knightly to be right but I couldn't deny it felt wrong. There was an unsettling quality to him that I hadn't encountered before. He may have ticked a higher than average number of boxes for first-date behaviour but he also presented loose ends which the control freak in me found impossible to ignore.

It was flattering that he had driven all the way from Bath to take me to lunch at a tapas bar in Notting Hill. Tick, tick. He'd had a haircut since we met and it was cut too short – why do men insist that they look more manly with a crew cut and the back of their neck weirdly shaved? – but I was able to surmount that because he was wearing nice linen trousers – his legs looked great – and he had expensive dark suede shoes. But I couldn't get over the fact that as we were leaving his car – a suitably sporty number – he grabbed a denim jacket from the back seat. My heart sank. I'm sorry but when you are fast approaching forty, you can't possibly go out with a man who wears a denim jacket and take your future together seriously, can you? I may have been open to new things but really! Apart from jeans, denim on a man who isn't a rock star or a documentary maker spells trying-too-hard up-for-a-lark irresponsibility. Even if I sneakily hated to admit that he looked pretty funky, this was not what I had in mind for myself. At all.

However, the ticks kept coming; he was an architect, (double plus of being studious *and* creative, while one day he'd be super successful and solvent, presumably?), he had a bachelor pad in Bath that he had redesigned (fabby for weekends away from London), he was single but had recently ended a lengthy live-in relationship (so he wasn't a commitment-phobe), he ironed his own shirts and liked to cook – beef and ale casserole being his forte (gloriously metrosexual) but then came the absolute kicker. A complete deal breaker. When I asked him how old he was, he asked me how old I thought. He seemed far more worldly than when we had met in the pool, so I said: 'Thirty-five?'

'I'm not sure whether to be flattered or insulted,' he smiled. 'I'm twenty-seven.'

Twenty-seven? At that moment, I wanted to pick up my

bag and my hopes, which were dashed across the floor, and leg it. How could I, at thirty-nine, go out with a twenty-seven-year-old? I felt all my old insecurities piling in. Get a grip Daisy. Get yourself a solid, solvent, sensible, soulmate not a sexy student look-alike who listens to bands you've never heard of and probably knows all sorts of indecent ways to get high. 'I think you ought to know that I am thirty-nine,' I said, sounding impossibly stiff.

He shrugged. 'So?'

'I am a divorcee with serious emotional baggage,' I continued. 'I haven't got time to play games any more, so I may as well be honest. I can't waste months messing around with a good time guy like you when I need to find myself a forty-something, six-figure-earning, BMW-driving, Alpha Male to settle down and breed with.' He lit a cigarette, took a drag, leaned back and smiled. 'And at my age, the last thing I need is to hang out with a guy who smokes and wears a denim jacket,' I concluded.

'Seems like you've got it all sussed,' he said. 'Only problem is, he sounds awfully boring, this forty-something guy.'

'Not necessarily,' I said, feeling strangely defensive for a man I had never even met, a figment of my imagination. 'He'll be more appropriate.'

'Ah, appropriate,' echoed Max, nodding. 'Appropriate on paper, no doubt, but what about here?' He banged his fist against his chest. 'What's appropriate in your head, doesn't always suit your heart.'

The waitress appeared and asked: 'Is everything okay?'

Max beamed at her and said: 'Yeah, we're at the stage where we're done with polite meaningless conversation and we're entering that delicate, raw, honest phase.'

The waitress laughed. 'I'll leave you to it, then.'

'No, feel free to join in.' As I watched them, I thought how incredibly attractive Max was. But I couldn't kid myself that he was anything other than Far Too Young. When he asked to take me home, I shook my head. 'Thanks awfully but no thanks,' I said.

Lucy asked me to lunch. It was the first time that I had been to her house since Edward had moved back home. Her girls were back at school after the summer holidays, so we had the place to ourselves. As I sat and watched her prepare roast-chicken salad, I sensed a fragile sadness, as if her aura had a shadow that she could not shake off. Even their house, which once seemed the epitome of luxury and style, lacked vitality. It was in the little things. I'd never seen vases with wilting arrangements and stale water before, or shrivelled grapes and manky pears in the fruit bowl. This wasn't a family fallen on hard times, it was a drowning marriage in which Lucy and Edward were fighting for air. There wasn't any energy left for anything extraneous to survival.

When she handed me a glass of wine, I asked, 'So how are things?'

She slumped on a stool by the kitchen counter. 'How do you think? Spending every single day with a man who has betrayed you is an appalling strain.'

Lucy Perfect Primfold; always beautifully dressed, coiffed and accessorised yet now beneath her matte make-up and semi-coloured lip gloss there was a lifelessness, like in her home. That's the price a woman pays to settle for the sake of her children; the toll of trying to cling on when inside she knows that there is nothing real to hold on to any more.

'Do you still love Edward?' I asked.

She shook her head. 'You can't love a man who doesn't support you or make you feel cherished. Not in terms of buying the odd bunch of flowers but in terms of taking you in their arms at night and knowing that they would do anything in the world to protect you.' She turned her head away. 'I've never felt less desired, Daisy.'

'So you and Edward don't sleep together?'

'Not since his affair. I've tried but I don't trust him enough to open up. Last week I had a massage and afterwards I lay in a lake of tears because it's not until you receive a kind, loving touch that you realise how bereft you are for the right sort of physical affection. Now I look at other couples who seem united and I don't feel jealous exactly, more incomprehension that they got it right when I got it so wrong.'

I laughed emptily. 'That's exactly how I used to feel when I looked at you and Edward,' I said. 'I thought you and Edward had it all.'

'So did I,' said Lucy. 'That's the heart-breaking thing. But we didn't, did we?'

I reached out and touched her arm. 'It's funny, isn't it? A woman can be successful, independent and powerful yet there is still that primitive side of her that craves support from a man. It's a horrible truth but no matter how emancipated we think we are, we still get validation that we're okay as women from a relationship.

'I remember that ghastly self-doubt after I left Jamie. How could I, armed with my top-notch education and solid degree, make such an appalling choice over a man? It rocks the core of you – that feeling that you can't trust your own judgement any more. But now I feel more philosophical. People change, relationships distort and life is both gloriously and dreadfully unpredictable.'

'Jess thinks I'm a fool,' said Lucy miserably.

'She doesn't judge you,' I lied. 'She just wants you to be happy. We all do.'

'Are you happy now?' asked Lucy.

I paused. 'I'm more confident, in the sense that I know I can survive on my own. I still have days when the fear creeps in and I think I'll be alone and childless for ever but I feel safer than I used to because I have a stronger sense of self.'

'So all that spiritual self-help stuff really works, then?'

I laughed. 'It doesn't numb the pain. If anything, the more aware you are, the more keenly you feel. The Buddhist books say that any spiritual initiation – an exceptionally difficult life passage that shakes your foundation and makes you question your purpose – is opportunity disguised as loss.'

'How could my situation be an opportunity?' Lucy looked incredulous.

'You could find the courage to leave Edward for good,' I said gently. 'Build a life for yourself and work on fulfilling your dreams.'

'I'm not strong like you,' said Lucy. 'And I've got my girls. They need a father.'

'Absolutely. But they also need a happy mother brave enough to fight for herself. In the end, if you stay, you build up a powder keg of resentment and regret.'

Lucy let her head drop into her hands. 'Shouldn't I stay here and honour my commitments as a mother and wife?'

'At what cost?' I said. She started weeping. I put my arms around her.

'Lucy, you've just turned forty. It isn't the end but it could be the beginning.'

# Chapter 8
# Premature We-jaculation

I was in the bookshop writing the meaningful missive of the day in bright cherry chalk: 'Happiness comes through doors you didn't even know you left open.'

Miles pretended to gag. 'Urgh, pass me the saccharine sentiment sick bag, please.'

'Miles, you emotional gibbon,' I said playfully, 'allow me to translate: all this is saying is that in order to be happy, we just have to be willing.'

'I'm always willing,' he said. 'Have you ever known me to turn down an opportunity to get plastered or get laid?'

'Willing to be open to something greater than yourself,' I said. 'It's like it never works if you look for love, you have to trust that love will find you.'

Miles stood back and surveyed me. 'You really believe in this, don't you?'

'Some of it,' I said.

'And where has it got you?' he said, a tad caustically.

'Out of a lame marriage.'

'But into it in the first place?'

Ouch. I couldn't help laughing. 'Oh, wait,' I said. 'On a happier note, it's got me another date with dishy younger man Max Knightly. He's invited me to Sunday lunch at his flat.'

Although my date with Max hadn't left me swooning, it had left me feeling something. Mostly, that here was a man keen to pursue me and on reflection, the age difference was flattering. When my male friends in their forties, like Miles, craved nothing but twenty-something pre-natal bullet-bodied babes – he was always harping on about 'young flesh' – the fact that a late-twenty-something guy was interested in the nearly forty *me* with my saggy boobs and squishy tops of thighs was quite a fillip. Also, the worst thing about having no one in your life – as the previous months had highlighted – is that you never get that bubble of excitement every time the phone rings or a text pops up. Being alone means that on an hour-to-hour basis, there is nothing to look forward to – apart from lunch with the girls, that is.

Lucy had asked Jess and me to meet her in a pub near the bookshop. It was a warm early autumnal day, so we sat outside at a table on the pavement, drinking Diet Coke and eating crisps. Lucy looked unusually plain for her – sure, her jeans were expensive and her T-shirt perfectly ironed and immaculately white, yet I noticed that she wore no jewellery. Even though she had a wan, tired look, she looked less adult than usual. Somehow girlie and afraid. 'What's up?' I asked.

'I finally plucked up the courage to leave Edward last week,' she said. 'Well, it's more of a separation really.'

'Thank fuck,' said Jess, raising her glass as a toast.

I shot her a look. 'What happened?'

'Edward didn't come home one night and something inside me just broke. I thought, "I can't go on like this any more always wondering where he is, doing what to whom." So the following morning, after I had dropped the girls at school, I went and rented a serviced flat in Chelsea. I spent all day there, getting it ready for the girls. Making up the beds with their favourite castles and fairy bed linen and putting their toys around, so it felt like home. When Edward got home and found out I'd gone, he called me on my mobile and asked "Where are my golf clubs?" Can you imagine? He didn't ask to speak to the girls or if we were all okay. He simply saw our leaving as an excuse for him to take a long golfing weekend.'

'Enough said,' said Jess, smugly.

'At first I was in shock,' Lucy continued, ignoring her. 'I was on automatic pilot, worrying about the children and keeping their routine the same. After I put them to bed, the anger would kick in. I literally felt consumed with rage; temper thudding through my body like a fever. Now, all I feel is grief. I want to lie around and cry all day.'

'Do you want to go back?' I asked.

'I don't want to go back but I don't want to go through this.'

'I know,' I nodded. 'When I left Jamie and the lawyer's letters starting coming, I lost my nerve. But I promise, you'll get through this and I'm not saying it is not hard but it does get better.'

'It's complete hell being a forty-something mother on your own,' said Lucy, bitterly. 'You have no idea what it's like. On Saturday morning I took the girls to Kew Gardens. I've never seen so many eager fathers with wedding rings playing with their kids, no doubt giving their wives a lie-in or the morning off to go for a Brazilian or get their highlights done ready for some romantic Saturday night.'

'Oh, don't buy into it, Luce,' shrugged Jess. 'Watch them closely enough and while their children play and they drink coffee, they're all madly texting. You can bet it isn't the wife at home they're getting textual with but the mistress they can't see until mid week.'

'For God's sake, Jess,' erupted Lucy, 'do you ever see any scenario in life that doesn't involve infidelity and a bit on the side? Just because you're the consummate mistress, it doesn't mean that there aren't women out there – wives and mothers – trying to live decent lives. Not every man is being unfaithful you know.'

'Wake up, Lucy!' Jess snapped her fingers in Lucy's face. 'Your husband has cheated on you. He's done it before and he'll do it again. And he's not alone. I just want you to find your self-respect and stop laying yourself open to further humiliation.'

'At least I've tried,' screamed Lucy, as a man passing on a bike swivelled his head to stare, making him swerve across the road. 'Unlike you, who's scared to ever risk any real feeling. I may be humiliated but I had the courage to put my heart on the line.'

Jess grabbed her handbag and stood up. 'And the dream is over, Lucy. It's all turned to dust. So who's better off between the two of us, now?'

Lucy stared at her, while Jess glanced at her watch, chucked the rest of her Coke into the gutter and stormed off. Before I could say anything, Lucy turned to me searchingly.

'Don't ask me,' I said. We sat in shocked silence.

After a while, Lucy said: 'The worst thing is that when Edward had his affair, I really tried to make the relationship work. Not in forgiving him but in keeping our domestic ship steady. I'd return from the school run and if the sun was shining, I'd think, "I love my girls, I love my friends, I love my house and garden and I love my life. So what if I don't love my husband and he doesn't love me? We don't make love but we don't fight either. I'm happy enough."'

'Oh Luce,' I said, forlornly, 'happy enough is not enough.'

'Isn't it?' She shook her head. 'I'm not so sure. Whatever Jess says, there's something to be said for marital stability.'

'Martial stagnation, more like.'

Lucy looked at her hands. 'It's true but I'm so lonely.'

'Loneliness, like fear, is a threshold emotion,' I said. 'You have to pass through it to conquer it.'

'I don't think I can,' she said.

'What are you going to do?'

'Go back to Edward soon, I guess.' She sighed. 'Hopefully, this will have given him enough of a scare. Daisy, please don't look at me like that. I'm not like you. You know that.'

All the way to Bath, I kept reciting: 'You have to give the water a chance to boil if you want to make a decent cup of tea.' Jess had sent me off to my Sunday lunch date with Max, this ringing endorsement in my ears, after my crisis of confidence the night before. We were tucking into pizza and Pinot Noir, when I began to wonder if there was any point in schlepping off to see Max after all?

'If you've met someone intriguing but you don't feel an immediate "click", should you get romantically involved anyway?' I asked.

'But you won't know if you click until you've kissed him,' said Jess.

'That's a chemical click,' I said. 'I'm not talking about that. I mean the "click" that involves a lightning strike sense of familiarity and an uncanny feeling of being understood.'

'Get real, Daisy, and just go on the date,' huffed Jess. 'Your expectations are so high that you constantly set yourself up for a fall. Just give the poor guy a chance. There's something called "a grower" where you feel neutral but you're open to it going either way.'

The thing about visiting a potential partner's pad is that you can't help doing a mental inventory to see if he could be the winning ticket to something better. It's not that I expected a man to support me financially, more that I wanted him to shoulder the emotional responsibility of me being me. As high as I could get on self-help, there were bleak moments when I felt I couldn't actually help myself and the weight of lugging all my anxieties around wore me out. The minute I walked into Max Knightly's pied-à-terre, I fancied him not because the pheromones were flowing but because it felt calm and safe.

Although I knew that Max was an architect, I hadn't stopped long enough to consider that he would have a zingingly metrosexual pulling pad. It was a modern, light, high-ceilinged apartment with thoughtful details that made hope soar. The bathroom – with glass partitions, a thundering power shower and stacks of thick oatmeal-coloured towels – was pure sex. Even better, when I went to the loo (not to pee but to check that my hair hadn't gone flat and fallen into an unflattering middle parting), I noticed that Max used Space NK products and even had a Diptyque candle burning. When I took a peek into his bedroom, I did a double take.

I would never, ever, forget the first time I saw Jamie's bedroom, so peering into Max's room was like being given another chance. When Jamie had taken me to his childhood room in his parents' house, that's when *I saw it all.* The blueprint of our marriage, of our complete incompatibility was laid out before my eyes. This was every public school boy's messy room and then some. The floor was overflowing with old school clothes, the bedside drawer had his Common Entrance papers stuffed in. The bed boasted a psychedelic, frantic-patterned duvet cover and nightmarish bottle-blue pillowcases. On the mantelpiece was every Valentine's card he had received and three Rubik's cubes. I remember trying to work out if the *pièce de résistance* was the teddy bear lampshade or the ceiling, covered with glow-in-the-dark stickers which read: JIM JAM LIVES HERE. I was so appalled that Jim Jam may as well have sprayed the walls with blood. Like a fool, I wanted to help him. I thought that I could force Jamie to grow up and into the man I had convinced myself I wanted to marry if I clutter-cleared his adolescent muckfest of a bedroom.

Instantly, I set about cleaning that room. I drove into the local town and bought scented lining paper for his drawers and rubber gloves. For the next eight hours, I literally 'shifted his shit'. When I caught Jamie trying to stuff a glittery cummerbund back into his drawers or hide a red holey jumper that sagged to his knees, I'd hold out the offending item and say: 'It's your choice. This or me?' Invariably I won but what sort of victory was that?

What I hadn't bargained for in my control-addled mind was that far from presenting me with a rosette of honour for hard labour, his mother would resent me. When she returned Lavinia Prattlock was so insulted you would have thought that I'd trashed the place.

Poor Lavinia. I wasn't what she'd envisaged as a daughter-in-law at all. She wanted some nice, uncomplicated, unemotional girl for Jamie, who had a little job as opposed to a career, doing something creative like stencilling frollicking rabbits around friends' playrooms or seashells on their bathroom ceilings. So the poor lamb was unable to hide her devastation when Jamie proposed to a neurotic, outspoken, bolshy career girl like me. The night we rang his parents to tell them that we had got engaged, they didn't even bother to ask to speak to me. A week later we met for 'drinkie poos' at their home, Manor Farm.

I often worry over the exact moment I knew I shouldn't have married Jamie but it was as if the faster the warning bells pealed, the more determined I was not to heed them. There was the language barrier that I dismissed because at the time I found it engaging and amusing and was quick to adopt it myself. Jamie was fluent in jaunty, Enid Blyton speech. An egg was a 'peggy weggy', a sock an 'ocky wocky', breakfast was 'brekkie-tuftal' and most hilarious – to me – a willy was a 'wonkle'. The Prattlock's large red brick house, like so many county abodes of their set, was filthy. The dishwasher door always hung open allowing their bloated Spaniel to lick the plates as he waddled past. The kitchen table was awash with debris; old newspapers, sticky jam pots, tins of shoe polish, some rotting fruit in a bowl and some dying roses in slime-laden water that stank. Yes, that was the point about the place. It was half-dead. Hardly breathing. Everywhere was stuffed with generation's worth of dust-filled clutter but none of it amounted to anything. It was as if anything beautiful like a wonderful piece of sculpture, or anything luxurious like a comfy chair with a cashmere throw, might be considered a weakness. Opulence was an irrelevance; a sign that you were stepping out of your circle.

We toasted our future happiness (or commiserated such an unholy alliance) with lukewarm 'cham-poo' and Pringles from the packet around the kitchen table. I sat facing the larder fixated on the over-crowded shelves. When we went to the local pub for supper, Lavinia took charge of the seating plan. Jamie sat next to her and I was placed across the table, next to Jamie's father, Gordon. It's one of the biggest regrets of my life, apart from accepting the blind date with Jamie in the first place, that I did not speak up then. I did not expect at my engagement dinner, which I had planned in my head since primary school, to be talking to Gordon about his golf handicap as I ate fatty duck through gritted teeth. Wasn't this the one occasion when I should have been able to sit next to Jamie and talk about me? Well, Jamie and me? About us?

I should have said: 'Oh don't be daft, Lavinia. Of course Jamie should sit next to me! This is our engagement dinner after all.' But I stayed schtum and hated myself for my compliance all evening.

Staring at Max's Zen room, with a futon, white bed-linen, vast window and window box filled with purple heather, felt like coming home. The contrast with Jamie was staggering. Here, clearly, was a sensitive neat-freak like me. The only picture, a large, hauntingly beautiful oil painting of Battersea Power Station made me fancy him more. Good taste, like the perfect dive into the sea, or an insider's knowledge of anything from vintage wine to obscure European authors, is an instant aphrodisiac. I quickly licked the back of my hand and sniffed it to see if my breath still smelled of garlicky pizza from the night before – phew, it didn't – and returned to the kitchen where Max was carving roast lamb. Again, the delight lay in the detail. The home-made red wine gravy, the toasty golden roast potatoes, al dente broccoli, claret breathing, a Kaiser Chiefs CD; suddenly I felt as if I was in this young, funky yet satisfyingly stylish world.

When Max poured me a glass of wine in a heavy goblet and gave me a sideways smile as he handed it to me, the chemical click clicked. I couldn't wait for him to kiss me.

All through lunch I could hardly taste the food as I was so

excited by the promise of what lay beyond. While he was talking – telling me about a block of flats he was pitching for the commission to design on a promontory in Malta – I was only half listening, as I was busy anticipating the moment that out lips would touch. Would he simply lean over and cup my face in his hands, or would he get up, take me by the hand and lead me silently to the bedroom? Not that I would have slept with him then, of course, because I had to get back to London that night for work on Monday and I wasn't about to break my steadfast rule that breakfast together is de rigueur following sex for the first time.

In fact, we had coffee on the sofa, sitting tantalisingly close. Suddenly jumpy and nervous, I starting talking too much, telling a deeply unflattering anecdote. I was explaining about a dating website that Lucy and I had logged on to for a laugh. We decided to answer the questionnaire to amuse each other and when the question was: 'Where are you happiest?' I suppose most people would, like Lucy, say: 'with my children' or 'with loved ones' or 'by the sea' but I said: 'In a five-star hotel when I'm not paying.'

As I was repeating this, I thought, 'Why am I telling something so deeply unattractive about myself?' It was a ghastly echo of my first post divorce date with Troy; I simply couldn't stop sending myself up in the most unbecoming way.

I thought that Max was looking at me like Troy had done – eyeing me either with benevolent amusement or could he have been trying to fathom if I really was that shallow? Either way, it gave me the jitters, so I leapt up and grabbed my bag and coat. 'Hey, Daisy, this place may not be a five star,' he said, 'but I've got some freebies in the bathroom. I'd love you to stay.'

I threw my hands in the air like I was a true ditz. 'I had no idea it was this late. I must get to the station.' I mouthed a strange fish-like kiss and left.

Miles found me sitting pensively in the stockroom the following morning.

'Why all the doom and gloom? What's happened?' he asked.

'I had lunch with Max Knightly yesterday,' I sighed. 'It was our second date.'

'Surely no man is that tragic a kisser?'

'That was just it,' I said, sinking into a chair. 'He didn't kiss me. He didn't even try.'

'Are you sure he isn't gay?'

'Miles, he lived with his last girlfriend.'

'Enough to turn any man to the other side.'

'No, I'm sure he's hetero.'

'Then the man's a moron if he has a penis and a pulse and didn't try to pull you.'

I looked him straight in the eye: 'What, like you, you mean?'

He shifted. 'Daisy, we have history. It complicates things. With a young guy like Max, a snog means nothing. It is like a handshake these days – it would be rude not to. Where were his manners?'

'You don't understand,' I said. 'He was too polite to try because I didn't let him.'

'So he did try?'

I shook my head.

'Oh crikey,' said Miles, sitting on the floor, 'I'm confused.'

'Max cooked this amazing lunch and afterwards we were drinking red wine on the sofa and sharing secrets and it was all too perfect, so I freaked out.'

'Still confused,' barked Miles.

'Not half as confused as poor Max was when I suddenly

leapt up and said I had a train to catch. I bolted and it wasn't until I was sitting on the train back to London that I realised my problem.'

'You'd left your door keys in his flat?' Miles gave me a friendly prod in the ribs. 'Oh come on Daisy, nothing's that bad. So you did a runner? Big deal. You'll get over it and he'll get his leg over some other chick faster than soon.'

'Don't you see?' I said. 'I'm too scared to let a man near me now.'

'Well, I'm sitting pretty close,' he said, inching nearer.

'Male intimacy, Miles. I just can't do it. After everything that's happened, I'm completely shut off.'

Miles stood up. 'I need a coffee for this.' He arched his back. 'Cappucino or espresso?'

'Cap with extra froth, please.'

When Miles returned with two large cups brimming with foam, I tried to explain: 'It's weird, as you get older, you develop an inverse relationship to pain. My tolerance to physical pain has gone up. Just grin, grit your teeth and bear it . . .'

'I thought you said you'd never had a Brazilian,' interrupted Miles.

'No, it's emotional pain I can't stomach any more. I've totally regressed. I'm like a child who can't bear the thought of getting hurt.'

Miles knelt beside me. 'You're the opposite of me, Daisy. I lay a lot of girls so I don't have to get emotionally involved. All you want is emotional involvement, so you don't lay anyone. We're both commitment-phobes, in our way.'

'Unlike you, I want to commit,' I said. 'I want to be brave enough to get close to a man but I'm petrified of being disappointed.'

'Yeah, disappointment sucks.' Miles stood up and shuddered. 'Well, that's enough touchy-feely for me. Get back to work, bitch! Go and write your clap-trap meaningful message of the day. That'll cheer you up.'

I decided to write something that would goad Miles and make me laugh. 'Whereas a promiscuous man is dysfunctional, a promiscuous woman is merely browsing.'

I stood back to admire my handiwork in purple chalk, when the door opened. I swivelled round and as he walked towards me, I inwardly cheered. Max Knightly smiled and said: 'I've got three questions to ask you, Daisy Dooley. One. Do you want to go to the cinema on Saturday night? Two. If not, why not? Three. If you can't do Saturday will you have dinner with me on Friday?'

'Yes to numbers one and three,' I said.

When you've spent months alone, the thought of great sex is a positive charge but the reality of sharing a bed afterwards is a downer. While I had lain alone at night, fantasising about Max running his artistic fingers across my body, the practicality of revealing my naked flesh made me dither.

Even getting ready for our dinner generated fresh anxiety. With youth on your side, there is nothing more thrilling than enjoying a prolonged pre-date pamper. The long oily bath, the careful application of make-up, the slow side-show as you put on your sexiest underwear admiring your reflection in the mirror. Then, casually throwing on a waft of next to nothing – a silk dress, perhaps? When your overall goal shifts from looking sexy to the serious business of looking younger without trying to be something you are not – i.e. a flighty babe able to wear a sheer top and skinny jeans and look effortless, not poured in – the whole event becomes more of a trial than a triumph. In the end (after an expensive blow-dry and some fancy skin serum, which was supposed to give me an instant face lift but made me look shiny as opposed to 'glowing') I passed muster, according to Jess. She popped her head around my bedroom door as I was preparing to leave. 'Hey! Not bad, you go girl!' She was already in her dressing-gown. For a moment, I was seriously tempted to strip off my well-cut black trousers, painful high heels and a low cut floral top and put on my towelling robe for one of our nights in watching reality TV on the sofa. 'No way,' said Jess, when I suggested it. 'I've got company myself, later.'

When Max walked into the restaurant, I felt a burst of pride that he was there for me. I hadn't seen him in a suit before and he looked sleek and urbane. Tie-less but sporting good Italian loafers (twenty years on, the latent Sloane Ranger in me still has a thing for a man in loafers) he definitely cut it. After a cocktail or two, I couldn't help asking the obvious: 'Why are you here with me when you could dangle any pretty young thing off your arm?'

He leaned back: 'There are lots of advantages in dating an older woman.'

'Give me a break.'

'No, actually you are much sexier,' he said.

I frowned: 'Don't be ridiculous, there are masses of younger, prettier girls out there.'

'Twenty-something women have incredible agendas these days.' Max drained his glass. 'They either want casual sex the minute you meet or they want the job, the man, the house, the baby. They're too hard-nosed for me. What I like about you is that you are completely secure in who you are.' If only he knew. 'At your age you're more realistic about life,' he said.

'What, you mean we're just grateful for whatever we can get? Do you see an older woman as an easy lay?'

'Hardly, you're more discerning. You know what you want and you're not afraid to ask for it.'

'Well, that sounds just as hard-nosed to me.'

'No, it's different because it's sexy because you've weathered more, so you're softer.'

'No, just bruised,' I smiled. 'It means you have to tread gently because of past pain.'

Max leaned forward and kissed me carefully on the lips. 'Now, that didn't hurt, did it?' he said.

'Thank goodness you had a snog at last.' Jess punched the air. 'It's bound to loosen you up.'

'Unlike you, I don't want to be loose,' I said. 'I don't want to rush anything this time.'

'So was Max worth the three-date wait? Is he a good kisser?'

'Yes. Very.' Jess and I were spending the weekend at Mum's, who was away at a dog show with Archibald and I was manning the fort. Walking across the muddy fields, the autumnal wind high, I felt a surge of glee following my date. 'It was fantastic. We made out like teenagers for hours. I just wanted to press the pause button on life and stay like that for ever.'

'I bet he wanted to fast-forward to some serious action,' giggled Jess.

'Actually,' I said, 'we both agreed it was a perfect evening.'

'On my God, alert! Alert!' shouted Jess. 'Premature "we"-jaculation. Fatal. You may be trying not to rush things, but mentally, you've got him up the aisle before he's got you in the sack.'

'What?' I looked at her lamely.

'Oh Daisy,' she said. 'It's the oldest dating dysfunction in the book – where one member of the couple starts using "we" before the other is ready.'

I sighed. 'You're probably right. My fantasy life has been in over-drive lately. All I could think about when we were snogging was: halleluiah, now I've got a boyfriend, I won't have to spend New Year's Eve alone.'

'What about Christmas?' laughed Jess, 'I can't believe you didn't factor that in?'

'Well,' I said sheepishly, 'I did have a heavenly vision of us alone in his flat in Bath, opening our stockings in bed, then drinking champagne as he gave me a beautifully wrapped present and us being all cosy, post-coital and coupley.'

'Dream on,' she scoffed. 'Who has ever spent a Christmas as perfect and family-free as that?'

We laughed. 'Actually, I'm quite scared of sleeping with Max,' I admitted. 'At the moment it is safe and sweet but the minute you become sexual, you can never reclaim that innocence again. It's ironic, you spend your teenage years desperate to lose that innocence but later on, all you want is to preserve it.'

'But how long is a stud like Max going to wait before you deliver?' Jess lit a cigarette and took a pensive drag.

'We'll soon find out, I guess,' I said. 'Anyway, you can vet him because he's coming to dinner tonight and I've asked Miles as well.'

Max proved the hero of the evening as he volunteered to cook. (None of my friends ever let me loose in the kitchen as they knew what a domestic cripple I was.) He made fantastic roast pheasant with parsnip crisps, while I twittered about around him, like some silly, flirtatious sous chef. Miles sat in the old dog-eared armchair by the Aga, one leg flung across the arm and gently quizzed Max, whose openness was becoming. He was one of those modern men who didn't feel he had anything to hide. Even though he was a decade younger than Miles, he held his own and I admired him. They teased and joshed – and Max wisely deferred to Miles – letting him come across as the general expert – on everything, even me.

'I'll give you one bit of advice about Daisy,' said Miles, cracking open another beer. 'When you think you're most sure of her, that's the time to doubt. She's the most unpredictable woman I've ever known.'

'And you've known some,' I teased.

Max put his hands on my shoulders and gave them a squeeze. 'How does any man get a handle on you?'

I simply smiled enigmatically.

After dinner, the four of us drank copious bottles of red wine by the fire and roasted chestnuts. Max was funny and sexy and charming. At one point he theatrically quoted the poet Neruda: 'I'm tired of being a man,' before adding: 'especially if it means always paying and never crying.'

Miles fell about laughing. He seemed to genuinely like Max as they had that easy-going male banter where they called each other 'mate' a lot and kept re-filling each other's glass. Jess was on particularly buoyant form and I was sad that Lucy wasn't with us. But when I'd told Luce that Jess was coming, she said she couldn't face her after their scene and that she felt too unhappy and burdened to join us anyway. I remembered feeling that after I left Jamie; that awful isolation as if everybody else was leading their life on a lighter plane and you didn't feel that you would ever succumb to fluff and fun, let alone raucous laughter, again.

I watched Max expertly bank up the fire and I couldn't understand why I didn't want to disappear upstairs with him and fold myself into his arms. What was holding me back now? No. It couldn't be true, could it? What was wrong with me? Why now? Why *him*? Watching Miles roll a joint with Jess as they laughed in that easy-going, good time girl/good time guy way – as if they might as well enjoy the opportunity of being thrown together – their faces glowing in the firelight, I realised I was jealous.

When we finally made it up the stairs to bed, I was grateful that I was sleeping in the single bed of my childhood. Although Max had gamely elected to share it with me, grappling for space killed any erotic edge. Fortunately, he was drunk enough to sleep in spite of the discomfort, while I lay awake crushed beside him.

Jess found me early Sunday morning sitting in the lotus position in the dog's basket by the Aga, holding a torch towards my heart. Donald and Dougie were snuggled in my lap, resting against the worn flannel of my pyjamas.

'Meditative self-flagellation is one thing but to involve innocent canines is quite another,' she said.

'They help anchor my knees and force me to sit up straight.'

'What's with the self-interrogation?' she asked, grabbing the torch and shining it in my face.

'Ouch!' I blinked. 'The process of becoming conscious is like shining a torch on our soul. As we fill ourselves with insight and self-discovery, we move towards those hidden places deep within ourselves that are usually left dark and unlit.'

'Spare me the spiritual psychobabble and tell me what's going on,' said Jess, filling the kettle. 'You've got a gorgeous boyfriend upstairs but you prefer the dog-hair-coated kitchen floor? Do I take it that the lack of a lie-in means that you didn't get laid last night?'

I gently eased the dogs off and struggled to stand, just as one leg was hit by a spasm of cramp. I hopped over to Jess and sat beside her at the kitchen table, trying to kick the pins and needles out of my calf. 'I'm totally deranged,' I said.

Jess raised a knowing eyebrow: 'At last, some real self-awareness.'

'No, I've realised that I don't have commitment phobia, I just have a phobia about committing to the wrong man.'

'Same difference,' she said crisply, pouring coffee. 'How do you know if a guy is wrong until you've tried him for size? Anyway, Max Knightly seems pretty right to me. You couldn't ask for a sexier, funnier guy, could you?'

'That's just it,' I said, slumping forwards. 'He's pretty perfect which is what freaks me out. All night, I've lain awake, wondering what's wrong with me. Here's this great guy, who likes me and wants to get things on with me and all I could do was obsess about another man.'

'Oh, not Julius again,' Jess frowned. 'Honestly, Daisy, this pattern is getting so destructive; meet sexy bloke who offers chance of real future but derail everything and drag in first love who will never be more than Mr Futile Fantasy.'

'No, not Julius. Miles.'

'Miles?' Jess spewed coffee across the table. 'Miles?' she shouted. 'My God, you are deranged.'

'Shush,' I whispered. 'He'll hear you.'

'Miles? Miles!' she repeated incredulously. 'After twenty years you've suddenly decided that Miles – a man who would be incapable of fidelity on his honeymoon – is the man for you?'

'Yes, because what I've realised is that I don't want someone to love me, like Max could, I need to someone to understand me, like Miles does.'

'It's precisely because Miles does understand you that he could never fall in love with you,' said Jess, laughing. 'Sure, Miles loves you like we all do; because you're a batty old broad but he also knew you as an insecure, lanky-haired twenty-year-old student. Why would he suddenly fall in love with an insecure, full-head-of-highlights divorcee?'

'Actually, they're only lowlights and I'm not insecure, I've got emotional integrity.'

'Then use it and go back to bed with Max,' said Jess.

I leaned back in my chair. 'Don't you ever hunger for a permanent relationship?'

'No. I'm like Miles,' she said. 'In my book, there's only one thing worse than being on your own. Wishing you were on your own.'

'But you must get lonely?'

'Yes, but I often think when I wake up in the night worrying, would it be better to have someone by my side or would it be irritating? Mostly, I plump for irritating.'

The door opened and Miles walked in, all tousled hair, crumpled shirt and boxers. With a pang of guilt, I remembered Max lying in my straitjacket of a single bed upstairs, equally virile and leggy. Miles smiled: 'I can't believe it. Finally, I think it's happened.'

'What?' we chorused.

My heart plummeted. Was he into Jess?

'After two decades of vicariously living through your dating and marrying hell, Daisy, I finally like your boyfriend. Max is a top bloke.'

'And what about you two?' I asked edgily. 'Did you spend the night together?'

'Now,' Miles winked at Jess. 'That would be telling her, wouldn't it?'

Jess shook her head at me. 'You never learn do you? Miles may be gorgeous and a tempting shag but he is single and might fall for me. I prefer to sleep with happily married men because they don't want to leave their wives.'

'Exactly. My rule is to never sleep with unhappily married wives as they might want to leave their husbands.'

'You old romantics,' I teased.

Though curiously relieved, I looked at Miles playfully ruffling Jess's hair and wondered if maybe it would be better to be loved than understood after all.

Although I didn't let it show at the weekend, the friction

between Lucy and Jess disturbed me. They were in such different places in their lives, both emotionally and morally, and I was tired of trying to keep my footing as well as their peace as I stood in between them on most things. Also, my indecision over Max disquieted me, so I decided to take a breather from the strain of London flat-sharing life and visit my old friend Natasha – who had introduced me to Julius.

Natasha was now married to Peregrine and they lived in Norfolk. It was refreshing that Natasha and I had kept up our friendship when we'd made such different choices in life. She had plumped for the security of the known; a life in which outwardly little would change. She and Peregrine still went on the same house parties and holidays as they had done twenty years ago, it's just that these days they were accompanied by their dogs and well-educated kids. Yet even back then, during the languid summer of 1988 when we saw most of each other, I always knew that I'd never settle down to a comparatively easy life like hers. In those days it was heady, *Brideshead Revisited* stuff and for her and her set, it still was. The clothes may have changed – jeans, sparkly tops and stilettos may now be acceptable for drinks before dinner but on the whole the house parties, the black-tie dances, the concrete formality yet utter frivolity of the social whirl was exactly the same.

It could have turned my head, yet instead I went into a form of revolt. One too many evenings fixated on bowls of garden-grown sweet pea, the gleaming silver, listening to inane banter and braying hoots of derision twisted my gut. Why are the upper classes unable to discuss anything real? God forbid anyone should discuss anything as prosaic as a feeling. It's all about external heroics and nothing remotely internal. Some have no greater ambition than to bolt down the icy Cresta Run in Switzerland on a tray or drive across

Africa in a Ferrari. Elephant polo, anyone? Far too busy checking out their artfully floppy fringes, they never stop for a second to look within. I wrote them off as suppressed twits and consoled myself that I may have cocked it up when it came to men but at least I was able to access authentic feeling.

Sitting at Natasha's table, two decades on, I thought what a mistake I had made. Peregrine Sackville had turned out to be an exceptionally decent chap with a cracking career in the City. They have two gorgeous, glossy, hair-flicking girls in their early teens and live in a rambling, fiendishly cold manor house with topiary hedges and those posh chickens with fluffy feet. When it was suggested that we 'freshen up' before dinner, unable to face the icy bath, I sat at the kidney-shaped dressing-table in the spare room and stared at my reflection in the mirror. I didn't see the feisty, uncompromising chick I set out to be in my twenties, crusading for love, emotional compatibility and an intellectual challenge. I saw an unmarried, lonely woman who could barely keep it together on a good day. Where had my ambition, my angst and my anger got me? Had it got me a rock-steady marriage, a decent house without a mortgage, some seriously enviable antique furniture, well-mannered children and a considerate partner who loved me because my wrinkles were proof that we had gone the distance? It had not.

In my trance-like state I reflected that even their home was devoid of anguish. Sure, it was bolstered by quiet money but why hadn't I pushed for a life in that calm, untroubled air? Their home hadn't witnessed the door-slamming, roof-raising rows of my marital abode nor had it been privy to the vindictive verbal volleys that Jamie and I hurled low when we lived as husband and wife. Clearly, Peregrine and Natasha never shouted things like: 'You really are a spoilt brat, Daisy. Sometimes, I hate you.' To which I would counter: 'No you don't. Relationships are mirrors, Jamie. You hate yourself.'

I thought back to one of the worst lows of our marriage; when I invited my editor, Sarah, from my old publishing house, Ludgate Press, to dinner. I was hoping that she might be persuaded to let me return to work part-time, as I could see that not working was having a deleterious effect on me. I had spent ages laying the table – fighting my control freak urge to measure the place settings with a ruler – and arranging pale pink roses in symmetrical vases, ensuring the flat looked sufficiently *à la mode* for a *World of Interiors* spread.

As I was serving out the rosemary-infused lamb, mini roast potatoes and asparagus tips (all pre-cooked from a nearby deli), one of the guests, Alan, a fairly high-profile PR, announced that he was a vegetarian. No prob, I assured him, inwardly thanking my guardian angel that I had taken out a small mortgage on the cheese selection. Jamie insisted on fetching it and as we'd been given a state of the art Perspex cheeseboard and matching knife for a wedding present, it never crossed my mind that he wouldn't return with the cheese on said cheeseboard. While I finished serving the rest of the table, I was busy sending him psychic emails to the kitchen. 'Try not to knock the herbs off the edge of the garlic goats' cheese as you unwrap it, dear,' and 'Darling, please put the wedge of Stilton at an angle on the corner of the board next to the organic oat cakes.'

At what point do you finally wake up to the fact that if you are a control freak of criminal proportion and don't want to be disappointed by a man, you do a job yourself? To me, the correct course of action was so blindingly obvious that an alien would have got it right. But not Jamie. Or maybe this was another perfect moment for him? The chance to humiliate – worse, hurt – me as he knew how much I cared. He was fully aware that I'm the sort of anal saddo who can't eat a meal without a napkin, unlike him who used to happily rip chicken wings from the steaming carcass, then wipe his greasy hands on his jeans – or on our chairs to really bug me. So, it shouldn't have been any surprise to me that he arrived back at the table with an over-ripe brie oozing from its sweaty wrapper. No cheeseboard. Not even a plate. In a blatant act of defiance, or was it out of his misplaced sense of humour, he looked me straight in the eye, put the cheese on to our hand-made light maple dining room table and cut great hunks off the wrapper. As I watched the oily marks stain the wood, I realised then how little he cared about me or what mattered to me.

Later, as we thrashed it out after the guests had gone, I returned to my inevitable theme. Every single argument always led to my nemesis: Lavinia. Cheeseboard to Lavinia. Wrong route on country drive to Lavinia. What to watch on TV? to Lavinia. Tuscany or Tunisia for our holiday? to Lavinia.

'You are so cruel, Jamie,' I shouted over the noise of running taps.

He stood in the kitchen doorway, triumphant. 'Get over yourself, Daisy, it was just a lump of cheese.'

I swung around from where I was loading the dishwasher. 'But you knew the evening was important to me. I wanted it to be right.'

'No amount of sodding *etiquette*,' he spat out the word, 'is going to get you another job at Ludgate Press. Face it, you're finished. You've lost your touch.'

Yeah, I noted to myself, and look how thrilled you are at the prospect. 'Why do you always need to humiliate me in public? Are you that threatened?'

'*Threatened*?' He gave a smug chortle. 'By a nutcase like you? You're not right in the head.'

'*I'm* not right in the head? Actually, it's normal to put cheese on a cheeseboard but you wouldn't know that would you? The way you've been brought up.'

Jamie stiffened.

'You have absolutely no manners, Jamie.'

'Do you honestly think that my manners would make one iota of difference to this mockery of a marriage?' he yelled.

Jamie stormed from the room and slammed the bedroom door.

My God, how the truth hurts. It still hurt me sitting in Natasha's tranquil home to realise how tense and wound up I'd been. In so many ways, Jamie had been right. What did it matter where you cut cheese? On the sofa, the loo seat or the floor, if you were happy. But I was so unhappy and so afraid of my unhappiness that instead of saying to Jamie: 'Look, we both made a mistake getting married,' the cheeseboard took on monumental significance. That Jamie didn't put the brie on a piece of plastic didn't destroy our marriage. It merely made the marital time bomb tick faster and deafeningly loud.

I went down to supper and watched through a haze of regret as the Sackvilles interacted in an enviably interdependent way. Natasha didn't oscillate between knee-cringing neediness and isolating independence as I do in relationships. She learned early on that the fastest way to happiness is to accept and appreciate her lot.

It was a shock to me to realise that weekend that actually I was a fully paid-up member of the sneering metropolitan elite. I used to mock the basic goodness of people like the Sackvilles because they say grace before mealtimes and go to church every Sunday. However, as I sat in my pew beside them and watched the sun stream through the stained-glass windows, I felt ashamed of myself. It was as if the things that I once held dear had slid through my fingers and smashed to the floor. My past values had been horribly conceited and corrupt. What was the good of acid wit if it did just that? Corroded the skin of another? What was so superior about cleverness over kindness? The errant rogue male as opposed to the loyal, steady mate? Maybe I was finally maturing, maybe I was just tired of trying too hard but I could see that I was in danger of becoming a caricature of myself. While it's expected you'll make a mess of your twenties and acceptable to stumble in your thirties, it is plain pathetic not to prioritise in your forties. Hankering after funny but flighty Miles was just a tried and tested way of sabotaging my future.

Max rang me when I got back. 'Daisy, I don't want to mess you around but I can't wait any longer for you to make up your mind. I need to know: are we an item or not?'

Max and I ended up having one of those dreamy telephone conversations that you don't want to end. When he asked if we were an item or not, I told him the truth: I didn't know because I was afraid to commit too far down the line. If being an item meant lazing on my bed, talking to him as I was then with absolute hand-on-heart honesty, then I was happy to be itemised. If it meant inching further down the dating path and slowly unearthing intimacies about each other, I would sign my name on his calling card. But if it meant the sort of unspoken yet implied contract that could lead to something more serious, then it was best he left well alone.

'Don't you want to get married again?' he asked.

'I honestly don't know, any more.' I sighed. 'I know it sounds awfully Buddhist but I've been so disappointed by love and had my hopes dashed so many times, that I only believe in the power of now. We have to live in the moment because we can't change our past nor predict our future. I try not to hold on to anything any more and that includes expectation, so that I won't get disillusioned.'

'It sounds rather dreary,' laughed Max. 'Do you allow yourself to hope for anything?'

'Oh yes,' I giggled. 'My Buddhist better nature goes to sleep early and then I lie awake and sift through my dreams. Of course I pray that I'll grow old with a man who is more at home with being a man than any man I've ever known. A man who shoulders responsibility with deceptive ease yet could be moved to tears by the grace of ordinary everyday people.'

'Oh, so it's a demi-god you're after?'

'Yes,' I said, 'because he needs to be good at DIY – that is, he can replace a washer on a tap or re-position the ballcock in the loo but also be able to pick the perfect-sized, non-tarty lingerie.'

'That begs the question; thong or French knickers?'

'Chiffon boy pants.'

'No wonder you live in the present,' chided Max. 'You're impossibly hard to please.'

'Well, the difference between men and women is that a man wouldn't be put off by what underwear a woman was wearing, his main aim would still be to get them off. Whereas the minute I've kissed a guy, I go into a flap about whether he's wearing boxers or not because if he was wearing Y fronts, I'd be immediately and irrevocably repulsed.'

'That's not very Buddhist, is it?' said Max. 'I thought it was what was inside that counted? And I mean the size of his soul not his lunch box.'

Suddenly, his voice sounded amazing – dark and throaty, hinting at something naughty. 'Okay, Buddhist babe, so quote me some more of your life lessons,' continued Max. 'They're so strange, I find them quite a turn-on.'

'Do you want the practical "nothing valuable can truly be destroyed because nothing you learn is ever lost and no act of kindness is forgotten or wasted"? Or do you want the Daisy Dooley: "I'll know it's real love when the man I'm with asks 'what are you thinking?' and genuinely wants to know the answer"?'

'I'll go for your personal peccadillos as opposed to pious preaching any day. Give me three more.'

'Only if you give me four of yours afterwards.'

'It's a deal, Dooley.'

'Okay,' I paused for thought. 'I can't stand the way some people save a teabag for a second use and it sits like a little dried-up brown sack by the kettle. I loathe tepid, so I find it enraging if tea, coffee and soup isn't tongue-burningly hot. And I love autumn so much that sometimes the glorious burnt-red and orange colours make my heart leap.'

Max gave a soft snort of appreciation. 'Okay, my turn. Here goes. I love light bouncing off a great glass building. I hate tattoos on women. I love jazz and I hate the fact that you are the most original woman I've ever met yet it's impossible to get to grips with you.'

'What do you mean?'

'Look, Daisy, I get it that you've been burned by men but don't keep us all at arm's length. Let me in.'

'I don't know how to any more.'

'Come away with me next weekend and I'll show you, step by step.'

Jess was waiting for me in the flat on Sunday evening after my weekend away with Max. She even rushed out and got takeaway fish and chips, which we ate at the kitchen table, washed down by strong cups of coffee. 'So? How did it go? I've been thinking of you all weekend.'

'Not at all as I expected,' I grimaced.

I explained that by the time Max came to collect me to drive me to the hotel in the Cotswolds, I was almost dizzy with desire. Spending the week fantasising about being in bed with him meant that I couldn't wait to get there and rip off my born-again celibate skin. In my mind, I had fully embraced the perks of having a fling with a younger man – mind-blowing sex with an energetic toy boy was bound to take me out of myself, wasn't it?

As soon as we entered the hotel bedroom, I checked out the freebies in the bathroom – lovely lavender L'Occitane – then fingered the towelling robes to see how thick and soft they were – eight out of ten – and after a quick snoop in the mini-bar – they had those trendy vitamin water drinks – I stroked the cosy chenille throw as I lay back as alluringly as possible on the bed. Max smiled and sat beside me. 'God, you're really quite attractive,' he said.

'Don't sound so surprised,' I teased.

He slowly traced the outline of my lips with his fingers and when I thought I was going to expire, leaned forwards and kissed me.

'It was one of those perfectly charged moments,' I told Jess, 'because as he started to undress me, I felt sexy and safe and thin.' (I had given up wheat for the previous five days, so my stomach was unusually concave and I had splashed out on La Perla matching bra and pants. Not in over-stated black but in statement dusty pink.) I closed my eyes and, wallowing in the bliss of it all, waited for it to happen. The kissing and cuddling continued . . . and continued. It was some time before I cottoned on that the whole thing had fallen rather flat, so to speak.

'You mean he couldn't perform?' shrieked Jess, half laughing, half horrified.

'Yup,' I said. 'After a while he sat up and copped to the fact that it wasn't happening for him.'

'I hope you were sympathetic. Men get awfully over-sensitive about erectile dysfunction.'

'Actually, I was furious. I couldn't understand how he couldn't do it to me. It wasn't exactly a confidence boost, I can tell you. Although I tried not to show it, I thought, "Typical! Finally, I feel ready for some serious action and not a (solid) sausage."'

'Poor Max, what did he do?'

'Actually, he redeemed himself because he was pretty cool about the whole thing. He went straight to the mini-bar and opened an expensive bottle of champagne. He then came back to bed with two glasses and told me that it was precisely because he was so keen on me that he couldn't do it. He managed to laugh about the irony of wanting the weekend to be so perfect, that he had ruined it. He said it had never happened to him before and I believed him. In the end, we really bonded, giggling about our completely chaste dirty weekend.'

'Most men would have gone into a terrible huff and you'd have had to spend the whole time placating them,' said Jess.

'The weird thing was that it made me find Max more attractive because he was able to laugh so openly at his shortcomings. I thought that was pretty sexy and mature.'

'So did you get there in the end?' asked Jess, banging her fist on the table.

'Yes, early the next morning. We were both half-asleep and devoid of expectation. I think he was pretty relieved afterwards. And as it had been so long for me, I felt like I was losing my virginity all over again.'

'How was it?'

'Bloody fantastic,' I said.

# Chapter 9
# Hook-ups not Hold-ups

As I hadn't seen Lucy for a while and felt guilty about living with Jess during this impasse in their friendship, I decided to surprise her with a visit. She hadn't been answering my calls and I wondered if she saw my closeness to Jess as some sort of betrayal. I knew that she was usually at home between three and four in the afternoon as that was her quiet time before the school run. I bought a large bouquet of white roses with green foliage and a box of sugary pink cupcakes for her girls and told Miles I'd be back in the bookshop in over an hour.

Lucy opened the door and seemed genuinely relieved to see me. We gave each other a warm, heart-felt hug. She took the flowers and said: 'Thank you but what's all this in aid of?'

'Friendship,' I said. 'I've missed you.' I went inside and the house felt different. Calmer. Things seemed to have changed. I didn't remember seeing some of the modern art in the hall before.

Lucy led me to the kitchen and put the kettle on. Everywhere looked exceptionally tidy, as if everything was newly ordered and in control. The house felt emptier, yet less lonely than the last time I was there.

'Have you been redecorating?' I asked.

'More like major clutter-clearing.' Lucy came and sat opposite me at the kitchen table. She twiddled the diamond stud in one ear lobe. 'Daisy, Edward has finally left me. It's over. For good.'

'Edward has left you? When?'

'A month ago.'

'A month ago?!' I repeated, shocked. 'Why didn't you tell me? Is this why you didn't answer my calls?'

She looked around the room, as if buying time. When she spoke it was slow and deliberate, as if she had rehearsed herself many times. 'I didn't tell you because I needed time to digest it myself. Because I feared that you were getting compassion fatigue about my marriage ever since Edward's affair. Because I am ashamed to admit that I am a single mother as it sounds so flaky. Because when he left, I was so ready for him to go that I'm not as upset as people expect me to be and because I like the stillness in the house of the phone not ringing and of no one having to worry about me. It feels like I am living this private life and for the first time in years, after I've dealt with the children, I can fully concentrate on me.

'It's funny, apart from hating the "single mother" label and loathing the instant, slightly patronising sympathy it elicits from my family, as if "poor thing, now she has to cope with all this *on her own*", there's not one thing about Edward leaving that devastates me. Maybe I'm in a fog of denial or maybe it is because his moods had got so much worse than I allowed myself to register but when he left, this time I felt nothing but overwhelming relief.'

I listened, barely able to move, as she went on: 'He went after we had a row at four thirty in the morning because I had developed this nervous cough. I coughed in my sleep and he said I was deliberately trying to wake him. Suddenly it was like Vesuvius erupting. All this terrible pent-up pain and rage exploded and he leapt out of bed and said he "couldn't do family any more" and that he wanted to leave. I told him to pack his stuff then and there, which he did. I threw black bin liners at him and while he hurled his stuff in them, I unloaded the dishwasher and then put on a load of white washing.'

When Lucy told me this, I remember thinking that it is the tiny, aching details of people's lives that unite us and make us so frail and yet so strong; so human. Her husband was leaving her with two small children and not knowing what else to do, she put on a colour-coded wash.

'After he had gone,' she continued, 'I lay down on the bed and felt this incredible calm. I didn't cry, I just stared at the clock until it was time to wake the girls and take them to school. Then I went to a yoga class and my day continued as usual.

'The thing that I'll never forget about Edward leaving is that once he had packed up the car, he came back into the house and went upstairs. I thought he was going to go and look at the girls sleeping and that then he would feel remorse or something – anything – so I followed him. But he went into the bathroom and put gel in his hair. Somehow, that finished it for me. It was as if a portal to my heart closed and I looked at this man that I once adored and I thought: "You are nothing but a vain, spineless buffoon."'

'Do you think Edward has someone else, since Susie, I mean?'

'I expect so,' said Lucy blandly. 'Men usually leave because they do.'

I nodded: 'Yes, women tend to tough it out and learn to accept being alone, mainly because we are too hurt to contemplate getting close to anyone else, but men, driven by a terror they barely understand, always boomerang into someone else's arms or into some grateful bint's warm bed.'

Lucy smiled. 'I should have told you before. I knew you'd understand.'

'Understand? I could write the screenplay.' I gave Lucy's arm a reassuring squeeze. 'I've never seen you more certain, Lucy and I'm so proud of you. There'll be moments of panic but I promise you, hope will far outweigh regret.'

I decided to take Lucy to a party to cheer her up. Due to the success of my self-help list at the bookshop, my popularity was ripe among alternative publishing types. I dragged Lucy to the talk and launch party of a new American author, Chad Peace, whose book, *The Alchemy of Fate and Attraction*, was riding high in the US bestseller list. Lucy and I sat near the back and listened as Chad, a thin, remarkably suave and attractive author, clad in Gucci shoes and chunky oatmeal cashmere, spoke of the inner ache of loneliness that intermittently plagues us all. As he spoke, I kept nudging Lucy and whispering: 'See, this is *exactly* what we needed to hear.' Ever sceptical, Lucy remained unmoved, but I couldn't soak up his message fast enough.

'The yearning to feel heard, needed and important is so strong in all of us that we seek validation in whatever form we can get it,' lectured Chad, who I swear was holding eye contact with me. 'For a lot of people, having an affair is an affirmation that "really, I'm okay". However, an affair always conceals deeper pain. Most of us learn to live with that deep hurt by dismissing it but the point is letting it be there. Not numbing it in someone else's bed or obliterating it in a bottle of gin but by embracing it. It is only when you are free from past pain that you can ignite the alchemy of authentic attraction.'

'What a load of old guff,' huffed Lucy, grabbing a glass of wine when the talk was over. 'What's wrong with distraction anyway? I'd love to have an affair – in fact, finding a lover is top of my list right now – and so what?'

'There's nothing wrong with that but what Chad was saying is that you have to examine your motivation,' I explained. 'If you're having an affair to distract yourself from the uncomfortable fact that Edward has left you, then you'll have to deal with the real issues later. Do you want an easy ride or a deferred crisis?'

'I want to feel feminine again,' said Lucy.

'But why do you have to have an affair to have that? Didn't you listen to anything Chad said? He said that most people don't have the courage to hold out for more than an affair, especially if they've been disappointed in love before. Why don't you want to fall in love again?'

For a moment Lucy looked so exasperated that I thought she was going to throw her glass of wine in my face. 'Daisy, I'm glad your self-help addiction has given you a career but sometimes I could throttle you. Not all of us live in Daisyland, some addled fantasy world where cupid, the great saviour, is going to show up and sprinkle our messy, mundane lives with fairy dust. At forty with kids, the chances of true love showing up for me are about as high as suddenly discovering my boobs are back in the position they were before I breastfed.'

Before I could reply that actually I'd read that with so many divorces and career women deferring marriage these days, a whole new cycle of late-life love was opening up among forty- and fifty-somethings, I felt a tap on my shoulder. I looked round to see Chad Peace beaming. 'Are you Daisy Dooley?' I nodded enthusiastically. Meeting an author you revere is always unusually intimate because of that false sense of knowing you have just because you've been party – along with millions of other readers – to their innermost thoughts.

'I hear you're the girl to woo?' he said.

'Why? Are you single?' cut in Lucy, acidly. 'Or is there a Mrs Peace? Or even a missing piece to your agenda?' Such was Lucy's combative stare that I felt a surge of excitement as I was never one to shy from a scene. It was as if Edward leaving had unleashed her gall.

Chad batted his thick, curly eyelashes at her. 'Sure, there's a Mrs Peace,' he said slowly.

'Is Peace your real name or is that fake too?' asked Lucy.

'Real name, wrong original spelling,' he said. 'It was Piece, as in "piece of the action", before.'

'Why doesn't that surprise me?' spat Lucy as she flounced off.

'As I was saying,' Chad turned back to me, turning up the volume of his charm: 'I'd really like to come and see you at your bookshop.'

'Oh, that would be wonderful,' I said. 'I'll arrange a book signing.'

It was the morning of Chad's book signing and I was busy arranging copies of *The Alchemy of Fate and Attraction*. Suddenly, Lucy burst through the door, her cheeks pink with temper. 'You're the last person I expected to see,' I said. 'You do realise Chad Peace is coming in an hour or two?'

'I'd forgotten about that freak,' she said, wrapping her arms around me. 'Oh, Daisy, I'm so apoplectic with this deep, burning rage, I can hardly function.'

I sat Lucy down and handed her a stress ball to squeeze. 'Edward turned up at the house last night to take the last of his stuff,' she began. 'I was so relieved that I didn't feel anything when I saw him. I just looked at his scared, wan face and felt totally flat. There was no longing or grief over our lost love, just astonishment really that I once felt anything at all. When he'd gone, I realised that he'd taken the toaster. Can you imagine? No regard for the girls and their breakfast the next morning. It was so petty and insulting that it has ignited this fury that I wasted so many years on this man who has turned out to have no moral values or anything that I can respect at all.' She threw the stress ball hard and it hit the pile of Chad's books which began to topple over. 'Bull's eye,' she said.

'Don't you see?' I started to rearrange my Peace pyramid. 'It's so obvious that emotionally you've begun to let him go. He took the toaster because there was nothing else he could take.'

Lucy let out a blood-curdling gargle. 'Urgh, you're right. God, you realise that you don't know someone until you marry them, then you divorce them and you find out that you never knew them at all.'

'That's exactly how I felt when I left Jamie,' I said. 'It's as if you marry the man you marry because you like their version of yourself more than you like your own. Then, you divorce them and suddenly you stare back at this cold, angry stranger whom you simply can't stand any more.'

'At least you never had kids with Jamie, so you never had to see him again. I have to face Edward visiting the girls and all I feel when I talk to him is this uncontrollable dislike.'

'I don't think that lasts for ever,' I said. 'I used to lie in bed and obsess about how much I loathed Jamie and now I think that if I saw him, I'd feel nothing but genuine goodwill. In time you realise that what you had together wasn't nothing, it was lots of things and in your case, you've got two lovely girls.'

'I feel quite sorry for Edward and I always have done for Jamie,' boomed a male voice. We swung round to see Miles pop up behind the counter. 'Poor pathetic sods.' Miles jumped down and went up to Lucy and kissed her straight on the lips. After a moment, she pulled away, astonished. 'There!' he smiled. 'You needed that. I find that newly separated women have this inner coil of tension. On the one hand they are wary and raw and on the other they have this urgent desire for destructive, physical passion to blow the cobwebs away.'

'You're not wrong there,' gasped Lucy.

'So how come you never snogged me after I left Jamie?' I asked, put out.

'Oh, because your wariness and rawness far exceeded your physical need for a shag. Far from soothing you, it would have screwed you up even further.'

Later, after Lucy had left promising to return when the Chad coast was clear, I watched Chad signing copies of his book and flirting with every needy woman in the room – i.e. *all* the women who had come because they were intelligent and empty – and thought how full of heartbreak most people's lives are. These women had been buffeted by disappointment and bruised by duff expectation, so their craving for pockets of peace and fulfilment was almost feral in its sense of urgency. I saw a face I thought I recognised and when she turned to me, I realised that it was Susie.

'How are you?' I said, greeting her.

'I'm doing okay. Obviously I'm a bit more cautious when it comes to men after the Edward fiasco,' she said.

'Justifiably so,' I smiled.

'I can't believe I've never been to Miles's bookshop before. I didn't realise it was such a scene, here.'

'It isn't usually. Normally it's just me and Miles baiting each other on a daily basis.'

'I'm sure it does him good.'

Chad came up and I introduced them. Susie seemed to know a lot about Chad's work and I thought how much Edward must have underestimated her. She was so much more than a cold, beautiful, trophy mistress. As I mingled, I overheard Chad say to Susie: 'Conscience is the soul's way of keeping you out of harm' and I wondered how much she had told him about herself. I looked across and she winked at me.

I was pouring indifferent wine into paper cups and filling up bowls with tortilla chips, when Chad came up with a fifty-ish, academic-looking woman with dark curly hair. 'Daisy, meet my editor at Insight Publications. Jennie Skipwith.'

'Hello,' she said, extending her arm. 'You've done wonders with your list here. You seem to have an uncanny feel for what people want to read.'

I felt myself blush. 'Thanks,' I said. 'It's more by luck than judgement.'

'Oh, I doubt that very much.' She reached into her bag and handed me her card. I could feel myself swelling with pleasure as I was unaccustomed to professional praise. And yet, even as I took the card and she was saying: 'You never know, you might want to write something yourself one day?' I felt like a complete fraud. Supremely mediocre and untalented. Unlike someone like Chad Peace with his strong, knowing, original voice. Okay, so I could spot a few potential spiritual bestsellers because they spoke to me but that didn't really mark me out in any way, did it?

I looked up and saw Max Knightly walk through the door.

'Daisy,' he said. 'I've got to tell you something and I'm afraid you're not going to like it.'

My mind instantly flitted through various trifling scenarios but I wasn't unduly alarmed. He had a lengthy architectural assignment abroad so our relationship would now move into long-distance territory? But that could be quite fun. All those *Love Actually* ecstatic airport meetings, all that urgent hotel-room sex and those teary departures followed by days spent pining, with giddy texting and saucy emailing. No, he was quite wrong about that. That wouldn't faze me at all. In fact, it would dispel the bleak moments of domestic boredom that everyday relationships inevitably bring. If he was living in a hotel, there would be expense-account room service and laundry on tap, so no washing of grease-embedded pans after cooking roast potatoes and no seeing him throw his crumpled boxers in the washing machine. This could be a real blessing. Or was it something that might prove more of a trial? His mother had given him a hard time on the 'how could you do this to *me*?' emotional blackmail front and was disappointed that he was dating an older divorcee, as it wasn't sufficiently boast-worthy to her bridge group? These were the sort of safe, easily surmountable problems (after all, I didn't even know if his mother played bridge or was that suburban-minded at all, as I'd never met her) that I was sifting through while he pushed me towards the stockroom and closed the door. I sat on a box of books and looked up at him expectantly.

'Daisy, there's no easy way to say this,' he said, 'but I've met someone else.'

'Met someone else?' I echoed hollowly. Initially, I laughed inside. With my peculiar blend of arrogance and punchy charisma that belies rumbling low self-esteem, my first thoughts were: 'Don't be so silly. How could you have met anyone more unique and fun than me?'

Max knelt in front of me so that we were at eye level. 'Listen, this is the last thing I ever expected to happen as I was really keen on you and I was looking forward to seeing how things panned out . . .'

'Really keen?' My echo was less hollow and more caustic. 'Really keen? What happened to "You're the most original woman I've ever met but I can't get a handle on you? Don't shut me out. Let me in . . ."?'

'Yes, absolutely,' he faltered. 'I did say and feel all those things but I suppose, if I'm really honest, you were the most incredible challenge I'd come across and I was fascinated.'

I stood up, as bizarrely all I could feel was temper thudding through my thighs. Max leapt up too. 'Oh, so I was quite the challenge but once conquered, the frisson wore off? Once we'd finally slept together – and let's face it, it wasn't me who said "I like you too much and that's why I can't perform" you found yourself window shopping for another, racier model?'

'There's no need to sound so bitter,' said Max smugly, which made me want to stab him.

'Bitter? *Bitter*! Don't you guys get it? I feel like you spun me round and then threw a wet flannel in my face. I told you I was different. Damaged. But you wooed me. You convinced me that I could trust you and then the minute I let down my guard and showed you who I was, you told me I wasn't good enough.'

'I never said that,' said Max.

'You didn't need to. "I've met someone else" is the same as saying "I've met someone better."'

Max leaned against the wall looking drained and I thought what an intolerably low threshold men have to the emotional crisis that *they* ignite. 'It's just easier with her,' he said wearily.

'Because she's younger?' I asked.

'Partly, yes. There's no expectation. I feel I can just have a good time because she's too young to want to settle down and have kids.'

'But I never said I wanted to settle down with you and have your kids.'

'You didn't have to, but with a woman of your age it's always there. Isn't it?' Max ploughed bravely – and brutally – on. 'With an older woman there's all this silent pressure on a man to be the man that the others weren't. In the end, I felt I couldn't live up to that.'

'No,' I said, gutted. 'I can quite see that.' He hung his head and turned to go. 'You've changed your tune since you first asked me out,' I said, archly. 'I thought it was the twenty-something women you couldn't stomach because of their agendas?' He paused but didn't say anything. He didn't need to. You could tell by the look on his face that he was thinking: 'all bloody women have agendas'.

When Max left I flopped on to the stockroom floor. Although I was crying when Lucy and Miles found me, I was also acutely aware of the state of the carpet and how badly it needed to be hoovered. Maybe it's a form of self-protection the way the mind multi-tasks in crisis like that? Your heart may be splintering but part of your brain is transfixed by the pattern the pencil sharpenings make fanning out across the floor. Lucy scooped me into her arms. 'Don't upset yourself like this,' she said, 'no man is worth it.'

'She's right,' winked Miles. 'We're all flaky bastards pretending we want commitment when we want our end away with as little aggro as poss.'

'I'll remember that,' said Lucy, tossing her head.

Two hours later, when Lucy had collected her girls from school and dropped them at their grandparents' London flat, she whisked me up the motorway to see my mother.

'But she's with Archibald,' I said. 'She doesn't want a reminder of my miserable life to bring her down and make her feel that because I can't hold on to a relationship, she's failed as a mother.'

'She loves you,' said Lucy. 'Your pain is her pain. Anyway, I've already rung her and she's expecting us. She's got the sympathy in the oven and the TLC on ice.'

I smiled. 'So, how was the snog with Miles?'

'I had forgotten that another man's touch could be so electrifying. Just the feel of Miles pushing his fingers into the top of my jeans was heaven.'

'Yeah, the way someone touches you communicates everything. Mind you, all Miles is saying as he's running his fingers down your spine is: "How soon can I have you?"'

Lucy laughed. 'He kept whispering, begging me to come back to his flat and I would have killed to have gone but I realised that I had to collect the kids from school. I was so depressed standing at the school gate as it hit me that dating as a single mother is anything but spontaneous.'

'We need hook-ups.' Lucy looked perplexed. 'It's all the rage in the States,' I explained. 'It's where you hook up with a best friend whom you sleep with. Ex-boyfriends are perfect as they are a known quantity. It's not as slutty as a one-night stand and it's not as complicated as an affair as there is no emotional agenda. It's just about having someone whom you feel comfy with call you up and afterwards you amicably go your separate ways.'

'What happens if one party gets serious?'

'That's the danger with hooking up. You have to remain emotionally detached or it doesn't work. Also, it's about being able to keep the meetings on an ad hoc basis.'

'So why don't you hook up with Miles?' asked Lucy.

'Same reason as you,' I said. 'Because neither of us could

guarantee that we wouldn't fall for him. Miles is a devil but better the devil you know . . .'

Later, at home, Mum made a sterling effort to cheer us up. She enveloped us with a warm maternal wisdom that made me feel safe again. Archibald was nowhere to be seen – which was convenient because, regardless of how grown-up you are, you want your mother to be in mother mode. You don't want to think of her as some man's lover. Mum had lit the fire and bundled us in front of it with tea, homemade plum jam and crumpets. 'You can't change people,' she warned. 'You girls have to respect that. These men are what they are and you are what you are. You dance or you don't dance. Simple as that.'

'So how do you find someone who makes a good match?' asked Lucy.

'That man doesn't need to be exactly like you. The two of you only need to be like a key in a lock. A fit that works.'

'But how do you find him?' I wailed.

'You believe in him, which means you must believe in yourself. Then, you get really clear about what you do and don't want.'

'Oh yes, Chad Peace talks about this in his book,' I said, excited. Lucy threw her eyes to the ceiling. 'No, listen. We've got to write our future man a letter.'

'Before we've met him?' Lucy asked, incredulous.

'Yes. We're inviting him to show up in our lives. The universe acts as the messenger. Come on, what's to lose? Let's try it.'

'How specific do we have to be in these letters?' asked Lucy, mocking me. We were sitting in bed in our pyjamas, pad and pen to hand. 'Do we write things like "Please don't be disabled or don't be a good-looking dwarf but it would be fun if you had the odd A-list celebrity friend and please, no hairy backs, greying goatees or man bags and gold jewellery?"'

I giggled. 'I think we are supposed to focus on what we want, not what we don't want to attract into our life.'

Lucy sighed, suddenly serious. 'It's so much more difficult when you've got children because suddenly you're a package. A guy has to fall in love with you and the kids. All single mothers pray that they will meet a fabulous guy who'll be the right father figure. What the biological fathers forget is that while they may turn up for access visits with guilt gifts, they are no longer the hands-on father because they're not doing daily parenting. The new man becomes the rightful father because he's coping with the broken nights, the tantrums and he has to share Mummy and be patient, mature and loving about it all.'

'Well, write that down. All those qualities are vital,' I said.

We wrote our letters in amiable silence before Lucy asked me to read mine out first. Nervous, I took a deep breath. 'Dear Life Partner,' I began. 'This is not a letter that I ever thought I'd have to write because I've been married and I thought I'd fought the battle of loneliness and won. Now, it seems that my quest for love became the battle between us. I have been so misled by my heart that it would be the easiest thing in the world for me to shut down and give up. Learn to live a life enriched by everything except a true loving life partner. To have wonderful friends, to be able to see the beauty in simple, everyday things – a sunset, a spring flower, an inspiring song – these would be safe and worthy things to plant the seed of happiness on. But what is life if we do not share our journey with another? The sunset is still beautiful but it has a melancholy resonance when you stand alone because you know how much more it would bring you alive to watch it with another.

'I do not care how old you are (but much younger than retirement age please as I want you to be able to get it up and keep it up!) but I want you to have lived; to have felt the sea change of emotion that plagues us all, to have an understanding of the interior dialogue that feeds our fears and frees our dreams. I may seem independent to you and strong – and in many ways I am. But in my inability to compromise – and with my past immaturity – I have walked an isolating road. I have never trusted myself or another to fully open my arms and let in love and all that it entails. I want to be able to be defenceless with you. To let down my guard and let myself taste the fear but also the glory of adventure because it is boring and ultimately self-destructive and pointless not to be able to do that.

'Please, hurry up and turn up! I've had enough of the crying in the middle of the night, of going to parties and weddings on my own, of spending Christmas with my mum because I don't have a family or my own home. I'm sick of the sense that you are out there but not here by my side.'

'Oh Daisy,' whispered Lucy when I finished, 'you write this stuff really well. He sounds great. You deserve to find him.'

When Lucy read me her letter, there was one bit that stayed with me. Her voice trembled as she read out: 'I have two little girls. They did not deserve to be neglected by their father who has left us. Looking back, I realise that I have rarely stood and watched them play with him, able to bask in a bonded, familial glow. If you love me, please love them as your own. Cherish their sweet smiles, their brimming innocence, their innate kindness, their reserves of joy. Love us like the unit we are. Please don't leave us in tough times or walk away because it wasn't what you dreamed it might be. We may not look like we need you but we do and we have so much to give back.'

Her letter made me feel ashamed. Typically, mine was full of what I needed and what I craved. But generous to the core, Lucy's finished with what she could proffer. What decent man in their right mind could resist that?

# Chapter 10
# PTDS (Post Traumatic Date Syndrome)

A month later, I was leaving an evening yoga class, all bundled up in a Puffa jacket over my pyjama bottoms – to hasten the time from corpse pose to being comatose in bed, dirty hair piled on my head – when I heard my name called. I looked around to see a vaguely familiar man walking towards me. It was his deportment; the ram-rod straight back yet loose-limbed gait that told me it was Andy Benton, an old boyfriend whom I had not seen for ten years. I instantly thought of my letter; maybe this universal instant messenger stuff worked? Andy may not be the The One but he'd make an ideal hook-up. 'Hey, Daisy,' he said, smiling his inimitably suggestive smile. As he folded me against him and nuzzled my neck like an animal checking out a potential mate's scent, I realised that Andy was still the most overtly sexual man I had ever known.

He suggested a drink and as we walked to the pub, I mentally replayed our story. When I met Andy, an art director at a glossy magazine, at a launch party of a new gallery, I was twenty-seven and had never before encountered the purely sexual charge he ignited. It was different from Julius as there was no emotional connection. From the moment I set eyes on him, I wanted him to touch me. Yes, he was attractive with dark hair and a penetrating owl brown stare, but more it was his physicality that floored me. He was standing admiring the line of a piece of sculpture and the way he lightly ran his hand across the curved back of a large wooden bird, you knew that he had a heightened appreciation for form. It was a predictably lavish bash, with mini fish-and-chip canapés wrapped in tiny newspapers and puffs of Yorkshire pudding stuffed with rare roast beef and a dot of horseradish sauce. Everything, including the waiters dressed in black, the lacquer trays of champagne fizzing in jaunty flutes and the female guests staggering under the weight of their bouffant hair, shoulder pads and gilt-chain jewellery had an ironic, smug feel to it. An 'Aren't we clever to have come up with *this*?' riposte, when every party was exactly the same. It was all artifice and show. The men in expensive suits with flashy watches. Wealth with no substance. Everyone got pissed to disguise how pissed off they were because they didn't feel they had enough on display.

When Andy started talking to me, standing a cigarette paper away, it was immediately obvious that we had the sort of chemistry that makes you feel that you are coming undone. We were moving through the throng of the party when he suddenly grabbed me by the arm and pushed me towards a lavatory door. Inside, he slammed me up against the wall and kissed me, pressing his hands firmly across my body. It is one of the many regrets of my life that I didn't give into the thrust of my desire and let him screw me then and there. Instead, due to a weak nod towards propriety – after all, I didn't even know him – I pulled away. He looked at me and laughed and we both knew that the dance had just begun.

He had that polished assurance with women – holding you in a certain way, openly claiming you in public by tugging you towards him – that said it all. Sure, he was a serial philanderer but who the hell cared when for days and nights on end, you were the chosen one?

I swooned through the first few weeks of our affair, blissfully unaware of the trauma ahead. His last girlfriend, whom he had left before he found out, was pregnant with his child and when he told me, it felt like he tore a hole through my future. Any delusions I had entertained of us having a life together – let's face it, I had fantasised that I could be the one to tame him – shattered in an instant. As he never intended to go back to the mother of his child, we carried on seeing each other; his guilt and my shame adding to the intensity of what felt like an appallingly illicit liaison. We broke up the night his son was born.

Sitting opposite him in the pub, he looked almost identical, apart from the grey streaking his eyebrows. He was now forty-seven and I was thirty-nine, so the age gap seemed to have lessened between us. He no longer appeared decadently older and I was no more in his thrall. We swapped our tales of the intervening years with painstaking honesty, admitting our follies and laughing openly over our flaws. What struck me was not so much how sexy Andy was, but how well he had matured. Career success had afforded him poise and sophistication, while living real life as opposed to shirking responsibility had given him depth. He was now a committed, loving father to his ten-year-old son. He still lived a bachelor life in London during the week – working and womanising – but weekends were for his boy.

As I told him about my failed marriage and broken affairs, I could feel myself tensing. I wanted Andy to see the carefree, optimistic girl of my twenties, not the nervous, guarded wreck I had become. It wasn't that I was facing him make-up free and covered in a film of post-yoga sweat, it was the fact that I was mortified by how asexual I was. Knowing that he would sense it, I blurted out how scared I had become of physical involvement. That I was no longer capable of lying back and letting go, emotionally or in the sack. In his open, earthy presence, I felt shut down and strange.

Outside the pub, Andy took my arm and pushed me towards the bonnet of the nearest car. Then, he leaned over and kissed me hard. As his arms tightened around me and the weight of his body fell against me, it was as if something inside me began to thaw. 'I think you could loosen up in no time,' he whispered. 'And I think I'm just the man for the job.'

I was writing the meaningful missive of the day in the bookshop, when Lucy came up behind me and read it out: '"When one lives without fear, one can not be broken. When one lives with fear, one is broken before one begins to live."'

'Do you know what I fear the most in life?' I shook my head and guided her towards the coffee counter. 'My biggest fear is that Edward leaving has broken a part of me that will simply never recover.' She slumped in a chair. 'I'm so riddled with anxiety that I feel claustrophobic in my own life – do you know, often when I'm going through the motions of the bath, book, bed routine with the girls, I'm present but I'm not there. I may be passing the flannel, saying "wash your face, angel" but in my out-of-body mind, I am naked, running down the street, screaming. I'm so afraid that we have irrevocably damaged our daughters by upsetting their natural equilibrium that I dislike Edward more than I thought possible. Some days, I feel I'm going mad as the anger of his betrayal simply doesn't abate.

'Last week, the girls were asked to be bridesmaids for a cousin of mine. I drove them to the dress fitting after school, arriving late as the traffic was bad. Lily wouldn't try on the little fur cape that went with the dress and while everyone there was gently coaxing her and saying "Come on now, darling, just put on this lovely cape" I had to use all my restraint not to open my mouth and scream: "Just put on the fucking cape." I almost wish I had. I'm so stressed that the slightest extra strain can trigger an almighty reaction. Daisy, I'm afraid of losing it completely.'

I handed Lucy a frothy coffee. 'Most people live their entire lives in the track of fear,' I said. 'They stay in relationships because they feel they have to. It's better to be with someone who wants to be with you than someone who has to be with you. So, Edward couldn't go the distance but the vital thing is that you are going the distance every day for those girls.'

Lucy said: 'Don't be too nice to me. It'll finish me off.' I sat beside her and pinched her leg – hard. 'Ouch! Oh, the agony of being a single mother is that you are on duty every day, doing all the boringly repetitive parenting things and then Edward turns up for access and plays the loving father and I want to shout that a loving father doesn't leave in the first place. Do you think he ever acknowledges what a great job I'm doing, bringing them up? 'Course not. There's no note of thanks, no odd bunch of flowers, no recognition that I'm alone, night and day, shaping our precious girls.'

I looked at Lucy, tight with despair and there was nothing I could say. I knew that the only thing that alleviates the feeling you've cocked up your life is the knowledge that your friends and family would do anything to see you happy again.

Fortunately Miles bounced into the bookshop and hugged Lucy. 'Have you heard,' he said, 'Daisy snogged Andy Benton last week.'

Lucy turned to me, amazed. 'Randy Andy Art Man? The guy who set your libido on fire a decade ago?'

'I bumped into him after yoga last week,' I confessed.

'Has he called yet?' asked Miles, mischievously.

'Actually, we've had this amazing flirty banter,' I said. 'He gives very good email.'

'Why doesn't that surprise me?' said Lucy. I led her into the stockroom and opened my laptop. Andy had sent me an email two days after our encounter: 'Dooley, still sexy, still crazy. How can I fulfil your fantasy?'

After much deliberation I replied: 'Escape the monotony of life with me?'

'What a great reply.'

'His was even better,' I said, scrolling down my inbox. 'Darling Dools. Escape is good. Irresponsibility better. Twenty-four hours in the hotel of your choice?'

I told Lucy that I had booked a hotel in the country, then freaked out about the price. Would he consider £245 for a room excessive or water off a duck's back? As I hadn't seen him properly for ten years, I had no way to gauge his reaction. Also, what was the etiquette of paying? I couldn't expect him to pay as we weren't dating and if I paid, did it make him a gigolo? So should we split it? I sent an awkward email stating the price of the room, jokingly adding that it was more embarrassing to discuss the fiscal rather than sexual implications of our assignation. His reply was pure gold. 'Fun is the main thing, something to remember, so yes all that is fine. I think splitting the cost is cool too so let's get over that issue and do what we want with each other for a moment in time . . . looking forward. A.'

The prospect of our night away had added verve because until just before we met we didn't communicate. A brief email on Friday afternoon said: 'Dooley; Tom. 5 p.m.' – and that was it. It meant that our assignation had a charged air. It impressed that Andy was an adult; he simply wasn't interested in trifling texts and endless emails.

As I walked into the hotel, I got into a flap about how I should describe Andy to the receptionist. I couldn't say: 'Is my boyfriend here?' as he wasn't my boyfriend and it would have sounded pretty odd to have told the truth and asked: 'Is my ex-boyfriend but current hook-up here?' To use 'partner' was equally icky and I didn't have the sangfroid to say 'Has my stud muffin surfaced?' so I plumped for a conservative: 'Am I the first to arrive?' The receptionist confirmed that I was and when she asked what papers we would like in the morning, I blew it. I racked my brains to remember what Andy read and drew a blank. (Isn't it awful; I could remember his neck size – sixteen and a half – but not his political leaning?) Feeling pressured and in a tizzy, I blurted out: 'I can't remember what he reads.' So that was that. I had outed us as nothing more than a couple of light-weight bonking buddies.

I was shown to the room; a mismatch of modern styles with a good, firm bed but what looked like a trophy cabinet in the corner to house the mini-bar. The bathroom was redeemed by the Hermès products. It felt a bit *Belle du Jour* to lie on the bed and wait – even if I was pretending to be engrossed in Sky Movies – so I went downstairs to the bar and not without a throb of envy watched a genuine weekending couple feed each other cake and plan their next day's outing with a large map. Suddenly, I felt awfully tired at the prospect of being a faux couple going through the lovey-dovey routine and it did occur to me that Andy wouldn't show. Maybe that would be his elaborate revenge for me leaving him a decade earlier? Tickled by the thought of such a great twist, I ordered tea and a glass of reviving champagne. Warming to my theme, if Andy was going to be a no show, I might as well have a piece of cake, so I called the waiter back.

Trying to look composed in the corner, knocking back alternate mouthfuls of champers and cake, I could feel my angst begin to stir. I was sitting in a pretentious hotel waiting for an old boyfriend because I wanted there to be something more to life, something thrilling and transforming. But maybe the couple drinking tea opposite had the answer? They seemed to embody the notion that sometimes you stay together because you don't leave. But me? I got up to go.

As soon as I stood and walked to the door, he appeared. He came straight up to me and in full view of the discreet weekenders pretending not to notice, kissed me passionately on the lips. He then finished my glass of champagne and said 'Shall we?' as he motioned upstairs. Part of me was grateful that he was playing the role of fully fledged lover to perfection, the other part was furious. Why did everything in my life always feel like it was a charade? This wasn't real, was it? Or if it was real, it wasn't for keeps. It was a moment in time on offer to enjoy and even before it began, I was yearning for more.

We went to the room and once the door was closed, I felt like I was in *Sliding Doors*. It was as if two options lay before me as to the way that this could go and I was suddenly aware that the journey between what is out there in terms of possibility and what is in our prayers is considerable and it can be difficult to navigate one's way between the two. If I had been really honest, I would have said as Andy came towards me and pulled me into his embrace: 'Listen, I've made a mistake. I thought I could handle some no-strings sex but actually, I'm too attached to the outcome for that.' With that, I would have kissed him on the cheek and run.

But wasn't that my problem? My bolter instinct that took hold the minute my fantasy script wasn't on course and the lines I heard repeated back to me seemed to jar? So I let Andy hold me and when he sensed that I was taut, instead of pulling away, he tightened his grip. There was something about the way that he stood there, as if the warmth of his body was reading me like Braille, that enabled me to relax. We undressed each other in silence and when he lightly peppered my neck with the touch of butterfly wings, I realised how bereft I had been of that kind of gentleness. It seemed so long – like for ever – that a man had been that physically sensitive to me. With Max we never quite found our groove and it made me think that Jamie must have had a tenderness chip missing. Sure, we had good sex but somehow it wasn't intimate. I could have lain and wept but I was too mortified because Andy was next to me, tanned and toned, and I felt like a giant, white slug sprawled on the bed. I was also overcome with regret because I had eaten a garlicky stir fry for lunch and all I could obsess about was whether or not I had bad breath.

That's what drove it home to me that although Andy was an old boyfriend, we were actually navigating uncharted territory because a decade's worth of distance changes everything. In the worn-down comfort of a day-to-day relationship you can say 'Do I have bad breath?' without a moment's hesitation or remorse. But now I was acutely aware that by nonchalantly chowing down chilli prawns for lunch on the day of our meeting, I had over-familiarised things.

Andy was both known and a stranger to me, so it was rude of me not to adhere to early intimacy etiquette which dictates that everything smells sweet and every body surface is depilated and smooth.

In the end, tortured by the thought that as we were kissing, he was valiantly trying not to be knocked out by my garlic pong, I plucked up the courage to ask: 'Does my breath smell?'

When he said 'a little', I was mortified but as I got up to go and clean my teeth, he wrestled me back on the bed. He didn't care, making it feel urgent and alive. Later, he whispered, 'I've got a secret I want to share but I don't know how to tell you.'

Lucy had asked me to a party as her metaphorical hand-holding date and afterwards we were going for a girlie supper. Her handsome divorce lawyer, Mark, had invited her to the swanky do and as I stood in the middle of the lively throng, I looked at these bright, successful, somewhat dissolute men and thought that while they were convinced that they had it all, they actually had it all wrong. You could tell watching them flirt in that awful, self-congratulatory way that they considered themselves Big Swinging Dicks, yet all I could sense beneath their St Moritz weekend tans was an unbearable deadness. I wanted to stand on a table in the centre of the room and shout: 'Don't worry about being successful. Work towards being significant!' But maybe being spiritually bankrupt is easier in the long run? These macho adrenalin junkies filled every waking hour with the pursuit of money, power, status and scarily aggressive sex, never stopping long enough to see that they were running on empty. You would never connect with a man like that, I thought. You could entice him, flatter him, fool him even, but you would never know him. Like wild horses used to the run and freedom of a vast prairie or plain, these men of the boardroom are never caught. They marry, breed, have affairs and breed some more but they never commit because they don't know how to – or want to. Their biggest fear is meeting a woman (or worse a man) who might crack open their hearts. Worse than bankruptcy, redundancy or astronomical alimony is if things get messy emotionally speaking and they lose control.

It was liberating to observe without feeling self-conscious and I was vaguely aware that this made me stand apart. When not at a party like this where they are jostling to flex their competitive muscle, men see the power in lulls, in silence. A quiet room is not threatening to them, so in not talking to anyone, I became quite the magnet. A man past his prime called David approached me and began chatting me up. When I told him I was divorced, he said: 'Remarriage is an excellent test of how amicable your divorce was' and winked.

I wanted to say: 'David, five years ago, when your gut wasn't straining ever so slightly against your Dunhill waistband and when your wedding band didn't cut into your podgy finger, you could have been a dishy date. But you need to update your self-image, old boy, because flashing those yellowing tombstone teeth doesn't do it for me any more than your wafting stale breath does, even if wedged against the passport sized piccies in your wallet of your missus and kids, your Amex card is a reassuringly expensive black.'

When he said: 'May I have your card? I'd like to get in touch,' I was so taken aback, that I gave it to him. He put my card in his jacket pocket and patted it as if to say, 'It's your lucky day, sweetheart.' Then a colleague appeared and manhandled him in that proprietorial way and they walked off without a backward glance. Five minutes later, I went up to

David and tapped him on the back. He swung round, astonished to be interrupted. In front of the colleagues fawning round him I said, smiling faux-sweetly: 'I'm sorry, but in a fit of polite naivety, when you asked me for my card, I gave it to you. Actually, I've made a mistake as I feel sullied by the thought of it in your grubby pocket and the porno thoughts you might attach to it. So can I have it back, please?'

He raised his eyebrow, playing to the stunned group as if to say, 'We've got a right one here,' and laughed nervously. He pulled out my card and I took it. 'Well,' he joked, 'that's a first! That's never happened to me before.'

'Don't worry, it's bound to be the last time,' I said and swept off.

Thrilled, I searched the crowd for Lucy who was standing in a corner close to the dangerously attractive Mark. Like Edward he had those effortless, confident, public school good looks; the sort of man who had spent decades striding across summer cricket pitches looking dashing in his whites. Only Mark was slicker than Edward. It was as if his brain was keener, his ambition edgier and his charm more lethal. He was the type who radiated that he knew he was good in bed. I went up and whispered: 'He's married, remember? Time to go.'

As she kissed him goodbye and walked away, it was obvious by the way that he looked at her that his interest in her was more than professional. Trouble ahead? Please God no, I thought.

Afterwards, over dim sum Lucy said, 'It's so depressing because at our age only married men bored of their wives and too guilty to leave their kids hit on you.'

'You said it,' I said, thinking of the vile David.

'So?' Lucy said, perking up. 'I'm dying to know. What was Andy Benton's secret?' She poured me another glass of wine.

'Well, my escapism with Randy Andy was typical,' I said. 'Like all perfect things, there's always something wrong with it.'

Lucy let out a knowing snort. 'Yep, I'm learning to aim low in life. Expectations are resentments waiting to happen.'

'Luce,' I chided, 'we must deal with your cynicism. If there is a lack in your life, there's a lack in your thoughts.'

'There's nothing wrong with believing that in order to find a trustworthy and truthful man you have to have them vetted by a secret agent, is there?'

I told her what had happened with Andy. 'We were entwined, having the most open, unedited, post-coital chat. It was jolly, like being on a sexual sleepover. We lay for hours in the dark, teasing each other and talking, when suddenly Andy pulled me closer to him and lowered his voice. He starting stroking my hair and said that he had a secret to share and that he hoped it wouldn't make me angry. My mind went into turbo-charged panic. He was married? He had a committed girlfriend? A boyfriend? A criminal record? But do you know what he told me – *after* we had slept together using a condom? That he had had a vasectomy.'

Lucy burst out laughing. 'God, I bet that was a relief! I thought it was going to be something awful.'

'In a way it was awful. I was so taken aback, I didn't know what to say, so Andy said, "The reason I didn't tell you before is that I thought you would be disappointed." "Disappointed about what?" I asked feebly. "That I can't get you pregnant." "Why do you think I'd want that?" "Because I've found that women your age, who aren't married, often want the baby more than they want the man."'

Suddenly, I found myself welling up. Lucy reached out and touched my arm. 'Oh, Luce, I'm so tired of always being in that place before tears,' I said. 'I was grateful Andy and I were lying in the pitch black because while he was talking, I felt tears dribble into my ears.'

'I didn't know you were desperate for a baby?' she said softly.

'Nor me. Yet I was completely thrown by Andy's revelation. Part of me was mortified that he thought I might be out to trap him, the other part was stunned because in a sense him telling me that closed a door. He was making it clear that this affair couldn't yield anything but if we're honest, we are always looking for a little bit more, aren't we? Or what's the point?'

'You're the one always banging on about living in the now,' said Lucy. 'I thought you rated Andy and he was a short-term tonic. Sounds to me that he offers the sort of sexual healing that should be free to despairing divorcees on the NHS.'

'Yeah, he makes me want to share myself in a way that feels safe and understood. He's the sort who debunks the myth that you have to wear mascara in bed to keep a guy.'

'So go and get laid! Lighten up and let some lovin' in. Lord knows, you deserve it.'

'I want to be able to but every month that I'm messing around with Andy, I'm reducing my chances of meeting a man who does want to have my child, aren't I?'

'What does Andy want?'

'He wants us to keep seeing each other.'

'And you?'

'I don't know what I want. I need to go away and think seriously about the fact that I may never have a baby and decide if that's going to work for me.'

'You don't know how lucky you are, Daisy. I wish I could find an Andy.'

'But you've had your daughters, so your emotional

landscape is different from mine. Destiny isn't chance, it is choice and I've got some sober soul-searching to do.'

I met Jess for quick coffee near her surgery as she'd been working so hard that even though we shared a flat, we kept such different hours that I hadn't seen her for ages. She had usually left for work before I got up and returned long after I was asleep.

'So how are you?' I asked, as she dipped the end of her croissant in her skinny cap.

'Exhausted,' she groaned.

'Me too,' I said. 'But not from working. From dating. I've been out with Max and Andy and all I feel is drained, depressed and confused.'

'You've probably got PTDS,' said Jess, matter-of-factly. 'There's an epidemic among my divorced patients.'

'I've been pretty careful. Ever since Troy, I always use a condom.'

Jess laughed. 'No, it's not an STD. Post Traumatic Date Syndrome. It's a form of chronic mating fatigue, whereby you work yourself into an emotional frenzy before any encounter, then suffer the inevitable letdown of the actual date, followed by mild depression afterwards because you haven't found The One.'

'Then I definitely have acute PTDS.'

I told Jess about Andy's vasectomy. She merely shrugged and said: 'I've got just the answer. Have Julius's love child and let Andy help you raise it.'

'Are you mad?' I shrieked.

'Not at all. Hey, it's unorthodox,' Jess lit a fag, 'but at least it's modern. Isn't that what contemporary living is all about?'

'I think I prefer traditional,' I said.

'You tried that with Jamie, remember?' she said, exhaling.

'You were bored after two minutes. At least this would pose enough emotional drama to keep you engaged.'

'It's true that Andy is devoted to his son. Maybe he'd like being *in loco parentis* to another man's child?' I said, wondering.

'Life today is about working out what fits where,' said Jess. 'Not in terms of the perfect minimalist home, with sisal and free surfaces but in roles and relationships too.' Jess looked at her watch. 'Shit, running late. Gotta go.'

Catching my expression she said: 'Sure, it's messy but consider the possibility. Listen, Daise, at our age, hope without action is useless because it puts all the power in the magic wand. Your solutions always lean in favour of the fairy tale. I hate to tell you this but your single unmarried Prince Charming waiting to breed might not show in this lifetime.' She blew me a kiss. I sat in the coffee shop, stunned. Could I really have a child with Julius but a live-in relationship with Andy? Would that be utterly absurd?

Dad and I met, at my request, at our Thai dump, where, as usual, the steaming, stinking noodles made me want to retch. He was tucking in with gusto. 'Sit, Daisy. Eat!' he smiled. When I had helped myself to some steamed rice and vegetables, he asked me how things were going.

'Well,' I said, 'it's difficult doing everything for myself. I feel so alone.'

'That's because you *are* alone!' he guffawed. As always when he hit the bull's eye, I didn't know whether to laugh or cry.

'Yeah, well, I'm trying to change that. I'm thinking of taking Julius up on his offer to have a child.'

'Aha, time to breed at last? Excellent news. Good for you. I'll be interested to see what my grandchild turns out like.

Hmm, a Vantonakis–Dooley cross. Not that I like babies much, or even small children of course, but then that's the joy of grandparenthood. Not too much involvement and you hand them back to their mother.'

I was tempted to say, 'So no different from your version of fatherhood, then?', but Dad continued: 'So at last the great Julius has left his wife for you? You did say he was married, didn't you? To one of the Randolphs, if I'm not mistaken? I knew a Randolph in Boston not long after I met your mother. A queer Brahmin fellow. He kept a white tiger in a cage in the garden. But then the very wealthy, like Randolph Hearst at San Simeon, have always indulged in expensive, dangerous pastimes, haven't they? Yes, this man also kept a collection of . . .'

'Dad,' I said sharply, 'Julius hasn't left Alice Randolph.'

Dad looked up at me. 'You're thinking of becoming his *mistress*?' The way my father mouthed the word 'mistress', as if rolling his tongue around an expensive claret, it didn't seem totally shocking, more old-fashioned, exotic even.

'No. We wouldn't have any sort of on-going relationship, post conception,' I said, deliberately clinical so that his scientific brain could absorb the facts.

'I see,' he said, when clearly he didn't.

He carried on chewing noisily, staring into his bowl as if the answer lay beneath the layer of grease floating on the surface. After a while, he put his chopsticks aside. 'Life is not easy, Daisy, but I've never understood your desire to over-complicate things.'

'That's because, sadly, simple solutions seem to elude me.' I sighed. 'I know it looks odd but I've been doing a lot of thinking lately and often our scripts for life are limited and trip us up because we don't have the courage or creativity to implement an alternative.'

'Ah, no one can possibly accuse you of not being resourceful,' said my father. 'It is just that what is needed to survive life is a shared sense of suffering. If it is a dark moment, it is a dark moment together and when you come out of it, you are standing in the light together. It worries me to think of you always standing in the dark alone.'

'What, like you, you mean?' I said.

Was it the most incredible synchronicity or was it wilful – and wishful – thinking? Just as I was working up courage to contact Julius, I got his text: 'Alice had the baby last week. A beautiful boy. I need to see you. Call me. J.'

I immediately went into a tailspin of despair. Now that he had his own child and the primal bond with his son had been forged, why would he want to procreate with me? Regret piled in. I should have got pregnant the minute he suggested it. I shouldn't have let my disappointment win. I always did this: waited for the perfect scenario, praying for the quick fix of the illuminated moment and then when it finally dawned that nothing better was on offer, fell to pieces.

I was in the bookshop writing on the blackboard: 'Maybe it's not our lives we can't afford but our aspirations.'

Miles looked up from his stocktake.'Whoa, Dooley, don't tell me that the notion of compromise is finally entering your repertoire?'

I told Miles my plight; that I had been thinking of having a child with Julius, while contemplating living with Andy.

'Do you love Andy?' he asked.

'Too soon to say,' I said. 'I think we could fall in love. It's a promising union. The signs are there.'

'You deluded fool,' said Miles. 'Look, Daisy, I've known you for twenty years and there's only one man you've ever gone gaga over and that was Julius. You fell for him because he's always been unattainable and no man will ever match him.'

'That's because I've never met a man as manly as him.'

'Do you mean manly or rich?' Miles winked.

'Miles, any man can be masculine but not many men are manly. Masculinity is the opposite of femininity but manliness is the opposite of male weakness. Julius is never weak because he breathes authority.'

'Right, because he's stinking rich and money is power, you mean?' chided Miles, before adding, 'My father always told me that the definition of manliness is a man who's confident in a situation of risk. So if Julius is as manly as you think, just because he's got one baby with one woman, it isn't necessarily going to prevent him having another child with you, is it? It would be a badge of potency to him – let's face it, men on his stratosphere hardly abide by pedestrian two-point-four-kids-and-a-discreet-bit-on-the-side, do they?'

'I don't know,' I sighed. 'There's a question of honour and now that Alice is the mother of his child, she probably has a lot more influence.'

'Get real,' shouted Miles, jumping down from the counter and shaking me by the shoulders. 'Do you think a man like Julius, who married a young, malleable trophy, even consults her, let alone gives a damn what she thinks? Masters of the Universe believe they can buy anything they want in life and if that means a compliant wife, they'll pay for it. No, the real issue here is what Julius wants. That's what you should be worrying about: does Julius *want* another child with you or not?'

'Only one way to find out,' I said, reaching for my phone. I texted: 'Congratulations. When and where do you want to meet?'

An hour later, I got his reply. 'Off on a business trip tomorrow. Will call you on my return. Jxx.'

The next week had that taut, cooling one's heels quality. It's almost impossible to live in the present when waiting because everything is angled towards the possible future outcome. Time drags and fantasies take hold. I managed to avoid Andy's calls as I didn't want to confuse my head even more. Eventually, Julius texted back: 'Meet me tomorrow afternoon at my office. Looking forward. J.'

That night I lay in tumult. Was Miles right? Was my infatuation with Julius because he was emotionally untouchable in the way only the super-rich can be? True, he could buy himself out of most situations but that wasn't a ticket to happiness or trust, was it? If anything, that amount of money fosters fear because you're never sure if people love you or how much you've got. I truly loved him and that's what always frightened him. He once said to me: 'You don't even know how scared you are until you're not.' Looking at him I realised that no matter how much a man is worth, he needs to feel important. Women, on the other hand, need to feel important to a man. We can try to kid ourselves otherwise but we will always believe that the cat-call of loneliness can only be filled by the call-back of a worthy mate.

As I opened the curtains, I felt the familiar stab of anxiety. Would I ever be able to look back on parts of my life and think: at least I was happy then?

I read in Chad Peace's book that the way to connect with your inner wisdom and learn to let it guide you is to write a letter to your younger self, sharing everything you have discovered. I decided to write to my twenty-four-year-old self; to the ditsy girl that fell in love with Julius. I propped myself up against the pillows and began:

*Dear Daisy, Don't believe the negative propaganda that plays in your head night and day. All those niggling voices that try to convince you that you are not good enough and that you won't get what you want in life. These will destroy the fabric of your dreams if you give them breathing space and without hope, you have nothing. Hold on to what you believe in, honour your inner voice and if your gut says no, heed it. The greatest regret comes when you only have yourself to blame.*

*So you think that the tops of your thighs are fat? The chances are they won't change. You'll add a pound here, lose two pounds there but you'll never dramatically remodel who you are. External appearances aren't going to alter much in the next two decades so don't fritter precious time caring. Men don't notice how thin you look in your jeans; self-acceptance is what turns them on. Sex appeal comes from some bolshy place inside which radiates an unshakeable confidence yet, strangely, also hints at vulnerability. Some of the best times will happen when you can't be bothered to wash your hair. Don't try to be perfect because nothing and no one ever is.*

*Don't set yourself unrealistic defining deadlines. There's no rush. You don't need to be married by thirty, pregnant by thirty-five. If you have the courage to let it, life unfurls at an unpredictable pace. Don't be so impatient because by forcing things, you'll make mistakes. Better by far to wait in hope than live with regret. If you have one teensy doubt about a man, however painful it will be, leave him. If you commit and, God forbid, marry him, you'll feel a fool for ever.*

*The most important ingredient between a strong woman and any man is that he has a cast-iron sense of self. If you threaten a man, in time he will try to destroy you. Weak men cannot bear a feisty female to outshine them. Beware: they can be more vicious than the most aggressive Alpha Male. And don't bother with younger men. They may seem fun and alive and profess to understand you but in the end their immaturity will cripple your relationship. Passion dies – it always does – and you'll want a mature friend, a worthy shoulder to lean on, not a spoilt boy depending on you. Finally, there is only one source of pain that is worth it. Laughing until it hurts. The best feeling there is. Love Daisy.*

When I finished, I felt strangely elated. It was encouraging to discover I had some insight worth offering myself after all. All day I kept checking my watch. Finally it was time to go and see Julius. Just as I was leaving the house, my mobile rang. Typical, I thought, he's ringing to cancel. That's the thing about an Alpha Male; you're always on their schedule. An important meeting, a ball-breaking deal and you are jettisoned to the sideline faster than a rock in freefall. That's why a true Alpha alliance of two strong, successful people is so rare and tricky to negotiate – Alphas always expect the upper hand: in business and in the bedroom. When it comes to love, they can only operate efficiently if their partner loves them more because they can't stand a threat to their emotional equilibrium.

To my surprise, it was not Julius's number that flashed up. Instead, it was Edward Primfold's, Lucy's ex-husband. I'd never heard him so agitated. 'Where have you been? I've been trying to get hold of you.'

'I took some time out,' I said coolly, thinking, since when did I have to answer to you, arsehole?

'Is Lucy with you?'

'No. I haven't heard from her for a while. Is anything wrong?'

'Everything is wrong. She's disappeared.'

There was a tight pause. 'Daisy, Lucy has run away.'

I must have caught Edward's panic because by the time I put the phone down, my hands were trembling.

According to Edward, two days earlier he and Lucy had

had their first joint access with their children since their divorce. They went to Hyde Park and while Edward pushed the girls on the swings, Lucy sat on a bench nearby. When he turned around, she had gone.

For Lucy to leave her beloved daughters, I knew that something was hideously wrong. I was tempted to give Edward a piece of my mind – what man deludes himself that he is a loving father, then ups and leaves two small kids and his wife because *he* can't cope with the monotonous pressure of family life? But I held myself in check because he was a waste of space and all that mattered was Lucy. She wasn't with her parents – Edward had roped them in to do the childcare fast enough – and he'd rung around her entire address book and still no luck.

My first thought as I sank into a chair was why hadn't she rung me? It stung that she was clearly in a dreadful state and yet hadn't contacted me. Had I been so wrapped up in myself that she had presumed I wouldn't be there for her? I texted Julius: 'Sorry, can't make today. Something serious has come up. Will call you, Dx'. I felt a frisson of Alpha Female as I pressed send. After all, it would do him no harm to be stood up for a change.

I called Lucy's mobile. 'Lucy, where are you? What is happening? Please, forgive me if I haven't been around enough lately. I'm so worried about you. Nothing is too awful that we can't get through it together. I'll do anything for you. Call me. Love you, Daisy.'

I was terrified by the time I put the phone down. Distraught for her and disgusted by myself, I could see that Lucy had kept flashing the siren of distress before me but I hadn't paid attention. Thinking back, she was always mentioning the intolerable loneliness and exhaustion of being a single mother but because she seemed to perk up after a few coffees or cocktails, I assumed she was just airing surmountable surface stuff.

I stayed in all day and every time the phone rang, my heart shot sky-high. That evening, I received her text. 'Am in the Randolph Hotel in Oxford. Please come quickly. Lucy.'

When Lucy saw me and Jess standing in the doorway of her hotel room, she welled up and flung her arms around Jess. It had been the first time they had seen each other in months. 'Thank you for coming . . . I'm sorry . . .' she sobbed.

'You've got nothing to be sorry for. It's me that needs to apologise,' said Jess, unusually emotional. 'I misjudged you and how difficult it's all been. In many ways you were right. I am a tight-arsed, blocked off workaholic. Forgive me?'

Lucy nodded, then fell against me. I could feel the cut of her pain as I managed to guide her back into the room. Clearly, she had cried herself to hell and back. Her face was swollen yet wan; she was utterly depleted. What had happened to Lucy Primfold, the poster girl of our generation who never had a straggly eyebrow out of place and now looked a picture of untamed despair?

'What ever is it?' I asked, plonking myself on the bed.

'Oh Daisy,' she said, 'I can't live like this any more. I want to die.'

'You don't mean that,' I whispered.

'I do,' she shouted. 'The reason that I didn't phone you is because I knew you wouldn't understand. Unless you've been there, you have simply no comprehension how demoralising it is being a single mother. I'm so tired of the back-breaking effort, of counting the minutes until the kids' bedtime and then the gnawing loneliness that takes hold of you afterwards. There's no one to offer you a glass of wine, give you any praise or hold you. No one, apart from a clingy child pawing at me, touches me any more.' She threw herself on the bed and started crying again.

I moved nearer. 'Luce, I know I don't have a baby, so I don't know what that's like but I do know what it is to feel so devastated that your life appears not to hold any meaning any more. I've been where you are in feeling that the grief inside is so deep that you'll never surmount it.'

Lucy rifled through a mountain of tissues, while Jess said briskly, 'Let me order you some room service and run you a hot bath and you can tell us everything.'

Later, as we all sat on the bed eating club sandwiches and chips, she began.

'Edward turned up for our first joint access day with the girls, looking all chipper and rested, which I resented because I was so damn tired,' she said. 'We went to Hyde Park and all the way there, while the girls slept in the back of the car, he told me that the relationship breakdown was *my* fault, even though *he* had had an affair. "You pulled the trigger, Edward," I said and he looked at me with such spite and said, "But you loaded the gun". I sat on a bench by the swings as he pushed the girls and all around me were kind, decent, Knightsbridge fathers, arms around their honed and happy wives, discussing where to go to dinner and what cocktails they would drink. I felt so alone because these were proper families with strong bonds of understanding who seemed to be actively enjoying their lives. I started crying while Edward pretended not to see. It was as if in that moment I realised that our whole marriage was built on a lie because Edward can't ever have properly loved me or he'd never have done this to me. As I watched him playing daddy for that hour or two, I thought what a total fraud he was. Even as he was pushing the girls on the swing, he kept discreetly eyeing his watch. All I could think was soon he would drive us home and then he'd swan off, no doubt to screw some chick, and I'd be left with the bed and bath routine and two over-tired daughters. I kept looking at the buses in Knightsbridge and it was as if unseen hands propelled me forwards and I just walked away and got on one. I spent the next three hours walking around crying, then I found my way to the train station and next thing, I was here. I knew it was wrong to leave the girls but all I wanted was for Edward to feel the complete devastation of being left with two children.'

'Totally understandable,' Jess said.

'You don't think I'm a dreadful mother for leaving my girls?'

'Lucy, as mothers go, you're one of the best,' continued Jess. 'You're just chronically exhausted and you reached crisis point. Everything suddenly hit you. No big deal.'

'Do you think I'll ever feel like myself again?' asked Lucy, lamely.

'You're going to feel better. It's just when you're as tired as you are, life is bled of all significance. I'm diagnosing a break with complete and utter spoiling and rest. Just stay here for as long as it takes and hit the spa with a vengeance.'

'Thanks, Jess. I've missed your brusque doctor's orders.'

'And I've missed you too,' said Jess.

After Jess and I left – and I had got Edward's credit card number and forced him to pay, telling him it was cheaper than long-term childcare if Lucy ended up in the Priory – I rushed back to work. It wasn't yet closing time when I arrived but I found the main shop plunged in darkness, while a telltale stain of light was seeping from the stockroom floor. When I opened the door, I found Miles lying on the accounting spreadsheets in a haze of cigarette smoke, a can of beer in his hand.

'Are you mad?' I shouted, rushing across the room to

retrieve a joss stick. 'You're totally polluting the environment with your toxic energy. Last month I smudged the stock to enhance our good fortune.' I lit the joss stick and started waving it around Miles's head. 'Haven't you noticed that since my abundance ritual and my daily prosperity chanting, the takings are up?'

Miles batted the sweet-smelling oriental jasmine away, while slowly exhaling a series of nicotine-laden smoke rings. 'Nope,' he said casually, 'but forgive me if I prefer not to partake in the senseless spiritual smorgasbord that is your life.' He waved the beer in my direction. I was so frustrated, I took a swig. 'That's it, Dooley,' he grinned. 'Embrace your inner laddette. God knows, if anyone needs a drunken night out, followed by a curry, an obligatory pavement puke and a zipless fuck, you do.'

'What's got into you?' I asked. 'Are you having some sort of male identity crisis? Is this a pathetic attempt to beef up your manliness?'

Miles sat up and cracked open another beer. 'Actually, I have had a change of direction and I'm celebrating,' he smiled.

'Tell me,' I said, settling myself beside him in a cross-legged position.

'I'm done with casual sex,' Miles said. 'I'm ready to fall in love.'

I couldn't have been more shocked than if he had told me that he got his kicks squirting whipped cream across choirboys' cherubic faces.

'Finally, I feel ready for the beating heart, the gooey pillow talk, meeting the parents and possibly working up to the big day.' Relishing my stunned incomprehension, Miles continued: 'You see, Daisy, I don't know what it's like to feel crazy about another human being and I want to.'

'Has your latest trophy shag dumped you?' I asked.

'Worse,' said Miles. 'She stole from me.'

'Obviously not your heart.' While I wanted to feel pleased for Miles that he had seen the love light, I felt unsettled. A niggling disquiet wouldn't go away. As I helped myself to a beer, I couldn't help but wonder if I was jealous.

'So,' said Miles, 'have you got anyone in mind for me?'

'Funnily enough, I have. I wanted you to take Lucy out, then take her to bed but I suppose your new puritanical bent might prohibit that? It's just that if anyone deserves a sexual odyssey and to get that prat Edward out of their system, Lucy does and you'd be just the guy for the job.'

Miles let out a contemplative sigh. 'Yeah, Lucy's top totty and I'd love to comfort her but let's face it, it wouldn't lead anywhere and I've decided to turn my back on meaningless sex.'

'Why couldn't it mean something?'

'Jesus, Daisy, you're worse than someone taking a bottle of vintage bubbly to an AA meeting. I'm trying to tell you that I'm a recovering sex addict and you're dangling the prospect of Lucy Primfold before me.'

'Firstly,' I said, defensively, 'you're not a sex addict, you're a recovering commitment-phobe and secondly, why couldn't you fall in love with Lucy?'

'One word,' said Miles. 'Kids.'

'Kids?'

'Yeah, I don't want the hassle of being a father to another man's sprogs. All that responsibility without any natural authority. No blood ties. I want to start afresh with my own.'

'I had no idea you were a closet romantic,' I said.

'I'm not the emotional cripple you think I am. I was just biding my time until I was ready for the real thing.' Shaken by a sudden sense of insecurity that Miles was going to give some lucky girl a life that had eluded me, I decided to play the Julius card.

'I must text Julius,' I said. 'We're meeting to discuss him fathering my child.'

Miles looked me squarely in the eye. 'Forget him. Why not have a baby with me?'

When I asked: 'Is this for real or are your rampant beer goggles talking?' he gave a lopsided grin, leaned across and kissed me. After two decades wondering what it would be like to properly snog Miles, watching the steady stream of sluts and Sloanes come and go, I finally knew.

As Miles pinned me to the ground, instead of raw urgency and clichéd passion, I was struck by a growing tenderness. The way he looked at me and traced the contours of my face with his fingers completely confused me. I couldn't help wondering if this was part of his successful seduction routine and if any woman had the sense to go with it, rather than being as destructively analytical as me, she'd be in nirvana by now. But true to my erratic form, I was plunged into doubt. I kept thinking, 'I mustn't open my mouth too wide or he'll see my fillings.' Then, while he kissed my neck, I tried to smell my own breath by giving off little putts to ensure it wasn't off colour. The more he wooed me, the more uptight I became. That's the problem with studs. You know you're not the first and you doubt you'll be the last, so how do you know when it's genuine?

Miles was gently coaxing the buttons undone on my shirt when I pulled away. I ran my fingers through my hair. 'Come on,' I said. 'This isn't what you want.'

'It bloody well is.'

'It might be what you want right now but it's not what you'll want tomorrow.'

'You're the one always saying we must live in the moment,'

he said, 'why forsake today because you're frightened of tomorrow?'

'Don't you get it?' I shouted. 'If we did it now, it would mean something to me. And I couldn't stand it that it wouldn't mean anything to you.'

'It would mean *something*,' he said, reaching out to touch me.

'Okay, so it would mean something but it wouldn't mean enough.'

It was his turn to sit up. 'For fuck's sake, Daisy,' he said, crossly, 'how could you possibly know what it might or might not mean to me? You think you're so clever, talking your way round everything, but some things just happen. But you are so controlled and prescriptive that you have to analyse everything. Nothing is left to chance.'

'I know,' I said, sadly. If only Miles knew that I longed to give into my longing and let twenty years of sexual tension between us explode on that stockroom floor. But I didn't trust him or myself to let go. Obviously he'd treat me better than a one-night stand – he'd stay for the all crucial breakfast and would stomach the post-coital chat – but I couldn't bear to think of him pretending not to be anxious to get away, then avoiding me in the bookshop. 'Miles, we work together,' I said.

'Obviously, you'd get the sack for sleeping with the boss,' he smiled. 'But then you could sue me for sexual harassment and unfair dismissal, so we'd make up your salary in no time.'

He took me in his arms and held me. 'Daisy,' he whispered, 'you do mean something to me.'

# Chapter 11
# Karmic Debt

I left Miles in an alcoholic fug because I wasn't sure that in the flat, sober light of morning, he would feel the same about me. Somehow everything in my warped little world was going mad and I realised that even my plan to have a child with Julius was absurd. I needed to walk away from him and all the complications of my twisted past. To set myself free, I had to believe in myself and hold out for someone new and special. So the next day I emailed Julius and told him that I was ready to meet him. He replied that he had a meeting near Henley and he would arrive at four o'clock the following day to collect me. After the meeting, he'd take me out to dinner by the river. When I saw his car draw up outside Jess's flat and his driver emerged to ring the bell, my stomach tightened. This was going to be a tough call because when your knight shows up on his expensive charger, it takes willpower of steel not to become the damsel in distress. Mind you, there was nothing dainty and fainty about me and never would be. But to stand firm and send him galloping off in the other direction at the end of the evening would surely absolve me of past relationship weakness and leave my dating account in the black?

Julius was on his mobile when I slid into the back seat beside him. The smell of power, of soft buttery leather, of his Blenheim Bouquet aftershave and the general charge between us was intoxicating. I kissed him on his cheek as he carried on discussing some seismic takeover and his smiling eyes melted something brittle and controlling in me. When he finished his call, he discreetly took my hand. Knowing that the driver, Paul, was all eyes and ears, probably primed to report to Alice, added to the intensity. 'You look great, Dooley,' he said, giving my hand a squeeze. 'You look like you.'

All the old feelings came rushing to the fore. Compared to Miles, Julius was a grown-up. While a fumble on the stockroom floor with Miles had been frisky and fun, this was quite different. This, for me, was real. Who had I been trying to kid in thinking I wanted anyone new? Not Andy or Max – after all, I'd tried being with someone that wasn't Julius when I married Jamie. What I wanted, who I always wanted, was right here. His mobile rang constantly as we sped down the motorway and while I listened to his calm authority as he talked, I realised that being with him only reminded me of my loneliness. That was where the heartbreak lay. Suddenly, it hit me with a wodge of panic. Forget having a baby with Julius. I still wanted much more. I wanted a life with him.

Watching the way he pored over the menu in a seventies-style Italian restaurant filled with spider plants, packets of bread sticks and giant pepper mills, eager to source the perfect seabass or an unusual salad that would bring me pleasure, I realised that after twenty years of loving him, I didn't know how to give him up. How would I learn to be without the promise of the great big happy ending with Julius Vantonakis feeding my dreams? My greatest fear was that I would never feel this way about another man and that all that stretched before me was the familiar grind of joyless intimacy with some nice enough, poor unsuspecting sod, a Jamie mark two.

Julius looked at me tenderly. 'You were right all along,' he said.

'What about?'

He shifted uncomfortably. 'About me marrying Alice. She isn't a match for me and there are days when I almost loathe her for her emptiness.'

'She knew what she was getting into marrying you.'

'Yes and she's not the one who's disappointed.' He paused. 'She's not lonely.' The inference was 'unlike me'.

For a second, I saw a glimpse of the interior of this man and it was as if a silent flare went off. 'I always knew that I lacked a quality of connectedness with her that I feel with you,' he continued, 'but I thought that having a child would override that. But a baby doesn't fill the gulf between parents, however far apart as people they are. Having a child magnifies hair-line cracks into canyons.' He leaned across the table and rested his palm on my arm. 'Daisy, I still want to have a child with you.'

'Will you leave Alice?' I asked, fear backing up in every vein. My question hung in the air like smog. Suddenly, he stood up. He threw a couple of fifty-pound notes on the table – we hadn't even had our first course. 'Let's get out of here.'

I followed him towards the door, when he turned. 'No, let's go out of the back door. I don't want Paul to see us leave or he'll follow us.'

We walked into the small garden of the restaurant and

stood by the fence that separated a field to the Thames. It was getting dark and difficult to see. 'Shall we?' Julius jumped over the fence and I crawled through a middle section, snagging my top. The grass, heavy with dew, soaked my shoes. He took my hand and we ran down to the river, stumbling and giggling with childish pleasure to have escaped. I can't remember the last time I felt that spontaneous and free.

When we reached the water's edge, Julius took off his bespoke jacket and threw it on to the muddy grass. The extravagance thrilled me. We sat down on it and he said: 'I always wanted the sort of girl who would run for the bus or who would get up at six and rush down to the beach without putting make-up on and I never had her.'

'Trophy chicks daren't risk natural and windswept,' I said, thinking 'but you could have had me'.

We watched the mist rise above the river. It was a perfect moment; laden with romance, tension and promise. I could barely feel the cold settling in my bones. 'I feel like I'm eighteen again,' he said. 'We had so much hope then, didn't we? The potential of youth.'

'For all the mess I've made of the last twenty years, I'd rather be me, here, today. At least I know who I am.'

Julius turned to me: 'I know what you want and you deserve it.'

My request that he leave Alice lay between us like a shared bruise; we were both scared to touch it. 'I'm hungry,' he said.

'Forget the fancy dinner,' I suggested. 'Let's eat takeaway fish and chips in the car.'

'I love that.' He smiled. 'And you.'

I know, I thought, delighted and frightened in equal measure. But for Julius, was love a good enough excuse? As we walked back to the car, he put his arm around me and squeezed me tight. In the way he held me, I knew that whatever the outcome, no man would ever touch the core of me like Julius could.

Lucy was helping me in the bookshop as Miles had sent a text the day before saying: 'Man the fort. Disaster on the domestic front.'

'Probably some trophy chick has broken a nail or discovered a split end,' she said.

'Yeah, maybe Miles pulled her hair in the name of rough sex and now she's demanding he replace her extensions.'

'The cost of that would kill him. I never had Miles down for the generous type.'

'Few men remain generous when they've got what they want.'

'So how can you contemplate giving in to Julius?'

'Isn't that below the belt?' She shook her head. 'But I haven't slept with Julius for over ten years and certainly not since he married Alice.'

'That's what makes this situation more explosive. His marriage could survive the odd affair – Alice probably expects that – but it can't sustain real love beyond its tight little boundary. No marriage defined by a deathly sense of duty can weather pure passion.'

'It's awful waiting for Julius to decide between Alice and me.'

'I just don't want you to get hurt by that man – again,' sighed Lucy.

I put my head in my hands. 'I know, which is why he has to leave her for me, or I have to walk away. I've seriously considered the short-term fix of the heady affair but I know it would end in tears and they'd all be mine. I know where my love for Julius begins but I don't know yet where it ends.

There are so many normal things I want to do with him. Affairs are unrealistic because you get intense shots of the best of someone in hotels and snatched places, when loving someone means knowing all of them, every day, at home. I've decided that love is a language beyond words; a knowing that whatever fluff collects on the surface, there is something deeper for keeps. I want to watch Julius grow old, I want to see him get cross and be with him when he's tired and grumpy and I want us to have nights when we laugh ourselves silly. I want to lie next to him on holiday and watch him read. I want to walk into a room with him and feel the comfort of his palm in the small of my back, knowing it spells reassurance and pride in us. I want to ignite that spark in him which went out long ago but more than anything I want his friendship and I want it to last.'

'You really do love him. Then you're right to wait and see what he decides because anything less will be an insult.'

Suddenly the door swung open and Miles stood there looking weird. I couldn't tell if his body was contorted with temper or he was massively hung-over. I guided him to a chair. He sat down, let his head hang back and closed his eyes. 'This is my worst nightmare,' he groaned.

'You've got some girl pregnant?' I whispered.

'Got it in one. Every man prays that this day will never come but mine has and it's worse than I could ever have dreamed of.'

I put the closed sign on the door of the bookshop and dimmed the lights to deter any potential customers. Although it was only early afternoon, the pewter rain-sodden skies made it feel like evening. Lucy, Miles and I sat on the floor behind the counter and the conspiratorial air, shot through with the static of Miles's confession, made us feel like we were bunking off school. Lucy handed us mugs of strong tea and we threw in whisky from a bottle we found loitering in the stockroom.

Miles emitted an empty laugh. 'Do you know what my first thought was when she told me? At least I haven't been firing blanks all these years. Most of my mates have the war wounds of abortion from their early twenties and alimony from their late thirties and I could never believe my luck that I had escaped that fate.'

'Who she is?' said Lucy.

'You don't know her,' said Miles. 'She's just some chick.'

'They always are,' I replied.

'So,' asked Lucy tentatively, 'is she having . . . an . . . abortion?'

'Too late for that. She's already had the kid.'

'Bloody hell,' I shrieked. 'So you're a father?'

God knows how Miles felt because I felt like *I'd* been kicked in the gut. It was as if my insides came tumbling out. This couldn't be happening, could it? That even Miles had already had a baby with someone else? Why did I always feel that as soon as I got near to the top of the life queue, somebody barged ahead of me and I'd always be left behind? 'I feel sick,' I said. 'I just can't believe this.'

'Daisy, this isn't about you,' whispered Lucy.

'Typical Daisy,' smiled Miles. 'I'm cold, so you put on a jumper.'

'Are you going to marry her?'

'She's already married,' said Miles. Lucy looked pained and I could tell that she was shocked, while I soared with strange relief that Miles wasn't about to be claimed, after all.

'You slept with a married woman and got her pregnant?' repeated Lucy, crisply. 'How could you have been so stupid not to use protection?'

'I fell for the bullshit that she was infertile. She'd been married for five years and nothing.'

'What does her husband think?'

'He thinks Clara is his daughter.'

'That is absolutely appalling,' shouted Lucy. 'What kind of woman is this? Has she no moral code at all?'

'So the husband never knew that he was infertile?'

'He isn't. He has slow sperm, apparently.'

'Too much information,' said Lucy, getting up and pacing. 'How old is she?'

'Early forties.'

'Your little girl, I mean?'

'Six months,' said Miles, slowly.

'Why did she contact you now?' I said.

'I don't know. That's the confusing thing.' Miles grabbed the whisky bottle and took a slug. 'She rang and asked me over. I thought it was for old time's sake and suddenly, we were kissing and I heard this baby crying. She brought it in and told me it was mine but I couldn't tell anybody because of her husband.'

'What a nightmare,' said Lucy. 'What did you ever see in her?'

'She always seemed fragile and lonely. I felt sorry for her. I always thought it was safe to sleep with married women because they don't want commitment.' He paused, briefly broken. 'Sometimes, I'm so damn tired of being a single man.'

The discovery of his love child brought out a reflective, sober side of Miles that I hadn't seen before. He didn't have the energy to deflect his pain with wry comments and witty asides but wore his disappointment openly. It was as if the shock of suddenly understanding, post forty, that over much of life we have little or no control, forced him to grow in a way I never imagined.

We retreated to Mum's in the Cotswolds for the usual weekend panacea of dachshunds to stroke, stodgy nosh, long walks and vistas to clear our heads. Miles's vulnerability upset me. He had always been a good time guy living for today, so to witness him this upset made him seem lonely and bereft. Typical of his rampant appeal though, even his Little Boy Lost air was sexy.

We were lying on the sitting room floor in front of the fire. 'The thing is, Daise, I always thought I was an expert on women,' he sighed. 'I could tell the needy ones who'd be grateful and the haughty ones who looked like they were frozen solid yet the minute you touched them, would morph into back-scratching fire crackers. Yet everything has become so complicated emotionally. Women today are always three feet away from their hearts because they don't know what to do with the rules. The feminists tore up the manual and left them stranded.'

'I totally agree. Women of my generation are completely confused. We want to be high-earning Alpha Females kicking arse in the boardroom but we want men to nurture us at home. We want to rock up from work buzzing with our own brilliance and self-importance yet we want you to choose the wine, pay for dinner and open the door for us. We want to be able to dominate sexually in the bedroom if that does it for us yet after being on top we want you to hold us, stroke us and promise to protect us.'

'And where is love in this mess?' asked Miles. 'You always berate me for not believing in true love but I'm not sure that women today have any faith either.'

'I think we're all afraid. Men and women,' I said. 'No one wants to get hurt. I still believe that if it hurts when you're together it's not love and that only the fear of not being loved hurts.'

Mum came in with a tray of tea and shortbread and sat on the sofa beside us. Miles turned to her: 'For the first time in decades of listening to your daughter's clap-trap, I think she's got a point.' We laughed. Miles continued: 'The knowledge that I am a father has made me react differently. I could go in all guns blazing, claim my daughter and destroy a family but how would that help this little girl who is entirely innocent? I've thought of nothing else lately and in this case, loving means letting her go. I've got to wait, knowing that one day this situation will explode. Her identity won't stay secret for ever. But I'll be waiting and when she's ready, I'll be there for her. I can't say I love her because I don't know her but I feel this overwhelming sense of responsibility.'

'That's because you're a natural father,' said Mum gently. 'Already, you're putting your child's needs before your own feelings and that's the first rule of mature and loving parenting.' Miles seemed touched.

'Daisy,' said Mum, 'please think very carefully about getting entangled with Julius. As Miles will tell you, when children are involved the playing field is no longer level and Julius already has a child.'

She looked me and then Miles. 'My prayer has always been that you two would get together.'

A couple of days later, when I saw Julius's car pull up outside the bookshop, I did a mad, jerky dance of terror. Miles came over and put his arms out to steady me. 'Remember, Dooley, whatever you do, don't be tempted to bang his brains out. That'll just confuse you both.'

'I'm not like you, Miles,' I smiled. 'I don't use sex to stifle pain.'

'Nor do I,' he said, soberly. 'Well, not any more.'

I kissed him on the cheek. He looked at me with surprising tenderness: 'Don't forget this isn't a movie. Julius isn't Jerry

Maguire. He doesn't complete you. He completely messes you up.'

'I know. I know.' I blew him a kiss and turned for the door.

As I left he shouted out: 'I'll be here for you.' I wasn't sure that I had heard correctly so I turned around. He gave me a knowing nod. Did that mean physically 'here' for me, in the bookshop, or '*here*' for me? Miles wasn't seriously waiting in the wings, was he?

Julius took me to the bar at Blake's Hotel. Although it was dark and sexy, all expensive lacquer and black orchids, it was where you met for a secret tryst, not for a no-holds-barred, let-me-turn-my-heart-inside-out, life-changing conversation. As he ordered champagne cocktails, I felt pre-empted and put out. He clearly felt at home among the clientele; controlling men who couldn't burn their money fast enough. The air was ripe with promiscuity. Women, flattered by the opulence, flicked their highlighted hair, thrust out their assets and tittered. For me, none of it was a turn-on because it felt flat and dated. These people may be rolling in it but they were frauds because they were bankrupt, emotionally speaking. They didn't yearn for a meaningful partnership; for souls to recognise each other and grow together. In fact, the mere concept of anything like that would make them gag on their gin and guffaw. They wanted to use each other. To them, all partners were replaceable. That was part of the fun. The danger and the diversity.

Julius sat close beside me and put his hand on my knee. Suddenly, I didn't want flirtatious gestures or coy asides. I wanted truth and authenticity and anything that would help me in my ultimate goal to feel whole. It was as if time was running out and I couldn't waste another second on artifice.

'Why didn't you want to marry me when we were in our twenties?' I asked.

He didn't flinch. That's what I always liked about him – his control. 'We were too young. We didn't know what we wanted.'

'I did. I wanted you. From the minute I set eyes on you, I loved you.' I banged my heart with my fist. 'From here. Really loved you. But you? You couldn't trust your heart, could you?' He took an almost imperceptible intake of breath. But I heard it. His hesitancy. His shame. 'You still can't. Don't you think I deserve that, Julius? To be loved?' Tears were welling and I willed them away.

'I think about you all the time, Daisy. I can't get you out of my mind.'

'That's just it,' I shouted. 'I don't want to be in your mind, I want to be in your life. Inside you. To be part of you.'

An overly made-up, mini-skirted piece of totty in her twenties looked across and giggled. I shot her a look. Silly thing couldn't begin to understand where I was coming from if she tried.

'That's the problem,' said Julius, his voice low and grave. 'You always want too much.'

I stood up and made my way out of the bar, up the stairs. I couldn't stand that oppressive atmosphere a second longer. As soon as I reached the street, he was there, behind me. 'All I ever wanted was for you to let me love you,' I shouted. 'To make it real. Not just harbour some adolescent fantasy that lived up here,' I tapped my temples.

'Is this real?' he grabbed me and pulled me into his embrace. He tilted my face to his and kissed me.

'Don't, don't!' I tried to break free. 'Please don't do this.'

'Well, what do you want?' he roared, exasperated.

'I . . . I just want you to hold me.'

As he held me close, I wept into his suit lapel. I could feel myself unravelling. 'Don't cry,' he whispered into my hair. 'Please, don't cry.'

'I can't go on like this any more,' I said.

And then I heard him say: 'Neither can I.'

Before I knew it, Julius had whisked me into a lavish suite in the hotel. Not, he explained, for anything untoward but because we needed somewhere private to talk. In other words, he couldn't stand the spectacle of me crying in the street. I went into the bathroom and pressed my head against the cool marble wall. Emotionally spun out, I wanted to get into the vast tub with all those expensive unguents and let it all wash away. I ran the bath, trance-like, as the water surged forth. Sitting on the side, my head in my hands, I closed my eyes and thought that the crucial life question is not 'Why are we here?' but as Camus put it: 'Why shouldn't we kill ourselves?' Clearly deranged, I found this unbelievably funny and started laughing.

Suddenly, Julius was at the door, shouting. Water was gushing all over the bathroom floor. With the high pressure, the bath had filled in a nanosecond and a gully of water was charging for the cream carpet outside. While I switched off the taps, he slammed the door shut and threw towels on the floor, kneeling on them to soak up the water. What I loved about Julius was that there was no hint of censure – no tight look which read 'You stupid broad, we could be liable for thousands if the ceiling gives downstairs', and that wasn't because the money was no big deal. It was because he, like me, had a glorious sense of the absurd. We fell about on the soggy towels, rocking with laughter. Soon, someone was at the door and every time they knocked, we collapsed again, helpless.

Later, when apologies and credit cards had been dispensed, we lay on the bed in towelling robes, waiting for our clothes to dry. Side by side, on our backs, we were close but not touching. He turned on his side and was about to speak when I said: 'Don't. It doesn't matter because I know you don't want to leave Alice and the baby.'

'Oh, I want to,' he said, his voice filled with longing, 'but I can't. Every day I have this battle. My head says: "You've got a wife and a child. You must be responsible. You must do the right thing." But my heart says; "I can't. I love Daisy." So my head says: "You must, you must." Then my heart says: "But how can I go on for the next twenty years?" And my head says: "You must."'

As hard as it was to hear, because I loved Julius, I understood. 'Yeah, it's not the courage to leave we need, it's the courage to listen to our hearts,' I said softly.

Julius reached across and touched my arm. 'I'm not sure I can live without you.'

'You're going to have to,' I said firmly, 'because it'll destroy me to have to share you. I don't want part-time love, I want a full-time partner. I want us to be able to go on holiday together, to plan out our lives, to fill each other's stockings at Christmas. I'm so proud of the man you are, Julius, that I want to be able to openly claim you. To walk down the street freely, arms entwined. I can't do the sneaking off, the lies and the deceit. If it was just a short affair, it would be different. But this is the real thing and you can't compromise with love. That's the point.'

I started to get off the bed when Julius pulled me back.

'Bite me,' he said.

'Bite you?' I laughed, stunned.

'I want to have your imprint on me,' he said.

'Don't be ridiculous.'

'Then let me bite you.' He lifted the towelling robe up my thigh. Before I could stop him, he bit the side of my bottom. I let out a yelp of pain. His pressure was perfect; enough to bruise me but not enough to scar me. Was that like our love? We looked at the rising red welt and then at each other, speechless. In that moment, my heart had never felt more full.

'You can search the world but you'll never meet anyone like me,' he said.

'And you'll never meet another me,' I smiled.

Before I knew it we were devouring each other, seeking each other out. Kissing and clinging on as if each moment might be our last. Julius was instantly inside me and while everything in me knew it was wrong, nothing had ever felt more right. We may have made love years before but this felt different because it meant so much more. So this is what real intimacy was; that feeling that had nothing to do with physical touch? Oh, he was touching me all right. Running his hands all over my body, openly claiming me. He kept whispering; 'Daisy, we fit. We are the perfect match,' and when he looked into my eyes I knew for the first time what it was to be completely united. In that moment, there was no one or nothing else in the entire world that mattered. We came together and afterwards we lay in silence as he held me. After a while, with rising dread at the prospect of leaving and knowing that one night is never long enough for new – or in our case renewed – love, without saying a word, I went into the bathroom to dress.

As I stood by the door to leave, Julius said: 'Why do you have to be so absolutist? We could have a life together just not in the form you want. You think you're kooky and rebellious, Daisy, but deep down, you're so damn pedestrian and conventional.'

I didn't have the energy for a fight and I knew he was lashing out because he was scared too. 'I know,' I said. 'It's as much of a shock to me to find out that I want a stable, committed union with all the trappings, after all.' I threw my hands in the air. 'Look: you're married. You're never going to leave your wife. It is what it is, Julius.' I shrugged and walked swiftly away. As I stood in the lift, I felt myself recoil inside. Why did I have to make our parting shot so taut and unemotional? I sounded like a stressed accountant faced with a nasty spreadsheet when this was our *Brief Encounter* moment. Leaving that hotel was as poignant for me as Celia Johnson watching Trevor Howard's train chug out of the station. Yet I had none of her dignity. Her heart-rending aplomb. Oh, but we did share the same inner ache.

I walked out of the hotel, too afraid to feel how frightened I was. I wandered aimlessly around South Kensington, not sure what to do or where to go next. You don't realise how deeply you care about someone until you are faced with never feeling them touch you again. I held the image of Julius in my head as he stood by the door of our hotel room, looking suddenly older and knowingly sober. The way he hung his head to one side suggested that he, too, had had his dreams infected by the blight of unexpected events in life. There seemed to be a point in adulthood when you had to put your hand on your heart and admit that you never expected things to turn out like this. Maturity was about accepting and transforming disappointment, so was this my time to acquiesce with good grace?

I made my way back to Jess's, praying that when I got there, he would be waiting for me. The adolescent romantic in me just could not accept that he wasn't going to turn up and surprise me. I kept looking at my mobile. Waiting for that call or text which said: 'I'm coming for you.' But there was no message. No text. Unable to face myself alone in Jess's flat, I wandered to my local bookshop and fast-tracked to the self-help section, like an addict on autopilot for her fix. I picked up a book, opened the page at random, took a deep breath and read: 'When we listen with the ear of the soul, we hear stories that need forgiveness. When we listen from ego, we take these stories as truth.' So I couldn't blame Julius for not fighting for me, could I? For not disrupting his whole world in the name of our love. It didn't mean he didn't care enough, it just meant that it wasn't meant to be. Didn't it? Well, that was the positive spin to put on it, I thought bitterly.

As I sat in a coffee shop, unable to even taste my coffee, I reflected that being with Julius was like finding that your black-and-white life was suddenly in glorious technicolour and surround sound. How many men make you feel that vivid and alive? I watched people eating, drinking, laughing and loving and thought how flat and grey my life felt. And yet, even as I was going through the well-worn 'woe is me' routine, there was a part of me, like a tiny flame first ignited in kindling, that was alight. I was bored of twenty years' thrashing myself in mental self-flagellation, bemoaning when I was going to meet my romantic match. I could no longer face my eternal fear of 'Whichever way you turn now, it's a long journey to the oasis of happiness.' Now, on the cusp of forty, I wasn't going to let anything stand in my way. I was going to get out there and get my life right. I dug around in my wallet for Jennie Skipwith's card. I was going to contact her at Insight Publications as I'd had an idea. Then, I grabbed my phone and sent Julius a text: 'Darling Julius, If not this lifetime, maybe the next? I wish it could have been you but I understand. Be good to yourself and find the courage to be happy. You deserve so much and more. D. x'

# Chapter 12
# Immaculate Misconception

I wrote on the blackboard in stark, white chalk: 'The suffering that results from betraying our soul's call far surpasses any trite pain.' I sat back and sighed. It had been a couple of weeks since my last encounter with Julius and I didn't know how I was going to live without him. But I did know that I would continue to be true to myself. It was my fortieth birthday in ten days' time and I knew with complete conviction that I wasn't going to settle ever again in life. Not for a mediocre job nor a half-baked bloke because I knew from experience that hard-edged compromise – not a gentle tugging here and a little relenting there – cuts to the quick. That is when the soul goes into revolt.

Miles came up. 'Oh for goodness sake, Dooley, can't you write something a little more upbeat? It is December next week, and we need some festive cheer. We want happy, extravagant shoppers, not depressed dead ringers for Scrooge.'

'Okay, tomorrow I'll do a jolly "Yo ho ho, don't mourn the end of the year, let Christmas be your new beginning. Give birth to your own miracle by believing in your dreams."'

'On second thoughts, maybe I prefer the grim moralising.' He handed me the post and I started absent-mindedly flicking through it. When I saw a letter from Insight Publications, my heart did a leap of excitement mixed with fear.

Hands trembling, I quickly ripped open the letter, skim read it and let out a yelp of pleasure. I punched the air and shouted an orgasmic: 'Yes! Yes! YES!!'

Miles looked up. 'Don't tell me. Julius has sent you a copy of his decree nisi?'

'No, but this is second best,' I said, elated. I ran up to Miles and hugged him tight. 'Thanks for everything you've done for me. You're going to have to find some new sucker you can pay a pittance to and bait all day long.'

'Why?' Miles asked, surprised.

'I'm leaving you,' I said. 'I sent in a proposal for a book I want to write and they've commissioned it!'

I jumped up and down, elated. 'I'm going to write my own guide to surviving divorce. It's going to be called *Daisy Dooley Does Divorce.*' Triumphantly, I waved the letter under his nose.

Suddenly, it was as if decades of backed-up grief, of wondering when my moment was going to come, came forward. The relief of feeling that I was finally going to be validated for something I had to offer, that a small talent however quirky or offbeat was being recognised, made all the past rejection seem poignant and almost worthwhile. It was no less painful but in a funny way, even this success hurt because it made me realise how long I'd trudged on wondering if I'd ever find my place in the sun. I'd lived the loneliness of the outsider being cold-shouldered for so long that I hadn't realised until this moment what a strain it had been. Always being overlooked by the man you want or feeling that the creative fulfilment you crave eludes you numbs something vital inside. I had pins and needles and, while it stung all over, I felt excited and alive.

I sat on the floor, slowly re-reading the letter, overcome. Miles crouched down and said: 'Of course it'll hurt, leaving me and our happy little set-up. You'll never find a boss as easy-going and indulgent. Who else would actually encourage you to fiddle your expenses?' He paused, adding with genuine feeling, 'And you'll never find a boss who adores you more. Congrats, Daise, you may be a disloyal bitch for ditching me but I'm proud of you.'

'Really?'

'Really. You have no idea how loved you are, do you?'

I stared at him, nonplussed. 'Just because Julius hasn't turned up on some massive great steed waving a ring, it's as if nothing else counts for anything in your life,' he said, unusually serious. 'But you've got friends who would kill for you, you've got a book deal and for a batty, nearly menopausal broad, you're in pretty good shape. I'd shag you, you know that?'

'Thanks!' I said, adding jokingly, 'that means everything to me. Finally, I feel like a real woman at last.'

But Miles was partly right; just because I wasn't going to waltz up the aisle with Julius it didn't mean that the next phase of my life was devoid of meaning, did it? 'I'm so used to rejection and feeling a failure,' I explained, 'it's as if I don't know how to feel successful and happy any more.'

'You're gonna find out,' he said, 'because Insight aren't some tin-pot organisation, they're the real deal.'

That night Lucy and Jess joined us in the bookshop and we drank champagne and ate Chinese takeaway. Jess stood on a chair and made a toast: 'To our darling Daisy, who's finally found her vocation. She did it the emotionally punishing way, of course, as the only thing she over-worked were her tear ducts, but her pain is now lucrative pain because she understands all the screw-ups out there looking for love who over-dose on spirit-lit and therapy-lite! Please, my good friends and potential fuck buddy,' she said, eyeing Miles keenly, 'raise your mugs of warm Moët to Miss Daisy Dooley, the only woman we know about to enter her fifth decade who still believes in guardian angels yet managed to make it to her honeymoon before it hit that she'd married a prize turkey. To the only woman I know to defy medical fact by claiming she got pregnant while "having her period" on the only one-night stand of her entire, sexually insignificant little life. Yet we must not forget that she did remember to use a condom with a man who'd had a vasectomy. To a woman who has kept us entertained for two decades with her will he/won't he Julius saga and who has – thank you God or possibly her guardian angel, at last! – put him to bed by banging his brains out. And finally, because she believes in feeling every feeling; she's a woman who cries when she's happy and cries when she's sad. She cries when she's horny . . .'

'And she cries when she's hungry,' cut in Lucy.

'Oh God, you're not one of those awful chicks who cries when she comes, are you?' asked Miles.

I smiled. 'That, my friend, you'll never know.'

'So, to Daisy deranged Dooley,' continued Jess, 'our best mate and the most wonderful source of inspiration because however bad our lives may be, we only have to look at hers to feel a surge of hope.'

'To Daisy deranged Dooley,' chorused Miles and Lucy in unison. 'Author-to-be of *Daisy Dooley Does Divorce*!'

After I had thanked Jess and told her that as soon as I had the first chunk of my advance from Insight, I'd be moving out and getting a deposit down on a flat of my own, Lucy said softly, 'You never told me you shagged Julius.'

'Because I knew you wouldn't approve and I didn't plan it, it just happened.' I shrugged. 'Look, I don't feel great about it but the weird thing is I don't feel guilty either. It felt right, so it was clearly meant.'

'Still Daisy, still in denial,' said Lucy.

'Listen, Luce,' said Jess. 'There are lots of ways to get over someone. The most pleasurable is simply to shag him out of your system.' Lucy pursed her lips.

'Now, now, you two,' I said. 'Anyway, it was far more than that. For the first time I know what it's like to make love as opposed to merely having sex.'

'There's no "merely" about having sex, you romantic fool,' said Miles.

'Well, all I hope is that you practised safe sex,' said Jess. 'We don't want a repeat of Troy Powers.' She looked at me. 'You did use a condom, didn't you?'

'Of course we did,' I lied.

If it's possible to know the second you get pregnant, then in the back of my mind, in some teensy place in my body, like an intermittent throb in my psyche, I knew. I didn't allow it to fully surface but as soon as I got the book offer, I heard something inside say jauntily: 'Oh, and I bet you'll be pregnant too.' I waited until the morning of my fortieth birthday to do the test because I wanted it to be meaningful, to me at least. I was only a few days late but it was no real surprise. As I peed on the stick, I didn't feel cold and sick as I had before. I felt secure. I watched the blue line appear and it was a wonderful relief to feel myself expand with joy. This was a life, a fresh start for me and a baby – and Julius, too, if he wanted it – and nothing on earth was going to persuade me to throw this shot at happiness away. I felt unusually calm and clear. I knew exactly what I was going to do. I wasn't going to shout it from the rooftops and get everyone's opinion, then let myself be swayed. For the first time in my life I was going to do what I wanted to do.

I put the pregnancy stick in my handbag and walked to work. I stopped at a post office and bought a jiffy bag and sent the stick to Julius. There was no need for a note. I got to work and Miles was waiting with fresh croissants, coffee and champagne. Christmas carols were blaring from the stereo and while I drank my coffee and pretended to sip the fizz, I couldn't remember ever feeling this relaxed, as opposed to the usual volatile tension that ran through my veins. My secret gave me a feeling of being at home in my own skin in a way I'd never known before. It wasn't that I wasn't scared of the future, as I was. But for once I felt as if destiny was a galloping horse and the only way to control it was to let go of the reins. Then there is nothing to pull against.

Later in the morning a courier arrived with package for me. 'No doubt it's some ghastly gadget from one of my mother's catalogues,' I said to Miles as I signed for it. 'Last year I got a cherry de-stoner, so maybe this is an avocado de-pipping device to mark my fortieth?'

I opened the brown wrapping and saw the pure, duck-egg blue colour of a Tiffany box. 'My God, she's excelled herself,' I said. 'Finally, my parents have coughed up for a piece of statement jewellery.' It was the sweetest thing but immediately I thought: If I'm having a girl, I can pass it on to her.

I opened the box and inside lay Julius's Fabergé egg. As I stared at it I literally felt my heart lurch. I lifted it out, twisting it in my trembling hand and opened the mechanism so the bejewelled butterfly rose up and the light bounced off the precious stones. 'Bloody hell,' said Miles, as he stared at the glinting rubies, emeralds and diamonds. 'You're only celebrating your fortieth. Not your coronation. How the heck did your Mum afford that? Or is it a fake?'

I shook my head. 'It's not from Mum,' I said, slowly. 'It's from Julius. And it's a real Fabergé egg.'

'How do you know it's from him? Is there a note?'

'No,' I said, swallowing hard. 'He doesn't need to leave a note.' I closed the egg and carefully put it back in its tissue nest in the box.

'What's this then?' said Miles, handing me a small envelope that I hadn't noticed. I opened it and read in Julius's tight scrawl: 'Remember that butterflies are fragile survivors. They exhibit virtually no parental concern for their offspring, save choosing a safe place to leave their eggs.' I put the note in my pocket and hurried to the loo. I locked the door and stood against it in a bid to catch my breath. God, he must love me, I thought. But was sending me his ultimate symbol of undying love Julius's way of saying that this was the most precious thing I could ever have from him? How would he feel when he opened his post and saw the symbol of the egg I was keeping safe for him?

Dad and I always had a pre-Christmas and post-birthday celebration lunch combined. This year he offered to take me anywhere I wanted but in a daft way, I had grown almost fond of the ritual of the yucky Thai Temptations. It looked incongruous in festive mode with silver plastic Christmas trees and garish pink flashing lights. For once I was there first and as I sat in our usual booth, I felt my nerves plucking. I hadn't heard from Julius and it had been nearly two weeks since he would have received my package. As it was Christmas at the weekend and he was probably going away to the Caribbean or skiing in Gstaad with his family, the signs weren't promising. He knew how much I loved him, so he knew I'd keep the baby. I wasn't in any doubt over that but the longer he stayed away and kept silent, the stronger my worst fear that he didn't intend to get involved. He wasn't going to get all heavy and threatening like Troy had done but it looked like he wasn't going to give me his blessing or be by my side, either. I had tried not to let any heartbreak in because I didn't want any of it to infect our baby but deep down of course I had prayed that this would be the rallying call for him to come to me. To us. Once and for ever.

Dad bustled in wearing a flasher mac that was probably at least half a century old. His face looked raw from the cold and the skin around his mouth was cracked and peeling. Because he considered central heating an extravagance, he always had that bluey frozen look in winter, as if he slept on the street.

'Ah, Daisy,' he said, dry-rubbing his hands as if warming them in front of a fire, 'let's order some of that hot and spicy soup. That will de-thaw us.' As soon as the soup arrived, he said, mid slurp: 'How was your birthday?'

'Lovely, thanks,' I said. 'I had a quiet celebration. I went out to dinner with Lucy, Miles and Jess.'

'Yes, I expect you didn't feel there was much to celebrate? I suppose being forty and single and childless and with a job instead of a career, it was a bitter pill to swallow, eh? Life rarely pans out in the way we dream. I mean, I look at myself, past seventy-five now, and I think, "I didn't expect to be on my own but then again, I didn't expect to enjoy being on my own so much either."' He let out a hearty chortle.

I looked at my father, at his watery blue eyes and couldn't work out, as usual, if he was being deliberately crass or trying to be kind. 'Actually, Dad, I've got plenty to celebrate,' I said, unable to keep my combative tone at bay. 'I've got a book deal from Insight Publications to write a guide to surviving divorce and to cap it all, I'm pregnant!'

Dad put down his spoon and stared at me. 'What a terrible blow,' he said. 'I'm so, so sorry.'

Was I hearing straight? 'What about? Being paid to write a book or having a child by Julius? A man I truly respect and love.'

'Well, you can't accept a deal to write a book if you've got a deadline and you're going to have a baby, can you? You'll have to tell them the truth and they might think you won't be able to deliver in time, unless you're not going to have the baby that is?'

'I'm having the baby and I'm going to tell Insight about it. It is possible to do both. That's what modern women and working mothers do nowadays.'

'And Mr Vantonakis? Is he doing the decent thing? Is he going to stand by you?'

'I don't know,' I said wearily.

'Well what does he say about it?'

'I don't know. I haven't spoken to him.'

'You haven't spoken to him?' echoed my father. 'Does he even know?'

'He knows.'

'Ah, so you've written to him? How very Jane Austen. Imagine the shame of illegitimacy in those days. At least today the stigma is less and by the time your child is at school, maybe you'll have married him or someone else, so the poor little bastard won't feel embarrassed when they're asked in the playground why their mother and father aren't married . . . I do think, Daisy, that however progressive one claims to be, a father figure is still vital . . .'

'Like you were?' I said acidly. My adversarial glare gave Dad a jolt of surprise. 'You may have been there during my childhood but were you really present? It felt like Mum did all the parenting and all the loving on her own. Sure, my situation isn't perfect but tell me, Dad, what is? And I can tell you that I've realised that I'd far rather be having this baby on my own than having had a baby when I was married to Jamie. Because however good or "legitimate" it might have looked on the surface, being with the wrong person makes you feel much more lonely than being on your own.'

My father seemed to shrink back into himself, as if trying to protect himself from my hostile glare. 'I've never seen you more certain,' he said at last. 'So you're having this baby at exactly the right time, unlike so many, myself included, who discovered that they were going to be parents and felt unsure. But we went ahead anyway because it was the right thing to do. That's what I most admire about you Daisy. Finally, you've learned to do what feels right on the inside, not what looks right on the outside.'

Lucy, Jess, Miles and I met for pre-Christmas drinks in the bookshop two days before Christmas Eve. Miles was going to his parents' after closing time on Christmas Eve, Lucy was taking her girls to her parents' the next day and Jess was coming to spend Christmas with me at Mum's after she had finished at the surgery.

This time it was my turn to stand on the chair. I cleared my throat and said: 'Eh-erm, I'd like to say a few words.'

The others settled into their seats and looked up. 'Please, spare us from any psycho-crap or hypno-speak,' said Miles.

'I promise, I'm not going to say anything offensively spiritual but this is from the heart.'

I looked at Jess, still wild and promiscuous, still searching in her slutty way to overcome her deep loneliness and find something meaningful in her life apart from her career and I thought how much I loved her. I looked at Lucy, still beautiful and still hurt by Edward, her aura seemingly for ever fractured by his betrayal and I felt my heart go out to her. And I looked at Miles, still gorgeous, still irresistible yet recently scarred by what life had thrown at him and I thought how much I'd always adore him. These were my closest friends and here we were after more than twenty years together, struggling like everyone else in the world to make sense of our lives.

'I just want you guys to know that I couldn't have got through the last shitty year without you,' I said. 'However, I'll need you more than ever in the shitty nappy-filled years ahead because I'm pregnant. It's Julius's baby and I'm having it.'

'You liar!' screamed Jess. 'You didn't use a condom, did you?'

'Nope. I openly and wantonly lied,' I giggled.

'When are you going to learn that sex without protection equals a baby?' laughed Jess.

'And are you ever going to be tempted to risk it?' I asked. She shrugged, still smiling. It was the first time I'd seen her waver. Maybe she was considering committing to something deeper, after all?

Everyone hugged and congratulated me and they all readily agreed to be godparents. 'Great, if it's a chick I can seduce her when she's sixteen and if it's a boy I can take him to his first hooker at fifteen,' said Miles.

'Fifteen?' said Jess. 'Isn't that leaving it a bit late?'

'And Julius?' enquired Lucy gingerly. The room fell silent.

'Truth is, I don't know,' I said. 'He knows I'm pregnant

because I sent him the pregnancy stick but I haven't heard from his since.'

They eyed each other knowingly. No one said it but I knew what they were thinking: no surprises there, then.

Mum had decorated the tree and Archie seemed to have a tray of eggnog permanently stuck to his hand. Wherever you went in the house, he'd pop up and beam: 'How about a snifter for Santa?' Home felt especially festive because it was Mum's first Christmas with Archie and she was having his children and grandchildren over on Boxing Day. She was in a terrible flap but I could tell she was relishing every second. She looked madder than ever, wearing a festive red silk kaftan under her green sleeveless Puffa jacket and mud-encrusted wellies. She was plastered with make-up and her neck was strung with her fattest pearls and I couldn't ever remember seeing her this happy. Archie was equally cheered in his cherry-red cords and tweed jacket. With his bushy white eyebrows and sprouting of nostril hair, he seemed, unlike my father, incredibly jovial. He may not have had the quiet insight of Dad but he didn't have the melancholy either. It was obvious by the way he watched Mum, stuffing her arm up the turkey's bum with gusto, that he simply adored her. I loved him for that.

When he went out to fill the log basket, I put my arm around my mother's shoulder and said: 'I've got something to tell you.' I was terrified that she was going to freak out and that I'd wreck her Christmas by announcing I was going to be a single mother, so I got it over with as fast as I could. 'Mum, I'm pregnant and it's Julius's baby and it wasn't planned and he knows all about it but he doesn't appear to want anything to do with it but I am going to have it and I'm pleased and scared and excited but I pray you'll be happy for me too.'

Mum stood statue still, holding her hand covered in turkey stuffing and grease in the air, as the tears began to roll. Oh Christ, I thought, here we go. I was willing Archie to return because I thought at least she wouldn't go off the Richter scale in front of him. Just then the doorbell rang. Thank God, Jess had arrived. She'd get my mother under control.

'It's Jess,' I said.

Mum took me in her one free arm – the other was sticking out as if she was hitching a lift – and wailed: 'I can't tell you how long I've waited for this moment. I never told you how much I envied my friends who were grandparents before because I thought it would upset you.'

Just then Archie entered the room. 'You've got a visitor,' he said.

'Archie,' screamed my mother, kicking her legs to the side in a little jig, 'I'm going to be a grandmother! Can you believe it?' I left them half-dancing, half-embracing and I could hear him say: 'Diana, that's marvellous news,' and then in a loud whisper: 'whose is it?'

I ran to the front door, relieved to see Jess, a sure-fire beacon of sanity. But she wasn't waiting in the hall. I rushed into the drawing room. But she wasn't there either. And that's when I saw him. He was standing with his back to me, staring into the fire but I recognised him immediately.

When he heard me enter, he turned around and as our eyes met, he came towards me.

Julius held out a jar of green olives.

'Because I know you can't stand black olives,' he said.

# Glossary of Dooley Terms

**Dating Dharma** As we get older, we get the face and the body we deserve. We also get the dates we deserve. Don't want to kiss another frog? Then get your inner bitch under control.

**Dick Delivery Boy** Being sexually serviced by a one-off or regular stud muffin at your place. Best enjoyed with post-coital take-out pizza.

**Emotional Contagion** The ability to pick up on your partner's feelings without speaking.

**Erotic Intelligence** Skilled flirting. A Double First in seduction.

**Hook-ups** Sex on an ad hoc basis with a male friend. Emotionally safe as there is no dating agenda.

**Manscaping** When a man pays extra attention to pruning his pubic topiary and sculpting his chest hair.

**Married Singles** Husbands who have convenient amnesia

about their wives and kids when poised to score. Permanent bachelors during the week, dipping into daddydom at weekends.

**McSex** A fast-food coupling – quick shag – that leaves you feeling empty and slightly nauseous. No emotional fulfilment on the side or to go.

**Mercy Jump** When your best male friend sleeps with you out of pity. Can it really have been that long?

**Post Divorce Date (PDD)** That all-important terrifying first date when you have to get back into the dating saddle having been bucked to the ground and had all your confidence shattered by divorce.

**Post Traumatic Date Syndrome (PTDS)** Obsessive rumination and mild depression, coupled with chronic mating fatigue following a date when you haven't found The One.

**Premature We-jaculation** A dating dysfunction where you start referring to 'we' before he has acknowledged that you are a couple.

**Radical Acceptance** The maturity to realise that life sucks and your ability to shoulder existential disappointment. So he was a total shit? Deal with it, drop him and move on.

**Rasa** Your sweet spiritual nectar. The essence of who you were before he broke your heart and poisoned your future.

**Sattvic Strength** That strong, silent, inner peace that is the answer to all your problems and endless, destructive mind talk. One part discipline, three parts trust. What you are speaks volumes louder than what you say.

**Sexual Sorbet** First person you sleep with after a break-up. A sexual palate cleanser to remove the taste of a bad, broken relationship.

**Shrink-wrapped** Therapied out.

**Sperminator** A man who serves only one purpose: to fill your tank with his fertile seed.

**Spirit-lit** A form of spiritually informing literature and therapy-lite to help you access yourself and survive the crippling disappointment of divorce. See all of the above.